Church Security
and
Outreach

Church Security and Outreach

A Spirit Led Strategy to Pursue the *One* and Protect the *Ninety-Nine*

by

Jason White

XULON PRESS

LedSecurity.com

Xulon Press
2301 Lucien Way #415
Maitland, FL 32751
407.339.4217
www.xulonpress.com

© 2019 by Jason White

All rights reserved solely by the author. The author guarantees all contents are original and do not infringe upon the legal rights of any other person or work. No part of this book may be reproduced in any form without the permission of the author. The views expressed in this book are not necessarily those of the publisher.

Scripture quotations taken from the Holy Bible, New International Version (NIV). Copyright © 1973, 1978, 1984, 2011 by Biblica, Inc.™. Used by permission. All rights reserved.

Printed in the United States of America.

ISBN-13: 9781545662182

Dedicated to
my wife Heather and son Wes.
Thank you, Lord, for blessing me with this family.

Endorsements

My friend Jason White breaks important new ground for the Church with his new book! While keeping the Great Commission central this security expert Biblically and logically offers a practical and full orbed approach for church leaders to protect God's people under their leadership and care. Read and implement this book!
    Dr. Pete Alwinson, Executive Director of FORGE

Jason White is highly esteemed by many as a mighty man of courage and faith with a stellar security background! This book astutely outlines vital church security matters from a primarily biblically based perspective. A comprehensive source of amazing Godly insight and wisdom addressing the current escalating security concerns in and around churches. It provides methodically sound strategies and action plans to implement. The balance presented of protecting the flock and reaching the lost is paramount! Absolutely spot-on! "Spirit Led Security" rightly stresses the importance of sharing security responsibilities with church members to maximize a safe church environment while avoiding interference with the sensitive and spiritual move of God in services. An extremely relevant and beneficial book for pastors, church staff, law enforcement personnel, first responders and all church members.
    Psalm 127:1 KJV
    Joseph J. O'Neill
    Assistant Special Agent in Charge
    U. S. Secret Service – (Ret.)

In *Church Security and Outreach*, Jason White tackles a subject few understand as he reveals the importance of church security. Readers will want to underline and highlight the pages of this book. Jason effectively teaches the balance of protecting the church and reaching the lost that many thought was not possible. I love the practical approach he navigates the reader through for this very complex subject. You will discover that this book is filled with thought provoking yet practical words of wisdom to protect your church and ministry. The pages are filled with insight that comes from years of experience and from the heart of a man who loves people. I cannot think of a more important book for the culture we live in today for the protection of our churches. We need this book in all of our churches today!

It has been my privilege to be Jason's pastor for many years. The truths he shares in this book I have seen him implement in our church and even around the world. I would consider him to be an expert in this arena. If anyone can honestly tell you how to protect your church and still reach people, Jason can. This is a brilliant must-read manual for security and protection.

Norm Dubois
Lead Pastor
East Coast Believers Church

My friend and partner in ministry for decades, Jason White, has developed content and instruction that is a must for every church to apply. His unique approach to security, is not only thorough, but its accomplished through a Gospel lens! You have to read and apply Spirit Led Security with your team. Not only will your church feel safer, but the kingdom of God will be strengthened and advanced!

Nathan Wilder
Lead Pastor
University Baptist Church

Endorsements

Jason White's remarkable professional expertise in the public safety, tactics and security field is eclipsed only by his love for God and his constant work to ensure God's word is delivered safely to all people! This book is rooted in the Word of God while seamlessly providing a current look at the dangers that besiege our churches. Biblically insightful, tactically intelligent and Spirit inspired... this book is the blueprint and a must-have for any church leader or staff that desires to truly protect God's people while maintaining a safe and uninterrupted environment of worship.

Dr. DeAngelo K. Brown,
The Peace Makers Group, Director of Operations
Lieutenant U.S. Navy Reserve, Intelligence Officer

Disclaimers

*N*either the author, editors, ConvergenceNow, references to Spirit Led Security in any form, or affiliates implies or expresses warranties of the material contained in this book. No recommendations contained in this book or otherwise are meant to be legal advice. The aforementioned are not liable under any circumstances, including but not limited to negligence, for a special, consequential, or incidental damages, that may result from the use of these materials and concepts even if a representative has been advised of the possibility of such damages. The use of the materials and concepts contained within the book are at your own risk. The intention of the material contained within this book is to be informational, useful, offer general recommendations, and foster discussion. Always remain within the laws that govern the location of your church and operate only on church property. The use of the materials and concepts are not warranted as being able to ensure the safety of the church, persons in it, property, premises, or others related to the area covered. No representation is made that the information herein is applicable for all locations and times.

All contents provided either orally or written are for informational purposes only. The materials and concepts contained are not warranted as being in compliance with any or all federal, state, regional, or local laws, statutes, ordinances, codes, or another standard. The accuracy, reliability, or correctness is not warranted and the reader and user accept the entire risk for their use, adoption, and adaption.

The information provided is done so with the understanding that neither the author, editors, ConvergenceNow, references to Spirit Led Security in any form, or affiliates are engaged in rendering legal, accounting, psychological, medical, or other professional services. If legal advice or other expert assistance is required, the services of a competent professional person should be sought.

The author, editors, ConvergenceNow, references to Spirit Led Security in any form, and affiliates are not liable for damages or injury, including, but not limited, to damages or injury caused by the use of these materials or concepts, whether resulting in whole or in part, from breach of contract, tortious behavior, negligence, or otherwise.

None of the information provided arises from, or is associated with the official duties of the author. It is not, and should not be inferred that any current or previous employer, volunteer organization, philanthropy organization, or entity including that involving the United States Government reflects an endorsement of the information provided in this book or by any other means.

Logo Created by Gabriella Owens of Think Bird Design

© 2019 by Jason White

Contents

Introduction: Pursuing the One and Protecting the Ninety-Nine 1

Chapter 1: The Problem and Proposed Solution 19
The Pastor's Paradox
Spirit Led Security
Actions to Deter, Avoid, and Mitigate

Chapter 2: The Biblical Basis 49
Foundation of Prayer
Pillar of Wisdom
Pillar of Controlling Fear
Foundation of Stewardship
Pillar of Action
Pillar of Vigilance

Chapter 3: The SLS Strategy for a Security Ministry 79
Security Ministry Basic Training
Sheep, Wolves, and Sheepdogs
Situational Awareness
Conditioning the Mind
Cognitive Blueprinting
The OODA Loop: Observation, Orientation, Decision, Action

Conditioning the Body
Christian Warrior Mindset

Chapter 4: Target Hardening **133**
Making Your Church a Hard Target
Establishing an Emergency Preparedness Plan
Cameras and Radios
Functional Design
Advanced Training from External Sources
Internal Investigations

Chapter 5: Creating a Safety Team **160**
Establishing the Safety Team
Consulting Security Experts
Recruiting or Discovering Team Members
Great Commission Worshippers
Commanded and Commissioned Warriors
Security: Gifts and Talents
Developing Leaders

Chapter 6: The SLS Tactical Strategy **195**
Strategy and Tactics: The *Who* and the *How*
Hired Law Enforcement
Force Multipliers
The Safety Team
Overt Deterrence - Covert Observation and Communication

Chapter 7: Red Flags **256**
Red Flags – Pre-Assault Indicators

Chapter 8: Safety Team Operational Training 268
Concept
Formal Training: Stewardship, Outreach, and Discipleship
Operational Training Exercise (OTX)
Tactical Considerations

Chapter 9: Outreach to First Responders 305
Strategy
Outreach: External Ministry- *poreuomai*
Outreach: Maximize Existing Relationships
Outreach: Taking Ownership
Outreach: Internal Ministry- *koinonia*
Education: The Mission, Audience, and Training

Chapter 10: Active Shooter 325
Evade
Hide
Fight
Recover

Conclusion 339

Bibliography 343

Index 347

About the Author 353

Preface

A desire to protect others and draw closer to the Lord guided me into a career in law enforcement and to His ministry. Decades of growth in both areas has placed me in a position to address the complexity that the church faces as it seeks to be open to all, while defending itself from potential attacks. The protector in me says, "fortify the church to be safe," while the pursuer says, "let's go rescue the lost." But, what if our pursuit of the lost increases our vulnerability to attack? How do we overcome this?

What does the Bible say? How can we functionally do both? Are there strategies and tactics that will allow us to enhance the safety of the church while also providing a warm, welcoming, worship environment for members and guests? How do we protect ourselves from attacks such as thefts, robberies, active shooters, and unmerited lawsuits? The purpose of this book is to offer information and recommendations that will answer these questions. It addresses the roles and responsibilities of everyone serving by providing a strategy to enhance the safety and security of the church during worship services and church events.

I am personally indebted to my wife, Heather; Gator; the entire Firebase Combat Studies Group; two international mission's organizations; two specific missionaries (to remain nameless); Joe O'Neill, U.S. Secret Service (Ret.); and "J" for the knowledge, skills, and insight provided in making the Spirit Led Security strategy possible.

I am grateful to Lead Pastor Norm Dubois and the entire staff of East Coast Believers Church. You continue to move people from the position that they are in toward the place God has called them to be. It is an honor to be part of your commitment to plunder Hell and populate Heaven by leading people to Jesus.

Thank you to Pastor Nathan Wilder for your friendship and letting me be a part of your passion to bring the love of Christ to every community that you touch.

To my family (both on my side and my wife's side), thank you for your love and heartfelt prayers. Finally, thank you *May May*. This book would never have been completed without your diligent work and faithful prayers!

Introduction

*J*esus said: "I have told you these things, so that in me you may have peace. In this world you will have trouble. But take heart! I have overcome the world" (John 16:33).[1] When Jesus said this, He commanded His followers to have courage when facing trouble. Just like the members of the early church, we live in a corrupt world filled with tension, strife, and violence. The same type of threats that the early church faced persist today as our contemporary church finds itself under constant attack in both the spiritual and natural realms. The origin of these attacks is an evil that seeks to steal, kill, and destroy the only entity proclaiming the hope for the world. Together we must stand against those attacks as we continue to share the Gospel.

Just as Jesus warned His followers of the trouble that would threaten them, He also commanded believers to honor Him, love their neighbors, seek the lost, and be responsible stewards of what He has placed under their authority. While we cannot ignore the threats that have relentlessly presented themselves against the local church, we also recognize that we

---

[1] Unless otherwise noted, all Bible references are taken from the New International Version.

are commissioned to seek the *lost* and are responsible for the protection of the *found*. Therefore, in ministry it is important that we not only pursue the lost but also protect those who are within our congregation. Make no mistake, we will be held accountable for our effort in each area.

Leaders are to be faithful stewards over *the church* as we pursue the lost abroad and within our communities. This is where the security ministry comes into play; our stewardship includes providing for the safety and the protection of the congregation. Unfortunately, some local churches' efforts to protect the congregation have led to isolation from the community. Other ramifications of ill-fated efforts have resulted in overzealous intimidating security teams, misguided hyper-vigilance, pride, and being so security focused that the church ignores the people outside the walls.

Striving to reach the lost and protect the congregation can be a difficult task. This is because seeking the lost requires locating them and inviting them into the church. After all, as Christians this is what we want to do. We offer a welcoming invitation to those who do not have a relationship with Jesus. However, by inviting everyone into the church we complicate our ability to protect the existing congregation. Therefore, by being open to all, we may find ourselves welcoming in the same people who *may* pose a threat to the very congregation we are responsible to protect. The very same person we invite in may turn out to be the person who harms a member of the church. Despite this reality, we are not going to shut the doors to the masses who are desperately in need of the Savior. We have to be missional while embracing the stewardship responsibility of protecting our people.

In essence, the local church has a fundamental question to answer: How should it protect the congregation while openly pursuing the lost? This question poses a uniquely Christian dilemma. When looking for answers, it doesn't take long to determine that the secular solutions fail to address the fundamental problem. They are not concerned with the lost. Secular approaches focus on securing buildings, people, and possessions. They say, "build a castle, secure it, and protect everyone within it!" From a worldly point of view, this makes sense. The priority in their opinion is to secure the congregation and cut off any potential threats. However, this position excludes biblical commands and the commissioning given by our Lord. Therefore, the secular solution presents an extreme view that is not a viable option.

It is important to recognize that there is an additional extreme which is equally flawed. This opinion comes from the opposite end of the spectrum and originates from within the church. This extreme says, "ignore the threat, focus only on the lost." It is a position that purposely disregards the stewardship responsibility leaders have to protect their congregation. It in essence abandons the congregation to whatever fate befalls them.

Both views are polar opposites. Fortunately, most churches find themselves somewhere in the middle of the two in their attempt to address this dilemma. Each one of us has to consider how successful our local church is in balancing the command to reach the lost and responsibility to protect the congregation. Retrospectively, we must ask: Are we doing enough?

Stewardship over the local church is demanding. It requires responsible oversight of church activities and events. On a day when an emergency situation occurs, the demand placed on leaders may become overbearing. An emergency situation (also called a critical event) is an unexpected state of crisis that poses a threat to someone at the church. These situations can cause physical and mental damage both during and after the event.

The damage inflicted upon the church can continue well after the culmination of a critical event. Just because the chaos has appeared to have stopped does not mean that further problems will not ensue. Even when "wounds" are being healed, other forms of attack can be launched. This can happen in the form of physical injury, mental damage, and lawsuits. Of these three types of attack, it is the last one, *lawsuits,* which many local churches fail to prepare for. That is why it is imperative to recognize that every time an emergency situation occurs, litigation looms.

Therefore, leaders must account for the legal issues that the church may face after a critical event. The event will be reviewed and the church will be scrutinized by unscrupulous people seeking profit from tragedy. We must actively protect the congregation well before a critical event occurs. We, as good stewards, cannot afford to overlook safety issues or the fact that we will be held accountable for both our action and inaction. Just as wrong decisions may invite lawyers, inaction can also lead to litigation. Thus, churches should go the extra mile and manage risk to avoid undesired litigation. A key way to ensure this is to make a diligent effort to provide a safe environment and properly *document* the actions that you have taken. The church may do everything right, only to find itself in legal peril due to a lack of documentation. This increased legal concern further complicates the aforementioned dilemma.

This quandary is endemic to the church. No other entity, business, or governmental organization sincerely invites in the same people who may pose a direct threat to it. Only the church has this type of responsibility. Spirit Led Security (SLS) calls this dilemma the *Pastor's Paradox.* The Pastor's Paradox identifies the stewardship responsibility to manage the congregation and the commissioning to seek the lost knowing that they may pose a threat to the very congregation we are responsible to protect. It articulates that too little security leaves the congregation vulnerable while too much security inhibits reaching the lost.

How do you balance these seemingly contradictory responsibilities? For leaders in the church, failing in either part (security or outreach) is not acceptable. Therefore, *action* must be taken to fulfill the responsibility and due diligence required for security and outreach. There is no perfect solution, cookie cutter plan, or simple fix where all of the lost will be found and everyone in the church will be safe and secure. Jesus warned us of the trouble we will face and we are facing it today. Just as some who hear the Gospel will not accept it, not everyone we want to protect will find safety. This is the reality of the corrupted state of the fallen world we live in. The fight is on and we must take action to overcome the Pastor's Paradox.

† † †

This book offers the SLS strategy as a solution to the Pastor's Paradox. The SLS strategy affirms that the stewardship obligation to enhance the security of the church can be achieved while remaining faithful to the Great Commandment and Great Commission. This is accomplished through a biblically based and tactically practical strategy. At the heart of the SLS strategy is the Safety Team. The Safety Team is a vetted group of individuals focused on *stewardship* (protecting the church), *outreach* (perusing the lost), and *discipleship* (spiritual growth). Members operate covertly as they observe and communicate information to enhance the overall security and safety of the church. The team uses *Actions* to *Deter*, *Avoid*, and *Mitigate* (ADAM) threats without creating a distraction or disruption to the worship service or church event.[2] Members also take ownership over a sustained outreach ministry to first responders. If you do not have a security strategy that is functioning to seek the lost and protect the congregation, it's time for a new approach.

The recommendations in this book rest upon a biblical basis and have a practical application for *everyone* serving.

---

[2] Actions to Deter, Avoid, and Mitigate attacks (ADAM) is a system of action created by the author to counter the threats and attacks that occur in both the spiritual and natural realms. It will be explained in detail in chapter 1.

Many churches negatively affect their ability to enhance the safety of the church because they limit the responsibility of security to a designated team. Security is a ministry that every member serving at the church must participate in. The SLS strategy focuses on the comprehensive application of *Actions* to *Deter*, *Avoid*, and *Mitigate* threats. Although everyone serving has a role to play in the overall security of the church, the Safety Team is the core group of men and women who operate covertly to assess threats. They do so by utilizing exceptional tactics that have been proven in military, intelligence, police, non-governmental, and missional organizations around the world. Although they are applied in the local church with a different purpose, they can achieve equal effectiveness. When the tactics are employed correctly, they provide security coverage without creating a distraction or disruption to any part of the service.

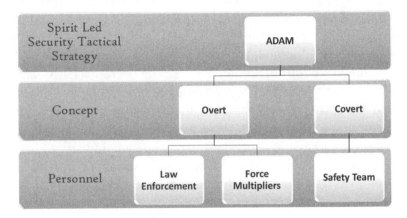

The Spirit Led Security Tactical Strategy

The SLS strategy involves a security ministry focused on *stewardship*, *outreach*, and *discipleship*. The Safety Team is the heart of the ministry. It functions to enhance the physical and spiritual security of the church while serving with a focus on stewardship over the congregation, outreach to first responders, and discipleship within the Safety Team. The team disciples one-another while pursuing the lost *one* and protecting the *ninety-nine*. The Safety Team operates by observing and communicating information relating to suspicious activity and threats, providing aid in emergency situations, and functioning as an outreach ministry targeting first responders. The team also trains other ministries and church staff (Force Multipliers) in their roles in providing a safer worship environment. Together, the Safety Team and Force Multipliers look for *anything* that presents a safety concern and take the appropriate action to address it. Examples of safety concerns can range from a person acting suspiciously --- to a coffee spill on the floor. Each presents a safety concern that must be addressed.

The SLS strategy will not sacrifice the mission and vision of your church, nor will it create an intimidating security force that causes distraction during service. Therefore, the change you will see is one where your people become empowered in their giftings. This happens through: 1)- assessing your current mindset; 2)- establishing a Safety Team that utilizes sound tactics that not only enhance church security but do so without being a distraction to the congregation; 3)- producing a sustained outreach ministry to first responders; 4)- creating a detailed Emergency Preparedness Plan.

This book will provide you with many recommendations on how to accomplish each of these tasks. They involve building a foundational SLS mindset which appreciates that protecting people (security) and leading the lost to Jesus (outreach) are not mutually exclusive. Church security can be enhanced while following the Great Commandment and Great Commission through the use of a Safety Team augmented by the Force Multipliers. If you have a congregation where people are serving and seek to discover their talents and calling, then you have what you need to accomplish this right now. Before you consider spending money on technology, focus your attention on the people around you. They are what the Lord has provided. Then, consider technology as it fits into the vision of your local church and supports the security ministry.

† † †

I was inspired to create the SLS strategy by Luke 15:3-7, the Parable of the Lost Sheep:[3]

> *Then Jesus told them this parable: "Suppose one of you has a hundred sheep and loses one of them. Does he not leave the ninety-nine in the open country and go after the lost sheep until he finds it? And when he finds it, he joyfully puts it on his shoulders and goes home. Then he calls his friends and neighbors together and says, 'Rejoice with me; I have found my lost sheep.' I tell you that in the same way there will be more rejoicing in heaven over one sinner who repents than over ninety-nine righteous persons who do not need to repent."*

This parable provides an example of the persistent love God has for humanity. It is a love that does not change. Even when people wander, even when they hide, even when they run away, the Lord pursues them; His love is truly relentless.

---

[3] The parallel recording is found in Matt 18:10-14. "See that you do not look down on one of these little ones. For I tell you that their angels in heaven always see the face of my Father in heaven. What do you think? If a man owns a hundred sheep, and one of them wanders away, will he not leave the ninety-nine on the hills and go to look for the one that wandered off? And if he finds it, I tell you the truth, he is happier about that one sheep than about the ninety-nine that did not wander off. In the same way your Father in heaven is not willing that any of these little ones should be lost."

The Parable of the Lost Sheep also provides an example of the thunderous rejoicing that rocks Heaven when the lost are rescued. Lives are changed when people are broken from bondage. Those of us who have been rescued and carried back to the flock are not only saved but commissioned to spread the Gospel of the Lord who saved us. Therefore, we cannot forget about the others who remain lost. As Christians who have been freed, we must intentionally pursue the lost inside and outside the walls of the local church. Admittingly, for most Christians this is easier said than done.

The Parable of the Lost Sheep not only addresses the lost, it also speaks of the ninety-nine who were left in the open country. What happened to them? What is their status? Did the shepherd abandon them? If he abandoned them, does he not care for them? If the shepherd represents the Lord, does that mean He saves us spiritually only to abandon us naturally? Of course not!

The following verses from the New Testament refute the idea that the ninety-nine sheep are abandoned by the Lord. Scripture from the New Testament says that God will *never leave nor forsake* His people (Heb 13:5). Jesus said, "surely I am with you always, to the very end of the age" (Matt 28:20). Furthermore, the Lord has provided us with the Holy Spirit. Jesus said, "I will ask the Father and He will give you another Counselor to be with you forever- the Spirit of truth. The world cannot accept Him, for He lives with you and will be in you. I will not leave you as orphans; I will come to you" (John 14:16-18). Additionally, Paul declared that nothing can separate His people from the love of God (Rom 8:35-39). In the same way that the Lord persistently seeks the lost while remaining with the ninety-nine, *we must pursue the lost, while protecting our ninety-nine.*

A glance at the Old Testament reinforces the belief that the Lord will not abandon His people. Moses said that the Lord goes before, is with, and never leaves or forsakes His people

(Deut 31:8). Joshua affirmed that the Lord will be with you wherever you go (Jos 1:9). Isaiah proclaimed that the Lord is present; He will strengthen and uphold you (Isa 41:10). It is also written that the Lord will not abandon or destroy you, He is merciful (Deut 4:31). Even when others forsake you, He receives you (Psa 27:10). The Lord loves the just and will not forsake those who are faithful (Psa 37:28). Finally, in 1 Samuel it is written that the Lord will not reject His people, He was pleased to make them His (1 Sam 12:22). These verses refute the argument that the Lord abandons His people. Even in His relentless pursuit of the lost sheep, He is with the flock. The love for all His children is affirmed in these verses. The ninety-nine have not been nor will they ever be abandoned.

We must emulate Christ when it comes to pursuing the lost and protecting the found. Our Lord never leaves His people. Even as He relentlessly pursues the lost, He comforts the found. This is evident through our relationship with the Holy Spirit. It is Jesus who empowered believers through the presence of the Holy Spirit (John 14:16; Acts 1:8; John 16:5-8). It is the Spirit who testifies with our spirit that we are children of God (Rom 8:15-16). Through the power of the Holy Spirit we are comforted, counselled, and convicted. We are a new creation made to glorify Him.

As a new creation we are blessed with various gifts and talents that come from the Lord; He is with us (1 Cor 12:4-11). The spiritual gifts are given to glorify God, express our faith, and encourage the faith of others. For some people, this spiritual gifting includes a concern for the security of the flock and ability to steward over their protection. People with this gifting are able to serve, teach, encourage, and lead others in pursuing the lost *one* while protecting the *ninety-nine* (Rom 12:3-7).

In the Bible there is a rare occurrence of a term that has a high significance in the SLS strategy. This is found in Job 30:1 where the author mentions the *sheepdog*. This is a designation that is commonly used in contemporary military and law enforcement circles. It is a title attributed to people who are *wired* to protect others. If you are in line with this trait, you will find it easy to identify with the sheepdog. Knowing what a sheepdog is will assist you in identifying like-minded people serving at your church and within your congregation.

A sheepdog is an amazing animal. It remains loyal to the shepherd and is a guardian of the flock. The sheepdog will never hurt the sheep. Rather, it is wise, vigilant, and fearless in its devotion to protect the flock. When something doesn't look right, the sheepdog acts even if it means placing its own life in danger. Sheepdogs have a purpose, they protect the sheep from the wolves. Sheepdogs are the watchman that stand guard against evil attacks.

There are sheepdogs within the church who walk with the Lord, love the flock, and are concerned about the lost. They have gifts, talents, and a calling waiting to be discovered by church leadership. As a leader in your church you must discover people with this calling. Encourage, uplift, and organize them. Their purpose is to serve the Lord by pursuing the *one* and protecting the *ninety-nine*. If you know your flock, you will discover who the sheepdogs are. These servants will play a vital role in enhancing the security and safety of your church.

† † †

This book presents recommendations on how to enhance the security of the church and create a sustained ministry to first responders. It is written to those in ministry who are concerned with the *one* and the *ninety-nine*. These individuals have an understanding of the dual responsibility to protect the church while pursuing the lost. The primary emphasis of enhancing the security of the church is through the SLS strategy that can be applied during worship services, baptisms, funerals, weddings, concerts, and other special events. Concerning outreach, the primary focus of the ministry is to target the first responder community. This includes all of the members of the law enforcement community, fire department, and other emergency medical services (EMS).

SLS recognizes that everyone's gifts and talents are to be used for the Lord's glory. Our gifts and talents are diverse in nature and in maturity. For example, some people reading this have a strong call towards seeking the lost sheep, while others will have a greater focus on the protection of the flock. I, for example, have a stronger gifting over protecting the flock than pursuing the lost. Protection comes naturally to me but, that does not mean that I am not to seek the lost. To the contrary, I am *commissioned* and *commanded* to do so. For me, evangelism entails more discipline in pursuing the *one* than stewardship requires in protecting the *ninety-nine*. I am naturally more likely to pay attention to a suspicious person walking towards the children's ministry than to randomly walk up to a person in the parking lot and ask them, "do you know Jesus?"

For you, the opposite may be true. You may find that stewardship over security is more difficult than evangelism. The idea of *security* may make you feel uncomfortable. Do not let this derail you. The responsibility of *evangelism* makes most Christians uncomfortable! Together we must overcome any discomfort and fear in order to be good stewards of security and proclaim the Gospel.

We have to be obedient to our stewardship responsibility over both *security* and *evangelism*. There is nothing wrong with either of us as long as we recognize the biblical requirements in the stewardship of protecting the congregation *and* in evangelism. The natural distribution of gifts and talents among believers allows us to serve together for the benefit of the church. We are stronger when we are united in the body of Christ. As this book will demonstrate, these endeavors are not mutually exclusive. Our obedience to the Lord requires effort in both areas to overcome the Pastor's Paradox as we serve to protect the *ninety-nine* and rescue the *one*.

I have organized this book with two purposes in mind. First, to point people concerned with enhancing the safety and security of the church to Jesus. Second, to offer information that can be used as a training manual for instruction. The main security focus of the book is the enhancement of the safety of the church during service and events. Although it provides information that will assist the church in its overall security throughout the week, the primary concentration is a strategy to be employed during the worship service and special events.

The SLS *Tactical Strategy* was created to enhance the safety of the church. It establishes a security ministry that, at its most basic level, needs only people committed to serve to fulfill this purpose. It does not require cameras, radios, weapons, or additional costs. Of course, any and all of these can be properly added to the SLS strategy when they are deemed to be appropriate. Those topics will be covered in this book and it is up to each individual church to determine what it needs to adopt and adapt to its unique condition.

Since everyone serving has a role to play in enhancing the security of the church, the intended audience is the people serving. This includes the lead pastor, church staff, and all of the volunteers helping during a worship service. Everyone serving requires the *Security Ministry Basic Training* principles presented throughout the text. Their individual roles in the enhancement of the security of the church are defined throughout the book. These men and women are the *Force Multipliers* to the Safety Team.

Each chapter in this unique focus builds upon the preceding ones. The goal is twofold. First, it is to enhance the safety and security of the church in a way that is cost effective and does not create a disruption to the worship environment. Second, it effectively does this while creating a sustained outreach to the first responder community.

Chapter 1 identifies the dilemma facing the modern local church and proposes a solution. The chapter is focused on the

Pastor's Paradox and the SLS strategy to enhance the security of the church and foster outreach to the first responder community. In addition, Chapter 1 introduces the ADAM acronym. This is an abbreviation for a process I created to counter the ongoing threats to the church. It requires taking *Action*, to *Deter, Avoid,* and *Mitigate* threats.

Chapter 2 presents the biblical basis of the SLS strategy. A biblical basis is needed in order to keep the SLS strategy Christ-centered. It is the biblical foundation of Security Ministry Basic Training. Therefore, all aspects of the SLS concept rest upon a foundation of *prayer* and *stewardship*. From this foundation rise four pillars which lead to the SLS strategy. Those pillars are: *Wisdom*, *Controlling Fear*, *Action*, and *Vigilance*.

Chapter 3 may be the most empowering chapter of the book. It sets the tactical foundation of the Security Ministry Basic Training. Chapter 3 focuses on how everybody can greatly improve their overall security. This is not just for the Safety Team, it is for all ministries at the church. Everyone serving can make a difference if they are educated and empowered. Empowering individuals who are serving will increase the effectiveness exponentially. One of the great things about this chapter is that it will raise each person's personal security inside and outside of the church. Therefore, those who adopt the mindset offered in Chapter 3 will not only increase their ability to survive an attack, but be better equipped to avoid an attack all together.

Whereas Chapter 3 provides a practical application for individuals, Chapter 4 focuses on the practical application for the local church. This chapter offers insight into making your church a *hard target* including information on creating an Emergency Preparedness Plan. This section of the book will also discuss risk management which will assist the church in avoiding undesired litigation. Chapter 4 also includes instruction on documenting the due diligence taken by the church to create a safe worship environment.

The focus of Chapter 5 is the Safety Team. This chapter outlines the team structure, the vetting of prospective members and maintaining a Kingdom focused team. The Safety Team is the heart of the SLS strategy. Its members are the people committed to protect the *ninety-nine* and pursue the *one*. Therefore, the members of the Safety Team are serving as stewards over the congregation and missional towards the first responder community.

Chapter 6 delivers the strategy and tactics to be employed during service. With a focus on *overt deterrence* and *covert observation and communication,* this chapter demonstrates the multi-layered SLS strategy. It involves the use of hired law enforcement, Force Multipliers, and the Safety Team to increase the overall safety and security of the church. A salient element of the SLS strategy is that it enhances the security and safety of the church *without* causing a distraction to service. The strategy and tactics utilized have proven to deliver a safe and welcoming worship environment in small churches, megachurches, and satellite campuses.

Chapter 7 provides guidelines for training everyone serving in the various ministries throughout the church. This chapter discusses the important aspects of *how to* and *how not to* conduct scenario-based training. Chapter 7 also provides material on identifying the pre-assault indicators often exhibited by threatening people. Specifically, Chapter 7 looks at the common *red flags* that indicate suspicion that everyone serving should be aware of.

Chapter 8 lays out how to train the Safety Team. This instruction goes beyond *Security Ministry Basic Training* and focuses on *Safety Team Operational Training*. Generally, a church's Safety Team will be made of members offering their time to serve. Therefore, most of them will have careers that make scheduling team training sessions difficult. This problem is overcome by the combination of quarterly *formal training* sessions supplemented with continuing *on the job training*.

Chapter 8 also reinforces the SLS focus on *stewardship, outreach,* and *discipleship*. All Safety Team training sessions will focus on the team's responsibility to enhance the security of the church (stewardship), minister to the first responder community (outreach), and creating internal ministry and growth among the team members (discipleship).

Chapter 9 is dedicated to the establishment of a sustained outreach ministry to the first responder community. The strategy includes an ongoing effort throughout the year as well as creating a single outreach event that can develop into a sustained ministry to first responders. Since the Safety Team will be involved with first responders weekly, elements of outreach are interwoven throughout the preceding chapters. However, Chapter 9 specifically addresses the internal and external ministry, education, outreach events, and how to build upon the event.

Chapter 10 centers on surviving an active shooter. It is impossible to prevent one from happening if the assailant is committed to attack the church. If measures to deter and avoid being hit do not work, you must mitigate the damage. Chapter 10 teaches four ways to mitigate the attack. These are: Evasion, Hiding, Fighting, and Recovering.

† † †

The Pastor's Paradox presents numerous difficulties to overcome when balancing the need to protect the congregation and seek the lost. The SLS strategy provides recommendations that can assist church leadership in managing that dilemma. Right now, you should assess how well your church is providing a safe and welcoming worship environment while also reaching out to the first responder community. Could it improve in one or both areas?

The SLS strategy and tactical techniques have proven to simultaneously fulfill the shared responsibility of reaching the

Introduction

one, while protecting the *ninety-nine*. This book presents practical, cost effective, and biblically based ways to create a sustained ministry to the first responder community and enhance the protection of the congregation. In order to be successful, your church must first overcome the Pastor's Paradox. Ask yourself, how will you do this? How will your church pursue the *one* while protecting the *ninety-nine*?

Chapter 1

The Problem and Proposed Solution

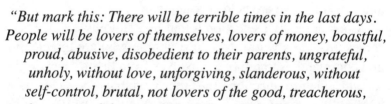

"But mark this: There will be terrible times in the last days. People will be lovers of themselves, lovers of money, boastful, proud, abusive, disobedient to their parents, ungrateful, unholy, without love, unforgiving, slanderous, without self-control, brutal, not lovers of the good, treacherous, rash, conceited, lovers of pleasure rather than lovers of God – having a form of godliness but denying its power. Have nothing to do with them." 2 Timothy 3:1-5

"'Love the Lord your God with all your heart and with all your soul and with all your mind. This is the first and greatest commandment. And the second is like it: Love your neighbor as yourself. All the Law and the Prophets hang on these two commandments.'" Matthew 22:37-40

"Therefore, go and make disciples of all nations, baptizing them in the name of the Father and of the Son and of the Holy Spirit." Matthew 28:19

"Be sure you know the condition of your flocks, give careful attention to your herds." Proverbs 27:23

"Obey your leaders and submit to their authority. They keep watch over you as men who must give an account." Hebrews 13:17

The Pastor's Paradox

These verses from Scripture can be challenging to reconcile when filtered through a security lens. They command us to act in what would appear to be opposing ways towards people. For example, we are to love all, separate ourselves from some, provide for the protection of others, and relentlessly pursue those who do not know Christ. We are responsible to know the condition of the people we oversee and as leaders we are held accountable.

Look at the first selection found in 2 Timothy 3:1-5. These verses provide a warning against people who are threatening and command us to remove ourselves from them. Then, in the second and third selections, the Great Commandment (Matthew 22:37-40) and the Great Commission (Matthew 28:19) we find direction concerning our relationships with God and people. Here, we are directed to have a loving relationship with God and people while pursuing the lost. The next selected verse is Proverbs 27:23. This is where we in the church are reminded of our stewardship responsibility over those we are leading. Specifically, this means that we have the responsibility to know what is going on within our "flock," giving careful attention to them. We must ask ourselves: Are there threats among them? Are they vulnerable to attacks based upon our lack of action? These questions must be addressed because in the final selected Scripture, Hebrews 13:17 we are reminded of our accountability (for the status of our flock and for the way we lead).

The verses create a dilemma concerning the responsibility to protect the congregation and follow Jesus' commands to seek the lost. Without any doubt, seeking the lost includes having a local church that is welcoming. So, how do we do it? If our effort is not balanced, we lackadaisically allow threats into our church or we overzealously lock out the lost. Neither is acceptable.

We have the responsibility to provide good stewardship over those entrusted to us. But, how do we wisely discern who to have nothing to do with while remaining faithful to the Great Commandment to honor God and love others while following the Great Commission to seek the lost? Another way of asking the question is: How do you protect the congregation, the people that you love and are responsible for, while seeking the lost, a group which may include people who could harm the congregation? In the context of church security, this is the Pastor's Paradox.

The Pastor's Paradox demonstrates that too much security will inhibit the ability to reach the lost while too little security leaves the flock vulnerable. As Proverbs 27 and Hebrews 13 indicate, protecting the congregation is a matter of stewardship to which all will be held accountable. Therefore, we know that we have to do something to protect the congregation while sharing the Gospel. That means that we must not only go and seek the lost, but welcome them in as well.

In 2 Timothy 3:1-5, the church is commanded to *have nothing to do with* people who are described as abusive, without love, slanderous, treacherous, and rash among other things. These descriptions represent the people threatening the church. Robbery, burglary, theft, slander, threats to children, terrorism, and violent attacks including active shooters come from unholy actors who pursue selfish gain by harming others. These threats have to be acknowledged, dealt with, and avoided when possible.

The Bible tells us to avoid certain people. This is shocking for many believers because mainstream Christianity does not preach avoiding people. To the contrary, one thing that I have learned in ministry is that, if you are seeking church growth, avoiding people is rarely an effective technique. However, avoiding certain people can increase our effectiveness in reaching those willing to hear our message. Much wisdom is found in 2nd Timothy 3:1-5.

The Great Commandment found in Matthew 22:37-40 is where Matthew records Jesus' commands to love God with all our heart, soul, and mind and to love our neighbor as ourselves. This is quite a different position than what is found in 2nd Timothy chapter three where believers are told to have *nothing to do* with certain people. On the surface they appear to be conflicting positions. They are *not,* however, in opposition with each other. Reconciling these Scriptures requires us to make a distinction between those who we are to seek and those who we are to avoid. This approach requires applying a great deal of discernment when considering people's character and intentions.

This brings us back to the Pastor's Paradox. How do you do it? Is your church fulfilling the obligation to seek the lost and protect the people in attendance? The Pastor's Paradox is a dilemma that affects everyone who has a leadership position over others. Earlier, I said that *we* as leaders have a stewardship responsibility to uphold over protecting those entrusted to us. As Christians, all of us are leaders in some area. Obviously, each church is led by the lead pastor, but associate pastors, elders, deacons, small group, bible study, and ministry leaders also have a stewardship responsibility. Because of this, *all of us have to overcome the predicament of the Pastor's Paradox.*

All Christians are required to follow the commands in Matthew 28 which direct believers to share the Gospel with the lost. The problem is that some of the lost may pose a threat to the church. This means the neighbors that we are commanded to love may contain people who we are to have nothing to do with. Thus, as leaders we have the difficult responsibility of balancing *protection* and *outreach* without compromising the fundamental Christian principles found in the Great Commandment and Great Commission.

How do you protect the congregation, the people you love and are responsible for, while seeking the lost, a group that may include threats to the congregation?

The Pastor's Paradox:

The Pastor's Paradox demonstrates that too much security will inhibit the ability to reach the lost while too little security leaves the flock vulnerable.

The Pastor's Paradox

The Pastor's Paradox sends us on a mission where the risk can be great. Shepherds must protect the flock while seeking the lost. Making no effort to seek the lost is a failure in accountability. Neglecting the flock by leaving them vulnerable is a failure in responsibility. Ignoring the lost and neglecting the flock are both failures in a stewardship. Each endeavor contains risks and success is not guaranteed. But one thing is certain, failing to act is not an option.

Christians accept that there are risks associated with pursuing the lost. Since the time of the early church, Christians have been persecuted, tortured, and killed for sharing the Gospel. If you are a pastor, elder, deacon, small group leader, ministry leader, or team member, you, like I, must accept this fact. Acknowledging the threat is far from a cry for martyrdom; it is a prudent position to take. It allows you to better understand the reality that exists. Knowing this, we must make wise decisions as we seek the lost and protect those under our stewardship. Unfortunately, most local churches do a better job of pursuing the lost than they do in protecting the congregation. Regardless of which part you church is better at, effort must be made on both fronts.

Proverbs 27:23 requires that leaders be sure that they know the condition of their flock. In its simplest terms, this means that leaders must pay close attention to the people they shepherd. Protecting them and making sure that the treacherous are not among them is a responsibility that comes with Christian leadership. This is a stewardship issue and it comes with accountability. Therefore, effort must be made to know who is within our flocks and to keep the threats out.

As seen above, Hebrews 13:17 provides leaders with guidance *and* accountability.[4] In these verses, the author of Hebrews identifies leaders as those who watch over the people. The Scripture states that leaders will be held accountable and Ezekiel 33:6 hammers this point home: "But if the watchman sees the enemy coming and doesn't sound the alarm to warn the people, he is responsible for their captivity. They will die in their sins, but I will hold the watchman responsible for their deaths." As you can see from this verse, the protection of the congregation is a responsibility not to be taken lightly. As difficult as it may be for some to read, if you are a leader, you are either the watchman or in a position where you are managing over the watchman. So, the question is, what are you doing to look out for the safety and security of the flock?

The Pastor's Paradox demonstrates the requirement of the church to pursue the lost and protect the found. However, how does the church do this when they appear to be mutually exclusive endeavors? If we seek the lost, we may bring in people who threaten the safety of the church. In addition, if we close

---

[4] Hebrews 13:17 ". . . [Leaders] keep watch over you as men who must give an account." They will have to account for those whom they serve and for themselves as stewards.

the doors to outsiders in order to secure our congregations, we are ignoring our Lord's commands and commissioning to pursue the lost. On the surface it appears that we have conflicting objectives. Therefore, formulating a plan to pursue the *one* and protect the *ninety-nine* is a difficulty that every leader in the church must tackle. It is the Pastor's Paradox.

Spirit Led Security

Spirit Led Security (SLS) is a strategy I created to overcome the Pastor's Paradox. Therefore, SLS provides recommendations on how to protect the congregation without creating an overbearing or intimidating force that creates a distraction during service. As a ministry, the strategy purposefully pursues the lost while using a multi-layered approach to enhance the safety and security of the church.

The SLS strategy is people-focused. Therefore, advanced technology (such as radios, cameras, etc.) is not required. That does not prohibit the use of various types of technology when deemed as an essential investment. For *many* churches, these tools may be needed as part of their security strategy. However, when applied, the tools of technology must be utilized to enhance the team. If the tools do not support the vision of the church and the people serving, they are a wasteful purchase. This will be addressed at greater length later, but the salient point is that we must be good stewards over technological purchases and make sure they support the vision of the church.

As a people-centered strategy, SLS operates within the lead pastor's vision and maximizes the gifts and talents of the people serving within the Kingdom. People are naturally security conscious (albeit to different degrees). Therefore, if you have people currently serving at your church, they are *no-cost assets already in place* that can be trained and equipped to increase its overall safety. It is not a stretch to say that anyone can be used to enhance the security of the church because to some degree, everyone is already performing this function.

For example, when people arrive at church, a common security measure that they take is to lock the doors of their vehicles. This is an elementary example of how they act to avoid a vehicle break-in. Notwithstanding that this may be the extent of their security consciousness, it is a starting point for training them to be situationally aware. Everyone serving has a baseline of security and opportunity to grow in proficiency. Our goal is to educate and empower them to increase their basic abilities not only for their benefit, but also the benefit of everyone at the church.

Unfortunately, in most instances the people serving throughout the church cannot answer the question, "what is your role in the security of the church?" Think about your church, how well can the pastor, greeter, member of the children's ministry, or any other person serving define their responsibility concerning security? What do they do if they see something suspicious? Who do they tell? What do they do in an emergency situation? What is the church's responsibility concerning the safety of the church during a violent attack, severe weather event, or medical emergency? These are all questions that lawyers, the media, and members of the congregation may ask after a critical event occurs. Post event scrutinization is not the time to be formulating answers.

We need to educate and empower the people who are currently serving at the church. Since everyone has a role to play, *Spirit Led Security is a strategy, not a security team.* SLS outlines everyone's role and focuses on their gifting to enhance security. This creates a security ministry that permeates throughout the church. At the core of the ministry is a mission-focused Safety Team that partners with Force Multipliers and first responders to stand firm in spiritual warfare against attacks.

The Problem and Proposed Solution

The components of the security ministry.

Shockingly, 75% of churches do not have a ministry designated to protecting the congregation.[5] Despite this, there are numerous reasons why churches should be concerned with security.[6] One of the reasons that they are devoid of a security

---

[5] Jeffery Hawkins, "Five Ways to Prevent Crimes Against Churches," Police Magazine, April (2012): Accessed November 17, 2018. http://www.policemag.com/channel/patrol/articles/2012/04/5-ways-to-prevent-crimes-against-churches.aspx

[6] "Security" is a loosely used term. It has different definitions in different contexts. Even within military and law enforcement circles, security has numerous applications and definitions. In most military and law enforcement capacities, a security team is mission focused on providing security against a direct hostile threat. However, in the context of local church security, the focus of the mission is providing safety for everyone at the church. Safety includes assisting those who have medical needs, providing aid in emergency situations, observing and communicating suspicious activity, and enhancing the security of the church against spiritual and natural threats. Because of this, in the broad context of "security," the ministry team that works towards enhancing the security of the church is best described as a Safety Team. The responsibility to enhance security

ministry is because they have chosen to ignore the existing threats. They blindly hope that the probability of being attacked is low and in the end, it will work in their favor. This position is what will be later referred to as *condition white*. It is a state of obliviousness that says, "If I cover my eyes, I won't have to acknowledge a potential threat. If the threat does attack me, I am going to lose anyway so, why pay attention to it?" This is not a wise position to take. It regrettably leaves the church vulnerable. It is a blatant failure in stewardship by those called to protect the flock.

The constant threat of criminal activity against the church should move leadership to seek guidance in how to protect the congregation. Vicious crimes, including acts of terrorism and the increasing occurrences of active shooters in the United States, demonstrate the urgency for enhancing security.[7] Addressing the threat is not only a matter of biblical stewardship, but also risk management, liability, and most of all being responsible to a congregation that likely assumes that something is being done to protect them. The bottom line is this: threats exists and leaders in the church must *Act* to *Deter*, *Avoid*, and *Mitigate* them.[8]

SLS recognizes that every threat to the local church originates in the spiritual realm. All believers must pray against evil

---

involves everyone to some degree. The Safety Team however, is a select group of individuals who are called to uphold the responsibility to serve in this capacity including training other ministries to enhance the overall security of the church.

[7] Active shooters are defined by the U.S. Department of Homeland Security as an individual actively engaged in killing or attempting to kill people in a confined and populated area; in most cases, active shooters use firearms and there is no pattern or method to their selection of victims.

[8] Actions to Deter, Avoid, and Mitigate attacks (ADAM) is a system of action created by the author to counter the threats and attacks that occur in both the spiritual and natural realms.

attacks. Therefore, invite the entire congregation to engage in constant spiritual warfare against the evil forces that plot, and scheme, to attack the church. Everyone has a responsibility to be part of a safe worship environment and prayer takes the lead role in the spiritual battle.

The responsibility to counter these threats and to enhance the security of the local church is found in biblical stewardship. Church leaders are called to be good stewards over what they oversee and to do all things for the glory of the Lord. Therefore, as stewards over the church, leadership must address the evil that threatens the congregation both in the natural and spiritual. Ask yourself, are you actively combating the threat on both fronts? How about others at your church?

Being a leader does not mean that the burden is entirely yours to carry. Your responsibility in addressing the threat is dependent upon your position and calling. Your position within that calling is what you must focus your sights on. Do find yourself trying to fulfill another person's calling or micro-managing areas that outside of your lane of influence? This is important to accept because there is always someone up the hierarchy that can be blamed when one's responsibility falls short. Do not set yourself up to be the person blame is shifted to or the one who blames the person above for your failure. Be a good steward!

For example, if a critical event occurs and proper action was not taken, the congregation may blame to the ministry team(s) for any shortcomings. Any ministry team can redirect that accusation to its leadership. The shifting of accountability can continue as leaders then can point to the staff, the staff can point to the lead pastor, and everyone can blame the government, culture, and even God! This transfer of blame is part of a victimization mentality that solves nothing. In the above example, the blame is shifted upward. But it can originate anywhere, even with a staff pastor who shifts blame downward to volunteers serving. We cannot deceive ourselves and say that this does not happen in the church. In order to fight against this repercussion of our fallen world, each of us must strive to know our role and operate within areas to which we are called.

When it comes to stewardship, the burden of responsibility is not equally shared, but everyone has a part in it (Luke 12:48).[9] Your role may be relatively large or small, but no matter what it is at this time, (because it can change) your role is significant. You need to identify that specific role, fulfill it, and encourage others to be accountable in their roles.

Enhancing security is the responsibility of all the people who actively serve in the church (1 Pet 4:10).[10] To various degrees, every person serving is a steward of what has been entrusted to them. Take for example the people who serve as greeters. They not only welcome everyone who comes into the church, they naturally observe people. Greeters may not know it, but they can play a crucial role in enhancing the security and safety of the church. Greeters are knowledgeable in observing and welcoming people. Because of their experience, they notice when someone looks out of place. Often, when a greeter identifies a person as being out of place it is because they have observed a first-time guest. This, of course, makes sense because greeters have been trained to look for and identify first time guests.

Doesn't it make sense that as one of the first lines of defense in the church, greeters should be trained to identify threats and how to communicate those observations to the appropriate

---

[9] Luke 12:48 "From everyone who has been given much, much will be demanded; and from the one who has been entrusted with much, much more will be asked."

[10] Often, we find it easy to identify with others who have similar spiritual giftings. But some people may not understand a gifting that concerns security. Regardless of other's understanding of your gifting, 1 Peter 4:10 states: "Each of you should use whatever gift you have received to serve others, as faithful stewards of God's grace in its various forms."

person? Afterall, this is exactly what they are doing concerning first time guests.

To be efficient greeters, they must be educated on how to recognize threats and have clear direction as to what to do with what they have observed. Simply put, who does the greeter tell and how do they do it without creating a disruption? By no means does the SLS strategy look to transform a greeter into an embassy guard. Rather, SLS seeks to utilize the gifts greeters (and other ministries) have to observe and communicate suspicious activity to enhance the security of the church.

People serving in various ministries throughout the church (such as greeters) may not have a security mindset but their position provides them with an opportunity to observe and communicate suspicious activity. They may not be members of a security and safety ministry but they do have the responsibility to serve at their full capacity as a greeter. That means, with a little empowerment and training, the loving, smiling, welcoming greeter can also be an active enhancement of the security of the church. The SLS strategy encourages the members of every ministry to be trained in Security Ministry Basic Training to enhance security. Once trained, they become *Force Multipliers* of the Safety Team.

Stewardship over security goes beyond the education of the non-safety focused ministries. It starts with a decision made by church leadership that is implemented by those called to the ministry. For example, the lead pastor is called to be the lead pastor of the church. That role requires decision making and leadership. Lead pastors cannot get so bogged down in any one ministry that it takes away from their ability to lead the local church. Think of it this way, the lead pastor should be *willing* to change babies' diapers in the children's ministry but shouldn't be doing it if it takes away from leading the congregation. In the previous example, you can substitute any department in place of "the children's ministry." This includes a ministry centered on safety and security. The lead pastor's role is to be the lead pastor while being security conscious in that role. It is not running any specific ministry if that takes away from leading the congregation.

Your stewardship over security is defined by your calling and the role that you play within it. In the SLS strategy, everyone from the pastor to parking team member, must enhance their personal security, situational awareness, and responsibility to communicate suspicious activity properly. Being equipped to do this comes by the basic training that everyone serving will receive in becoming a *Force Multiplier*. As will be seen in the chapters to come, one of the responsibilities of the Safety Team is leading the training that transforms other ministries into Force Multipliers who enhance the safety of the church.

What is your role? Are you a leader in the church that is not going to be part of the Safety Team but will be a Force Multiplier? Are you a staff member, volunteer, or pastor? Whatever your role is, you must identify it and serve within that capacity. Regardless of the role, you can support the enhancement of the security and safety of the church by embracing the stewardship responsibility of keeping the congregation safe. You have a part to play in watching over the *ninety-nine*!

The lead pastor of the church will ultimately have to direct the enhancement of security by creating a Safety Team. More than likely this direction will come through the responsible delegation of duties. This will involve identifying and empowering people with the gifts and talents to serve as stewards of security. Therefore, when it comes to creating a Safety Team, the focus should be on discovering people with specific gifts and talents, not just recruiting people to fill spots on a roster.

The SLS strategy recognizes that protecting the *ninety-nine* is a matter of stewardship as is evangelizing the lost. There is no better group of people to lead the outreach effort to first responders than those serving on the Safety Team. That is why you must make it a priority to identify members of your congregation who have a calling to enhance the security of the church *and* facilitate outreach to first responders. Encourage team members to fulfill this dual responsibility. Failure to do so leaves the church vulnerable to attacks in both the spiritual and natural realms and it neglects outreach opportunities to the first responder community.

Regrettably, most churches consider enhancing the security of the church and conducting outreach to first responders as two mutually exclusive endeavors. This unfortunate view limits the church's ability to make it safer and reach first responders with the Gospel. It has been my experience that most churches fail to recognize that each area of ministry can effectively sharpen the other (Prov 27:17).[11] In the SLS strategy, the combination of security and outreach is essential and non-negotiable. Regardless of the size, location, or cultural makeup of your church, conducting outreach to first responders will enhance its security. Also, by enhancing the security of the church through interaction with first responders, outreach will occur. If you only want to increase security and are not concerned with outreach to first responders, the SLS strategy may not be for you.

† † †

SLS is a strategy that is Spirit led and therefore not secular. In both the spiritual and natural realms, evil schemes are constantly being devised to prey upon the church. Therefore, addressing church security cannot be limited to temporal conflict. The enhancement of church security must be founded on a biblical basis and engaged in spiritually. This biblical footing is essential to best equip the church in spiritual warfare and against temporal attacks. Therefore, members of the Safety

---

[11] Just as we can sharpen each other spiritually, working to secure the church will increase outreach opportunity to the first responder community. Through outreach to share the Gospel, we foster relationships that also enhance the safety and security of the church. Proverbs 27:17 says: "As iron sharpens iron, so one man sharpens another."

Team must be professed followers of the Lord or else their efforts will be limited to the natural realm.

SLS is a ministry that is very different than secular security. The tactical mission of the SLS strategy is to counter the constant threats against the church by taking strategic *Action* to *Deter*, *Avoid*, and *Mitigate* threats. The SLS mission begins in the spiritual realm, an area that secular options omit. Although there are many secular security resources available to assist the church in combating the temporal attacks, they unfortunately exclude God from their security equation. Thus, secular security is heavily restricted. A fundamental problem with that approach is its inability to address the need for securing the local church while remaining committed to the Great Commandment and Great Commission. Therefore, secular options do not have an answer for the problems presented by the Pastor's Paradox.

The main issue with secular security is twofold: 1)- It is not Christ-centered. 2)- It is not people-focused. Both SLS and secular security may sincerely act to enhance the safety of the church but the focus of the approach differs greatly. Whereas secular security is often fixated on keeping people out (like intruders), the SLS strategy presents a structure that seeks to bring people in (the lost). This is accomplished by maintaining a Safety Team with a focus on *stewardship*, *outreach*, and *discipleship*.

SLS will not sacrifice following the Great Commandment or Great Commission in order to enhance church security. It is a strategy to accomplish both. The core values of *stewardship*, *outreach*, and *discipleship* keep the ministry Christ-centered while empowering its ministerial ability.

As previously stated, a key part of the SLS structure is the establishment of a Safety Team. This team will create a relational partnership with first responders. That partnership makes the church safer and functions as a ministry. Secular security is not concerned with this type of relationship. However, the SLS strategy is Kingdom-focused and missional in its approach.

Every first responder who comes to attend the church through the outreach efforts of the Safety Team brings with them their professional knowledge, skills, and abilities to protect the *ninety-nine*. Security and outreach are mutually beneficial.

The Safety Team is the core of the SLS strategy. The team is practical concerning security and missional concerning the community. By employing concepts, tactics, and techniques that are covert, the Safety Team does not create a distraction during service. Internally, the team discovers, trains, and develops leaders who replicate its vision and operation which ensures the teams growth. Externally team members are stewards over outreach to the first responder community. They seek the lost while protecting the flock.

What is your role? Are you in a position to support the creation of the Safety Team? Are you a prospective team leader or member, are you serving in a different ministry that needs to be empowered as a Force Multiplier in security? Do you hear the call to pursue the *one* and protect the *ninety-nine*? If so, it's time to take action and get started.

Actions to Deter, Avoid, and Mitigate

ACTION: The ADAM acronym was designed to provide a framework for combating spiritual and temporal attacks. Like the innate call for self-preservation, it requires action to prevent, counter, and lessen the damage of an attack. The ADAM approach does not allow for inaction. Prior to a critical event you must be planning; during a critical event you must be executing.

In every situation take action! In times of preparation and in times of execution you must always do something! What are you currently doing to counter the threats you face and the threats the church faces? Do you have a plan, a designated ministry, or formulated concept? If not, start taking action now during the time of preparation.

Examples of *Actions* include prayer, training, tactics, and providing direction. Actions can be something as simple as moving out of the way of an attack or as complex as creating an Emergency Preparedness Plan. The ADAM strategy focuses on tactically combating spiritual and temporal attacks by taking *action* in the areas of *deterrence*, *avoidance*, and *mitigation*. Action, therefore is constantly required to strategize and execute plans.

There are many action steps you can take to combat threats. Some steps are simple and effective, others are more complicated and intense. Increasing one's *situational awareness* is a simple and very effective action step. Consistent prayer against threats is another positive action to take. Being a leader who inspires others to be situationally aware and engaged in prayer is an empowering action step. It is one that is greatly needed within the local church.

As you can see, taking action does not have a threshold that models the Hollywood imagery of a hero running through a burning building carrying a rescued victim while shooting endless amounts of bullets at the enemy. If that is your default idea of taking action, you are living in the land of make believe. Hollywood provides misleading presentations designed to generate revenue. SLS provides a practical application of skills that enhance security and reach the lost for Christ. Hollywood does not produce heroes or solutions to problems. They create fictional characters and alter reality to generate profit. Don't rely on fictional characters to formulate your action steps, look to professionals with properly conditioned hearts. I believe that you will find them in your congregation and through your outreach efforts to first responders.

Professionally, military and police members of the special operations and SWAT communities are involved in high risk missions throughout the United States and the world. Collectively they are a group of men and women who have been called to serve on the elite teams of their respective branches of government and agencies. A calling, selection process, and rite of passage precedes their designation as an operator or team member. The heart of that calling is a desire to serve where few others choose to explore and a commitment to those who serve alongside them. They rely on forged dependability, proper preparation, and securing victory. For these warriors, success in confronting violent threats begins in the heart with a call to be sent (Isa 6:8).[12] It is refined in proper planning, intense training, and the commitment to execute the mission. Their professional survival consists of constantly taking *Action* to *Deter*, *Avoid*, and *Mitigate* threats.

Even after these elite warriors leave their respective teams, units and departments, they still feel the call to serve in that capacity. Many say, "it is in my DNA." If you are gifted and "wired" this way, it is in you too. It is important to remember, *the call comes before the designation.* Therefore, your resume does not have to explain your calling. It can certainly demonstrate where you have applied it, but for some, that resume begins with being a warrior for the family, community, and church. Has He called you to a new designation?

The SLS strategy seeks Christian warriors but beware if this is "in" you. Embarking on a journey to fulfill your calling over the protection of the church brings with it a possible downside. Designation can result in pride. What starts out as a toehold can grow into a stronghold that assumes your identity. *Do not become a warrior for good when you are called to be a warrior for God!* Do not let your position or gifting become your identity. Never identify with the gift more than the Gift Giver.

My friends who are my brothers and sisters in Christ and have served in the armed forces, Central Intelligence Agency,

---

[12] Many men and women who serve in the military, police, and fire departments have a desire to serve. They are following a calling similar to that of Isaiah 6:8 which says: "Then I heard the voice of the Lord saying, 'Whom shall I send? And who will go for us?' And I said, 'Here am I, send me!'"

federal law enforcement agencies, SWAT teams, police and fire departments, and in emergency medical services know how quickly these careers can become one's identity. This too can happen at the local church within the security ministry. "Security" becomes a person's identity rather than a gifting. When this occurs, they must focus on the God that has gifted them and the people that they are serving. In *American Sniper,* Chris Kyle wrote: "It's taken a while, but I have gotten to a point where being a SEAL no longer defines me. I need to be a husband and a father. Those things, now are my first calling."[13] If you are going to be a member of the Safety Team, never forget your first calling and Who called you to it. To overcome the Pastor's Paradox, you must remain within the bookends of the Great Commandment and Great Commission as you serve. Love God, love people, and stand against evil and all its wicked schemes.

Former members of the military and law enforcement communities, especially those who were part of special operations units and SWAT teams, will struggle with finding a place to use their gifting after they have left that unit, team, or department. Although their priorities will change as they transition out of those capacities, their giftings can still be used for His glory. These men and women bring gifts and talents to your church that will enhance its security and reach other members of the military and first responder communities. The SLS strategy challenges you to discover these men and women and utilize their skills to empower your team.

Being in the military or a first responder does not have a monopoly over these abilities. You will discover people in your congregation and community who, like these operators, have a calling, commitment, attention to detail, and value of

---

[13] Chris Kyle, Scott McEwen and Jim DeFelice, American Sniper: The Autobiography of the Most Lethal Sniper in U.S. Military History (New York: Harper Collins, 2012) 375.

The Problem and Proposed Solution

others above themselves. Some will have experience as a first responder or member of the military, but most will not. If you seek first in prayer and in discovering the ones called to this ministry, then you are more likely to establish a Safety Team with Kingdom-focused members. Discovering the people called to the security ministry is a foundational action you must take in establishing your Safety Team.

Regardless of your role in the SLS system, with the proper heart and mindset, you can set yourself up for success by taking action. Proper preparation will correctly place you in the best position to prevent, counter, or lessen an attack. In order to be successful, you must execute proper planning and effective training. Appropriately done, this will prepare you to correctly determine the type of action that you will need to employ at your church before, during, and after a critical event. With a foundation of prayer and stewardship, a pure heart, and proper mindset you can avoid the paralyzing effects of fear and pride. Each of these can foster inaction which will ultimately lead to failure. Set yourself up for success; take *Action* to *Deter*, *Avoid*, or *Mitigate* threats now through prayer, planning, and preparation.

Action to:
Deter
Avoid
Mitigate threats

The ADAM Concept.

DETERRENCE: Every action should have a purpose. In the SLS strategic context, the first type of action to take is adopting a deterrence strategy against threats in the spiritual and natural realms. *Deterrence* begins with actions to prevent a threat from becoming an attack. This begins in the spiritual realm with prayer. It also involves creating an Emergency Preparedness Plan, a Safety Team, procedures to handle threats, and contingency planning. Deterrence includes training the Safety Team and church staff on how to respond to emergencies. It also contains measures to make your church a hard target by having an overt police presence, making other ministries overt Force Multipliers to the Safety Team, addressing the lighting and physical features inside and outside of the building, and considering other resources such as medical equipment, weapons, cameras, and radios. These are just some of the actions that you may choose to employ to deter attacks that will be covered in this book.

AVOIDANCE: Action to create deterrence is part of the due diligence you should take to counter threats. But, what do you do if the attack still comes despite your best efforts to deter it? The answer is, you must act and prepare for what is coming to avoid being directly hit. Make no mistake, there are motivated actors who are committed to attack the church. For this type of individual, most types of deterrence will not be enough. An extreme example is an assailant who assumes that he/she will be killed during the course of the attack. Think of a suicide bomber, an active shooter who plans on being killed during the attack, or people who intentionally seek to be killed during the attack (suicide by cop). The effectiveness of deterrence is close to non-existent when assailants do not value their own life.

Therefore, when you see that an attack is coming, you must act to *avoid* being directly hit. *Avoidance* is very different than deterrence. Whereas deterrence is a strategy to prevent a threat from becoming an attack, avoidance is taking actions to circumvent being directly hit. Avoidance only works if you see that the attack is coming. Therefore, the key to avoidance is situational awareness. If you are not situationally aware, the attack will blindside you. This is why proper mental preparation and training in situational awareness are necessary to be effective and are covered comprehensively in chapter three.

MITIGATION: Finally, if you are beyond the ability to avoid a direct attack and are engaged in the fight, you must have a *mitigation* strategy. Proper mitigating actions serve to reduce the detrimental effects of the attack. Mitigating actions also stop the bleeding, lessen the damage, and counter the attack. They are the last resort and a crucial element that must be planned for. The following examples are used to reinforce the point of employing *Action* to *Deter*, *Avoid*, and *Mitigate* threats.

Illustration 1: Imagine if you are going to take a late-night walk. In order to deter someone from robbing you, you decide to bring a flashlight. Walking with the flashlight provides the ability to illuminate the area around you. When you use it, others see it and it becomes a form of *deterrence*. This is an action you have taken to dissuade a person from taking advantage of the dark shadows of the night to rob you. Finally, it is an action that would not be out of place for anyone walking at night. Therefore, you are not creating a distraction by utilizing a flashlight. For everyone else who sees you walking with a flashlight, you appear normal.

In this hypothetical situation, imagine that a person is suspiciously standing in the shadow near a bench in the direction that you are walking. The way he focuses his attention in your direction prompts you to use the flashlight to fully illuminate the area around you. Despite your attempt to *deter* the person from threatening you, he begins to walk in your direction. He is rapidly closing the gap between the two of you. Immediately, you sense that this threat has transitioned into an attack.

Since the use of the flashlight as a *deterrent* was not enough, your next action is to *avoid* the oncoming attack. Therefore, you cross the street and begin walking on the sidewalk opposite of the suspicious person. Unfortunately, your attempt to *avoid* the attack fails and he crosses the street. He is now, once again closing in on you. Within a few steps he is upon you, challenging you, and you find yourself in the middle of the attack. It is now time to *mitigate* the damage.

Because you were situationally aware and perceived the attack before it started, you are able to dodge the first punch thrown at you. Rather than being hit in the head, you *mitigated* the damage to a glancing blow that impacts your shoulder. Situational awareness has bought you precious time to avoid being the victim of an overwhelming attack. In addition, it has allowed you to take action to protect your life. You swing the flashlight and strike the attacker as you run away. Therefore, you *mitigated* the damage of the attack to a glancing blow to your shoulder, you countered the attack, and you created an opportunity to escape. By following the ADAM acronym, you altered the way that this encounter could have ended. You were able to escape which is far better than being beaten and robbed.

In the same way the ADAM acronym was applied in this individual situation, it can be utilized to combat threats anywhere. Although this book is focused on the worship environment of the local church in the United States, the principles and techniques are equally beneficial for missionaries, and Christian organizations. The principles and tactics of Security Ministry Basic Training have proven to be beneficial for the workplace, in school, and out in public.

In this second illustration, you will see how the practical application of *Actions* to *Deter*, *Avoid*, and *Mitigate* threats is applicable to the local church.

Illustration 2: For this example, the setting is your local church on a Sunday morning. Imagine that service has begun and late arriving guests are making their way into the church. A car pulls into the parking lot, circles around three times, and eventually parks. The car sits there and no one gets out. Fortunately, part of your SLS plan for *deterrence* includes an off-duty police presence during service. If the sight of a visible police car deters a person from committing an attack, then the deterrent presence of the police officer was successful.

The overt presence of a police officer is a *deterrent* that attackers must overcome. Unfortunately, its success is not measurable because we generally don't know how many people see the deterrent and choose not to commit an act. Despite this, deterrence is highly effective. In this illustration, everyone hopes that the person parked in the car is deterred by the sight of the law enforcement officer. Upon sight of the officer, this suspicious person must recalculate their attack if they had not previously planned for it. The attacker knows that if he chooses to commit a crime, he has to face a police presence.

Ideally, once a person with criminal intent sees the presence of the police officer, he is deterred and chooses to drive away. However, for the purpose of this illustration, that does not occur. This person is committed to their evil act and is not deterred by the police presence. He gets out of the vehicle and proceeds toward the church entrance. As the suspicious person makes his way into the church, no one can tell if he is a first-time guest, lost, looking for someone, or a person with nefarious intent.

Fortunately, the suspicious person was observed by your Safety Team. They have been watching him since he was suspiciously sitting in the car. They have been surveilling him without being detected or creating a distraction to the worship service. Their surveillance began as he exited the car and continued as he proceeded to walk inside the church building. Neither the suspicious person nor the congregation knows that the Safety Team has been watching him and communicating his actions. They are covertly observing him.

The members of the Safety Team do not wear anything identifying them as being affiliated with the church. There is no security badge, lanyard, or clothing that links them to serving on the Safety Team. Their dress code allows them to look like church members. Because of this tactic, they are able to blend in and follow the person into the sanctuary without being detected. This is a low-visibility surveillance tactic.

While surveilling the suspicious person, the Safety Team communicates their observations with the ushers. Concerning security, the ushers are Force Multipliers for the Safety Team. They provide the Safety Team additional resources to conduct surveillance without anything appearing to be out of place. This allows the Safety Team and ushers to work together to effectively surveil the suspicious person. The tactics used by the ushers (overt) and Safety Team (covert) work well because they have trained together, know each other's role, and use proper tactics to observe and communicate suspicious activity.

In this scenario, the suspicious person has entered the building and sits down on an aisle seat in the sanctuary. His intentions are unknown but, his suspicious demeanor requires attention. He must be constantly observed. His description, location, and actions must be efficiently and effectively communicated to others. Therefore, the covert Safety Team members discreetly sit in areas where they can observe him while blending into the congregation. Thus, they avoid detection. Neither the suspicious person nor the congregation is disturbed by the low-visibility Safety Team. Most importantly, the service is not disrupted at all; no one in the congregation is distracted. Even at the height of the surveillance, nobody's worship experience is affected.

The ushers in the sanctuary have been advised of the suspicious person via coordinated cell phone text message groups that were pre-established. Without any interruption to the ongoing service, the ushers and the Safety Team have been able to focus on the threat and place themselves in advantageous positions. If the suspicious person decides to conduct any type of attack, they are covertly poised to respond. In addition, the Safety Team's observations have been communicated to the police officer working the security detail at the church. Before

The Problem and Proposed Solution

the attack initiates, the officer is informed and takes an innocuous position of advantage to respond if needed.

If the suspicious person does nothing, there is no disruption to service. Everyone returns to their responsibilities and the service is not disturbed. If this occurs, the entire event results in a successful surveillance of a suspicious person that will be documented. It is an overall victory for the team. However, for this scenario imagine that the following events occur.

Returning to the scenario, the suspicious man yells out an inaudible phrase and begins to run towards the pulpit. Since the Safety Team has positioned themselves in an advantageous way, they have prevented the suspicious person from getting far before being confronted. In addition, the police officer who had been alerted by the Safety Team immediately assists in the removal of the man. The police officer is no longer acting as a deterrent, *he is taking law enforcement action!* For the church, this is preferable as he is a trained professional able to handle the situation. This takes the burden of responsibility off of the Safety Team and the church when law enforcement action becomes necessary.

For the sake of the illustration, imagine that the attacker had a knife and planned on stabbing the pastor. Fortunately, the damage of the attack was *mitigated* away from injuring or killing the pastor to a mere disturbance during the service resulting in the arrest of the assailant. Early observation of the suspicious person and proper tactics led to a successful mitigation of the attack. In the absence of the Safety Team that identified the suspicious person early on and the presence of the police officer, the assailant would not have been identified until he lunged towards the pastor while wielding a knife. That result would have been catastrophic.

† † †

Actions to *Deter, Avoid and Mitigate* threats can be very successful. Is your church able to provide security like this?

Could it provide that type of surveillance without creating a distraction to the service? Can it do it while also fostering outreach to first responders? If a person perpetrates an attack like this, is your church prepared to act? If not, use the recommendations in this book to enhance the security of your church.

A great deal of effort is required to establish a Safety Team that operates as was depicted in the preceding illustration. Success demands proper planning, intense training, commitment, and the ability to act when needed. It is a Kingdom-focused, Christ-centered low/no cost way of enhancing the safety and security of the church. One of the first steps to take towards a functional security ministry is discovering and empowering people within the church who are called to be a part of it.

In the preceding example, the only financial cost to the church was to hire a police officer to be present during service. The entire Safety Team is a zero-cost group of individuals serving in the Kingdom. All you need to do is discover who they are and empower them. This book provides you with recommendations to get your team there. Your Emergency Preparedness Plan and Safety Team will be a product of your actions. If you develop them correctly, they will enhance the security of the church and foster outreach to the first responder community.

As good stewards of what God has provided, it is recommended you establish a comprehensive Emergency Preparedness Plan and Safety Team regardless of the size, location, or configuration of your church. By doing this, you are taking preemptive steps against the evil threat that lurks in the darkness prowling for prey (1 Pet. 5:8-9).[14] Never put your guard down and ignore the fact that the devil is always looking

---

[14] Together, we have the same enemy who is looking to attack. 1 Peter 5:8-9 says: "Be self-controlled and alert. Your enemy the devil prowls around like a roaring lion looking for someone to devour. Resist him, standing firm in the faith, because you know that your brothers throughout the world are undergoing the same kind of suffering."

The Problem and Proposed Solution

for an opportunity to steal, kill, and destroy the mission of your church (John 10:10).[15] This is why you must constantly *Act* to *Deter*, *Avoid*, and *Mitigate* the evil schemes targeting your church.

Your church is always under the threat of an attack. Changing conditions will raise or lower the threat level, but at any given time, an attack may occur. Therefore, you must continually *Act* to *Deter*, *Avoid*, and *Mitigate* threats. This is more than just growing in your understanding of the threat, action is necessary. James taught that listening to what has been said is important but of greater importance is following through with what you have been taught (Jas 1:22).[16] What is being said must not only be heard but accepted (Prov 4:10).[17] James explains that "anyone who listens to the word but does not do what it says is like a man who looks at his face in a mirror and, after looking at himself, goes away and immediately forgets what he looks like" (Jas 1:23-24). When it comes to *securing the congregation and reaching the lost*, don't be like that man who forgot what he looks like, listen to instruction and do not ignore it (Prov 8:33).[18]

---

[15] "The thief comes only to steal, kill and destroy; I have come that they may have life, and have it to the full" (John 10:10).

[16] Each church should look at the information provided in this book and adopt and adapt what is beneficial to the vision and mission of the church. However, to blatantly ignore responsibility is not acceptable. Ask the Lord to lead you in your discernment and application of the recommendations provided. James tells us, "Do not merely listen to the word and so deceive yourselves. Do what it says" (James 1:22).

[17] Proverbs 4:10 and 8:33 reinforce the point being made: "Listen my son, accept what I say, and the years of your life will be many" (Prov 4:10).

[18] Seek God first and His wisdom as how to overcome the Pastor's Paradox: "Listen to my instruction and be wise; do not ignore it" (Prov 8:33).

As a leader, listen to what is being recommended and avoid being deceived into a false sense of security. Adopt and adapt these recommendations to fit *within the vision of your church* and make sure you take *Action* to *Deter*, *Avoid*, and *Mitigate* threats. Finally, never forget that all of our gracefully-given gifts and talents (and those of the people around us) are not for our benefit; they are for others' growth and His glory. Therefore, use them to glorify the Lord by pursuing the *one* and *protecting the ninety-nine*.

Chapter 2

The Biblical Basis

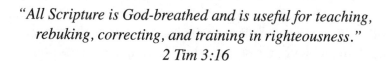

"All Scripture is God-breathed and is useful for teaching, rebuking, correcting, and training in righteousness."
2 Tim 3:16

*O*ur stewardship over security requires that we return to the core of Christianity for direction, sustainment, and purpose. The root cause of the malicious attacks on the modern church are from the same evil the early church faced. The modern church is armed with the Bible and the guidance of the Holy Spirit. We are at war in the spiritual and natural realm against the evil that causes injustice as it seeks to steal, kill, and destroy us. The Word is the weaponry we have been provided to use against this evil threat (Gen 1; John 1:1-3; 4:24; 3:6-8; Col 1:15-17; Heb 1:1-3).

It is very common to seek individual Scriptures to *inspire the troops in truth* as we go from battle to battle. For example, Isaiah 8:9-10 states: "Raise the war cry, you nations, and be shattered! Listen, all you distant lands. Prepare for battle, and be shattered! Devise your strategy, but it will be thwarted;

propose your plan, but it will not stand, for God is with us."[19] These verses are motivational as they convey the Lord's power and truth. However, this exclamation is not enough to form the basis for a security ministry. Additional guidance must be found throughout the Bible. Therefore, it is appropriate to look to the Bible with questions such as: what did Jesus model and how did the early church function concerning security?

The biblical basis of the SLS strategy has a foundation that consists of *prayer* and *stewardship*. Resting on this foundation are four pillars which represent four biblical themes to consider when addressing security. They are: *Wisdom*, *Controlling Fear*, *Action*, and *Vigilance*. On the prayer side of the foundation we *acquire* wisdom and an increased faith that overcomes fear. The stewardship side of the foundation *requires* our action and vigilance.

This section of the book will look at the prayer side of the foundation before moving on to the stewardship side. The prayer side of the foundation offers each of us the opportunity to acquire wisdom and faith; the stewardship side requires our action and vigilance. The following image contains verses that will aid in understanding the SLS biblical basis. These verses within the four themes have been inspirational to the SLS strategy and should help guide your security ministry and Safety Team.

---

[19] Here Isaiah provides us a warning and prophesy. Later in verse 17 he shows us that we are to trust in God's timing and not in our plans. "I will wait for the Lord, who is hiding his face from the house of Jacob. I will put my trust in him" (Isa 8:17).

Spirit Led Security: Biblical Basis

Wisdom	Controlling Fear	Action	Vigilance
• Matt 10:16	• Deut 31:6	• John 8:59	• Matt 10:17
• Prov 4:25-27	• Ps 27:1-3	• John 10:39	• 1 Pet 5:8
• Jas 1:5	• 2 Tim 1:7	• John 7:1	• Mark 13:33
• Jas 3:17	• 1 Pet 2:19	• John 11:54	• Matt 24:42-44
• 1 Corn 1:30	• Josh 1:8-9	• Acts 9:29-30	• Neh 4:9
• Eph 1:17	• Eph 6	• Acts 14:5-7	• Neh 4:13
• Prov 24:3-4	• Ps 91	• Acts 20:3	• Neh 4:22
• Jas 3:13-14	• Heb 10:23	• Jas 1:22	• Neh 4:23
	• Matt 5:16	• Luke 21:36	• Luke 22:36
			• Luke 22:38

Prayer — Stewardship

The SLS Biblical Basis.

Foundation of Prayer

"In the same way, the Spirit helps us in our weakness. We do not know what we ought to pray for, but the Spirit himself intercedes for us through wordless groans. And he who searches our hearts knows the mind of the Spirit, because the Spirit intercedes for God's people in accordance with the will of God."
Romans 8:26-27

Every endeavor in ministry must begin in prayer. Prayer is the first step in enhancing the security of the church. Security is as much (if not more) a spiritual matter as it is temporal. Therefore, comprehensive security cannot come from secular government or private actors alone. It must come from what the Bible has taught. Thus, a biblical foundation is necessary.

True security only comes to light through a Christian conceptual lens. The SLS approach is to establish a God-centered ministry engaged in prayer, rooted in faith (Jas 5:13).[20] Although your security ministry may involve entities outside of the church (for example: government, police, or private sector security professionals), it should never be exclusively a secular endeavor. A SLS ministry is centered on values of servanthood and outreach. This is a different approach than what is taken by secular security.

Secular security says: "be afraid and do something to prepare for the attack," whereas the SLS strategy says: "overcome fear with faith and *Act* to *Deter*, *Avoid*, and *Mitigate* an attack." Secular security begins its planning from a position of fear; SLS acknowledges fear, overcomes its negative aspects through faith, and begins its planning from a position of peace. This is not a position of arrogance but one that has resulted from the grace that God has provided. The Lord has given each of us a measure of faith and it is up to us to use it accordingly (Rom 12:3).[21]

Pillar of Wisdom

"By wisdom a house is built, and through understanding it is established; through knowledge its rooms are filled with rare and beautiful treasures." Proverbs 24:3-4

When building a house, an error in the foundation can set you up for disaster. The same can be said for building a security ministry. As you move towards enhancing the security of your

---

[20] James 5:13 tells us to always be in prayer and praise. "Is any one of you in trouble? He should pray. Is anyone happy? Let him sing songs of praise."

[21] Paul tells us, "For by the grace given me, I say to every one of you: Do not think yourself more highly than you ought, but rather think of yourself with sober judgment, in accordance with the measure of faith God has given you" (Rom 12:3).

church and establishing a sustained outreach to first responders, strive for godly wisdom to direct your decision making. Every step you take to enhance the security of the church should be preceded by prayer. This includes meetings, security planning, establishing and building the Safety Team, and in service.

Historically, the spreading of the Gospel has been met with rejection and violence. Fortunately, the same godly wisdom that guided the early church remains with the modern church through the power of the Holy Spirit. As you *Act* to *Deter*, *Avoid*, or *Mitigate* an attack, do so with the guidance of the Holy Spirit. When rejection comes, seek wisdom over ignorance, faith over fear, action over paralysis, and humility over pride.

Church leadership has to address the Pastor's Paradox and maintain a balance between security and vulnerability. Too much security will impede your ability to fulfill the Great Commandment and Great Commission, too little security will leave those you are bestowed to protect vulnerable. Because the stakes are so high, wisdom is necessary in determining the type and amount of security you will employ. Wise choices will allow you to remain Kingdom- focused and overcome the Pastor's Paradox.

Be wise to act but not over react. If churches become armed fortresses, like castles or embassies, how will they be able to openly welcome people in need? However, if church leaders do nothing to provide for the safety of the congregating, they are failing as stewards of what the Lord has provided. Seek wisdom to balance security and vulnerability while seeking the lost.

James gives insight on how to make wise decisions. He writes: "If any of you lacks wisdom, you should ask God, who gives generously to all without finding fault, and it will be given to you" (Jas 1:5). This underscores the importance of praying before action. Believers should always seek God first through prayer. *It is far better to pray ahead of what may come, than to rely on prayer as a last resort.*

In James chapter three, we find a description of the characteristics of godly wisdom. He states that "the wisdom that comes from heaven is first of all pure; then peace-loving, considerate, submissive, full of mercy and good fruit, impartial and sincere" (Jas 3:17-18).[22] Heavenly wisdom is not self-seeking. Your Safety Team's success will rest upon maintaining the characteristics outlined by James and remaining focused on *stewardship*, *outreach*, and *discipleship*. Nothing should be done out of selfish ambition or vain conceit (Phil 2:3).[23] When security is a matter of stewardship, humility becomes a characteristic of the team. Finally, the Bible tells us that deeds performed in humility come from wisdom (Jas 3:13-16).[24]

As you discover members for your Safety Team make, sure that their character displays humility and service. Being part of a group of like-minded individuals on a Safety Team can be very rewarding. But giving out the title of *Safety Team Member* can create an inflated sense of empowerment. Therefore, the battle against prideful empowerment should be waged early on during the team building process. Your Safety Team leader will play a vital role in the war against pride. This is why it is wise to

---

[22] Godly wisdom is the opposite of secular foolishness. James wrote: "But the wisdom that comes from heaven is first of all pure; then peace-loving, considerate, submissive, full of mercy and good fruit, impartial and sincere. Peacemakers who sow in peace raise a harvest of righteousness" (Jas 3:17-18).

[23] Security over the church is about stewardship and not self-gratification. Paul warns: "Do nothing out of selfish ambition or vain conceit, but in humility consider others better than yourselves" (Phil 2:3).

[24] James also warns against selfish ambition: "Who is wise and understanding among you? Let him show it by his good life, by deeds done in the humility that comes from wisdom. But if you harbor bitter envy and selfish ambition in your hearts, do not boast about it or deny the truth. Such 'wisdom' does not come down from heaven but is earthly, unspiritual, of the devil. For where you have envy and selfish ambition, there you find disorder and every evil practice" (Jas 3:13-16).

seek and discover the right person for the position. Do not foolishly plug people into positions that they are not called to be in.

Jesus warned His disciples about the evil that exists. He gave instruction on how to act as they departed to spread the Gospel. Jesus said, "I am sending you out like sheep among wolves. Therefore, be as shrewd as snakes and as innocent as doves" (Matt 10:16). It is not by physical power or might, but by the wisdom of the Holy Spirit that you will be victorious (Zech 4:6).[25] Only through the guidance of His wisdom shall the Safety Team deploy on this vital mission of confronting evil while following the Great Commandment and Great Commission.

Pillar of Controlling Fear:

"Do not let this Book of the Law depart from your mouth; meditate on it day and night, so that you may be careful to do everything written in it. Then you will be prosperous and successful. Have I not commanded you? Be strong and courageous. Do not be terrified; do not be discouraged, for the Lord your God will be with you wherever you go."
Joshua 1:8-9

Fear can destroy a team and an individual. The enemy uses fear to steal potential. Fear can cause church leadership to not want to create a Safety Team. It can attack by causing worry about financial cost or unmerited concern about what others might think the team may look like. Fear can attack in the form of a non-supportive congregation. Some may say that

---

[25] "So he said to me, 'This is the word of the Lord to Zerubbabel: 'Not by might nor by power, but by my Spirit,' says the Lord Almighty'" (Zech 4:6). It is the wisdom of the Holy Spirit, not a trust in human abilities, that we find the source of victory.

the church does not need to worry about safety, "God has it under control."

For individuals called to be a member of the Safety Team, the fear of serving can keep them from fulfilling their purpose. People may be reluctant to serve because of a lack of experience in safety and security. Finally, the fear can cause paralysis by inhibiting action before, during, or after a critical event. This is a destructive type of fear that can cost lives.

The SLS approach does not let fear direct or inhibit action. Since faith can conquer the negative effects of fear, SLS begins from a position of peace not fear. It is faith that defeats the negativity that fear brings. The Lord gave us a measure of faith as a weapon to use in spiritual and natural battles against the injustice of evil. Philippians 4:6 says, "Do not worry about anything, instead, pray about everything. Tell God what you need and thank Him for all he has done. Then you will experience God's peace, which exceeds anything we can understand. His peace will guard your hearts and minds as you live in Christ Jesus" (Phil 4:6-7).[26] Peace, not fear will guard our hearts. It is the condition of the heart that is the difference between SLS and secular security. SLS comes from a position of peace, secular security operates as a response to fear.

When fear emerges, you must take *action* and pray! Prayer is relational as it connects the person praying with God. And by God it connects the people praying together. Relational prayer produces a peace that guards the heart and mind of the believer and therefore is a foundational trait of the SLS ministry. This is how the SLS strategy starts from a position of peace and not one of fear.

---

[26] Note: Taken from the New Living Translation: "Don't worry about anything; instead, pray about everything. Tell God what you need, and thank him for all he has done. Then you will experience God's peace, which exceeds anything we can understand" (Phil 4:6-7 NLT).

The Biblical Basis

† † †

The members of the Safety Team serve by standing watch against evil attacks. The dangers that these threats bring are real and the damage that they may cause can be catastrophic. Therefore, effort must be made to control the effects that fear has on an individual or group. When danger lurks, fear will try to creep in and try to derail your attempts to counter it. Fear may come at the planning phase of the security ministry or during a critical event. Whenever fear attacks, be prepared in your role to counter it. That way, when the attack comes, you will be able to stand your ground and when you have done all that you can, you will remain standing (Eph 6:13).[27]

Fear is a cognitive or emotional label for nonspecific physiological arousal in response to a threat.[28] Members of the military and police do not deny its presence, they just do a good job of controlling their response to it. Fear is an automatic emotional reaction to a perceived danger or threat that is characterized by a high state of arousal.[29] Fear is the ultimate stress in that it can inhibit function. It can cause paralysis in ministry, marriage, leadership, and in developing a church security plan. The ramifications of not being able to control fear can lead to catastrophic consequences.

Despite all of this, fear also has positive attributes that cannot be ignored. For everyone, not just those in the military,

---

[27] "Therefore put on the full armor of God so that when the day of evil comes, you may be able to stand your ground, and after you have done everything, to stand" (Eph 6:13).

[28] Dave Grossman and Bruce Siddle, "The Psychological Effects of Combat," Human Factor Research Group (2018): 1, accessed on August 7, 2018, www.hfrg.org/wp-content/uploads/Psychological_Effects.pdf.pdf.

[29] Michael J. Asken, Dave Grossman, and Loren W. Christensen, *Warrior Mindset: Mental Toughness Skills for a Nation's Peacekeepers* (Millstadt, IL: Warrior Science Publications, 2010), 77.

law enforcement, or firefighters and EMS personnel, the onset of fear should be taken as a warning sign. It signals the need for caution and produces a readiness to respond.[30] Controlling fear means acknowledging the warning, replacing the influence of fear with faith, and responding with the appropriate action.[31]

This response is a wise and responsible counter to the attack of fear. It is not attempting to be fearless. Striving to be fearless is dangerous because a fearless person is a careless person. We strive to control fear, we acknowledge its warnings and make wise decisions. Do not ignore fear as doing so will create recklessness. Rather, face fear head on and control it. By doing so you will operate from a position that allows you to be courageous.

A strong theme throughout the Bible is the replacement of fear with faith, weakness with strength in the Lord, and paralysis with purpose. After all, is it possible to have courage if there is no fear? I do not believe so. We cannot attain courage without experiencing fear and then overcoming it.[32] The ability to overcome the detrimental effects of fear require us to recognize it, possess faith, and receive wisdom from the Lord. Then, wise decisions can be made and actions taken to fulfill a specific purpose. This is when a person becomes *courageous*.

Courage comes from the Lord's mighty power. With it, you can stand to confront the enemy and, in the end, remain standing (Eph 6). Deuteronomy 31:6 commands: "Be strong and courageous. Do not be afraid or terrified because of them, for the Lord your God goes with you; he will never leave you

---

[30] Asken, *Warrior Mindset*, 78.

[31] Note: In *Warrior Mindset,* Asken identifies six types of fear: Realistic Fear, Fear of the Unknown, Anxiety, Illogical Fear, Fear of Failure, and Fun Fear. Each type of fear can be addressed by psychological techniques which allow the individual to manage fear and its impact on decision making. See *Warrior Mindset* chapter four, Condition Black: Stress, Fear and Mental Toughness.

[32] Asken, *Warrior Mindset*, 77.

nor forsake you." Psalm 91, shows how God covers His people and under Him they find refuge. His faithfulness is our shield and armor that provides protection (Ps 91:4).[33] Our faith and His faithfulness can overcome the detrimental effects of fear. Therefore, we must do as the author of Hebrews says in chapter 10 verse 23 and hold on to our faith without wavering because God, the one who promised, is faithful.

Be confident in the courage that you have found in the Lord. This type of confidence is recorded in the Psalms: "The Lord is my light and my salvation; whom shall I fear? The Lord is the stronghold of my life; of whom shall I be afraid? When evil men advance against me to devour my flesh, when my enemies and foes attack me, they will stumble and fall. Though an army besiege me, my heart will not fear, though war break out against me, even then will I be confident" (Ps 27:1-3). In the New Testament Paul wrote, "For God did not give us a spirit of timidity, but a spirit of power, of love and of self-discipline" (2 Tim 1:7). Fear can become paralyzing, but your faith and God's faithfulness are the ultimate weapons forged to combat the negative effects of fear.

When courage overcomes fear, it places you in a position to help others and save lives. One way that God can use you is by placing you in a position to help others. But you have to choose to act. When we act to help others and glorify the Lord, He recognizes our actions. Others see it as well and that gives us the opportunity to glorify God. In the Gospel of Matthew, it is recorded that believers are the salt and the light of the earth. The Bible says that Christians cannot lose their saltiness or hide their light because of fear. Jesus said, "let your light shine before me, that they may see your good deeds and praise your

---

[33] In the theme of protection, the author of Psalm 91 promises the Lord's presence through times of danger. "He will cover you with his feather. He will shelter you with his wings. His faithful promises are your armor and protection" (Ps 91:4 NLT).

Father in heaven" (Matt 5:16). To lose one's saltiness, is to lose their flavor and value. In the end, this renders them useless (Matt 5:13).[34] Stay salty!

Fear that produces inaction renders us useless. To hide one's light, diminish it, or deny it when the situation becomes dangerous, can be a result of the inability to control fear. Its paralyzing effects can influence the decisions that we make. Therefore, rather than being led by fear, take action and let His light shine through you. Be strong in faith and in courage. Control fear, do not let it control you.

When fear creates an emotional warning that something dangerous may be ahead, listen to it, but do not be overcome by it. Controlling fear allows us to be ready to respond and that readiness places us in a position to be courageous and help others. We must make preparation, take action, and help the people who have been placed in our lives. This must be done even if that means confronting danger head on. Because fear causes paralysis, we must seek faith that empowers us to fulfill our purpose. That process begins in prayer. From a position of prayer we grow our faith, draw closer to the Lord, and find peace. Thus, *we start from a position of peace and not fear.*

† † †

As you plan, create, and begin to use a Safety Team, start from a position of peace. Reinforce the importance of keeping prayer a priority. It leads you down the path of controlling fear. In the SLS structure prayer must precede all security planning and remain constant in all things, on all occasions (1 Tim 2:1; Mark 1:35; Jude 20; 1 Cor 14:15; Eph 6:18). Prayer is

---

[34] If we are not affecting the world around us for His glory, what good is it? We must remain salty in both our pursuit of the lost and protection of the church. Matthew wrote: "You are the salt of the earth. But if the salt loses its saltiness, how can it be made salty again? It is no longer good for anything, except to be thrown out and trampled by men" (Matt 5:13).

essential in seeking the guidance of the Holy Spirit for discernment. It is through prayer that you receive the wisdom on how to best enhance security without sacrificing the vision the Lord has provided for your church. A Kingdom-focused security ministry is Christ-centered and engages in spiritual warfare by praying without ceasing. Paul advised the church in Thessalonica, "pray continually" regardless of circumstance (1 Thess 5:17). Prayer demonstrates that the security ministry is not controlled by fear. Rather, through a faith that produces peace and courage.

As Christians focus attention on security, they address the plethora of difficult situations facing the church. Any and all of them can cause fear. On any given day the attack may come in the form of an active shooter, domestic issue, robbery, theft, or disturbance during service. This is why believers must pray continually against these threats (1 Thess 5:17; Phil 4:6). The SLS Safety Team must be prepared to address all of the types of schemes and attacks that come in both the natural and spiritual realms. The Safety Team must be committed to the initiation of spiritual warfare in the spiritual realm and then transcend into the natural realm.

Prayer begins with a focus on God and His Kingdom. Oswalt Chambers once said that "we have to pray with our eyes on God, not the difficulties." Chambers does not ignore the difficulties, as some choose to do. Rather, he suggests that we stay focused on God through them. The security ministry must commit to focused prayer as a preemptive move against the threats that seek to steal, kill, and destroy the church. Through preemptive prayer we invite God into securing the church rather than just praying to Him as a last resort when an attack comes.

Believers are commanded "not to worry about anything." Instead, to "seek God in prayer about everything." Paul instructs: "tell God what you need and thank him for all he has done" (Phil 4:6 NLT). This is how believers can experience God's peace "which exceeds anything we can understand" (Phil

4:7 NLT). Although Paul is speaking specifically about a way to combat worry with prayer, it is applicable to the security ministry for combating fear. Both fear and worry steal our peace. We cannot afford for it to be taken from us. Peace is the state of mind that we seek to achieve before planning, taking action, or recovering after an attack. Obtaining peace comes through the refinement of the heart, overcoming fear, and preparing for battle. All of these start in prayer!

If you fail to train your team on the importance of prayer, you set the security ministry up for failure. The evil forces moving against the church demonstrate the need to pray *every day* against the schemes and attacks emerging from the spiritual and natural realms (Eph 6). But, no matter the circumstance, no matter the pending threat or attack, pray in faith with a focus on God (Jas 5:13; Heb 6:11). The best way to concentrate on God and not the threatening difficulties is to begin with reassured faith that leads to focused and undivided prayer. James states: "when you ask Him, be sure that your faith is in God alone. Do not waver, for a person with divided loyalty is as unsettled as a wave of the sea that is blown and tossed by the wind (Jas 1:6 NLT). It cannot be said enough how important that it is to begin every aspect of the security ministry in prayer. This includes praying against all of the evil attacks that have yet to occur and the schemes that are secretly being plotted against the church.

Pray with preemptive expectation; do not just rely on prayer as a last resort. Remember, prayer is the ultimate weapon and, in some cases, the only weapon that works. In Mark chapter 9, Jesus healed a demon-possessed man. Previously, the disciples were not able to drive the demon out of him (Mark 9:14-17). Later, the disciples inquired as to why they failed. Jesus said to them, "This kind cannot be driven out by anything but prayer" (Mark 9:29 ESV). This account reminds everyone that humanity is limited. However, through Godly focus and prayer, Christians can witness His supernatural work which exceeds human ability.

There are difficult situations that can only be resolved through prayer. Therefore, refusing to appeal to the Holy Spirit will leave your Safety Team wide open to difficulties that they are powerless to address. This is why secular security is helpless in many situations. Unfortunately, you too can become powerless if you do not invite God into every aspect of securing the church. For the SLS ministry, that invitation starts in prayer.

SLS constantly acknowledges its dependence on God. Prayer is where it maintains its perspective and acknowledges who sits on the throne. Through prayer, SLS emphasizes that it is not by our strength or might that we succeed, rather it is only by His Spirit that we are victorious. Prayer, faith, peace, and courage will allow you to overcome the fear trying to prevent you from creating a Safety Team, serving as part of a security ministry, or taking action when you are being attacked.

Foundation of Stewardship

"Each should use whatever gift he has received to serve others, faithfully administering God's grace in its various forms." 1 Peter 4:10

Security within the church involves stewardship at every level of leadership. It begins with the vision of the pastor and is delegated to responsible people who become stewards over the functional security ministry. This includes the staff, church leaders, and the people serving in various roles during service. It is a large responsibility to comprehensively cover the church with security. It requires efficient planning and dedication by everyone involved to be successful. Delegation of responsibility is required to function efficiently but is never an excuse to pass down the role you are being held accountable for. If handled correctly, the delegation of responsibility will model the principles that Jethro presented to Moses in Exodus 18.

Robert Welch, former Dean of the Southwest Theological Baptist Seminary School of Educational Ministries[35] looked at the role of the shepherd in *Serving by Safeguarding Your Church*. He used the example of Psalm 23 where the lone shepherd was described as being armed with a rod and a staff to ward off danger. He explains that once the sheep were brought in the shepherd became the "door" at the entranceway, even sleeping at the opening in order to secure the sheep.[36] From this example we can see how the shepherd is always serving. Even as he sleeps, he is a steward over his flock. The shepherd has many roles and responsibilities to fulfill but must focus on the specific role he is serving in at that specific time. When it comes to protecting the flock, failure in that role can be catastrophic.

The shepherd prepared himself with a rod and staff and took an advantageous position to protect the flock even as he slept. Like the shepherd, we should be ready to take on a protection role. The lead pastor is not immune from this. It is the lead pastor who has to decide how to manage all of the ministries of the church. Either it is managed directly or effectively delegated to responsible leaders.[37] The latter is the optimal solution for most churches. This underscores the importance of discovering leaders for the security ministry.

---

[35] Welch served in the United States Navy and received his B.S. in Biology and Chemistry from East Tennessee State University in 1960. He then completed an M.S. in Oceanography at the Naval Postgraduate School in 1967. After accepting his call to ministry, he earned both his M.A.R.E (1985) and Ph.D. (1990) from Southwestern Seminary.

[36] Robert Welch, Serving by Safeguarding Your Church, (Grand Rapids, MI: Zondervan, 2002), 16.

[37] In Exodus 18, Jethro, father-in-law to Moses, recognized that Moses was not efficiently leading. He suggested that he delegate work which allowed Moses to focus on the work only he could do. This delegation reduced stress and improved productivity.

All believers have a responsibility to serve. Therefore, the stewardship responsibilities within the church involve more than just the pastor(s) and staff. Every Christian's vocation, hobbies, talents, and gifts are avenues to serve the Lord. Within each congregation is a diverse pool of resources to draw from to fulfill the vision God has provided the pastor for that church. Leaders within the church like the pastoral staff must fulfill their calling to serve and do so while holding themselves to a high standard.

Biblically, holding oneself to a higher standard is found in the priesthood of the believers. In 1 Peter 2:9, Peter identifies believers as "a chosen generation, a royal priesthood, a holy nation, a people for his own; that you should show forth the praises of him who has called you out of darkness into his marvelous light." As a royal priesthood, Christians are to conduct themselves with a benchmark that is higher than others. This is not exclusively to those whose vocation is in ministry, it is for all of us seeking to be more like Christ.

We, as believers have been gracefully blessed with gifts and talents to be used for His Kingdom. Therefore, we should seek to model a gracious personal character as we oversee others who serve with us. Titus 1:7 explains that "an overseer, as God's steward, must be above reproach. He must not be arrogant or quick tempered or a drunkard or violent or greedy for gain" (ESV). Therefore, everyone entrusted with being part of the Safety Team must conduct themselves at the highest standard while seeking to live beyond reproach. Yes, this is easier said than done, but it is the standard we seek.

Regardless of the size or makeup of your church, the ministries operating within it can enhance the security and safety of the church. There are no lines of division drawn between the different ministries; no single one is more important than another. For example, the Safety Team is no more important than the hospitality team. Each has a specific function to perform within the Kingdom-focused vision of the church. There

Church Security and Outreach

truly are no secular "workers," only servants of the Lord. Security is in no way an exception to the rule. Everything is done with equal importance for His Glory. Therefore, no ministry can be secular. *Just as the church does not provide secular childcare, it must not provide secular security.*

If you have a gifting that can be used to help secure the *ninety-nine,* then you must use it. No matter what your position is, as a God-centered, Kingdom-focused leader, you must make a diligent effort to manage and care for others. By providing security over those entrusted to you through direct management, delegation, or serving on the Safety Team, you are a good steward over the church.

Everyone has some degree of skill and talent that can enhance security. We all have giftings. Your gifting may be as a staff pastor who oversees the Safety Team, or it may be as a Safety Team leader, Assistant Team Leader, team member, or Force Multiplier. Regardless of the position that you currently occupy, you have a specific purpose. Your God-given gifts cannot be withheld from those who need it (Prov 3:27).[38] When it comes to the safety of the church, we need it and have a role to play in providing it.

The stewardship responsibility over safety and security requires that we consider all options available. A common question concerning church security is: what about utilizing secular options? This is a valid question because, despite the obvious problems, there are many secular avenues into security that may be beneficial. The government, private corporations, and other entities offer many opportunities for the church. Many of them have good concepts and ideas. But, as a responsible

---

[38] We cannot avoid or delay from doing good. "Do not withhold good from those who deserve it, when it is in you power to act" (Prov 3:27).

steward, you have to ask yourself, does a security strategy that is *not* Kingdom-focused work within the vision of the church? Is the system they advance one that will hinder the church's unrelenting focus on the Great Commandment and fulfilling the Great Commission? Finally, will the secular security approach require the church to sacrifice its missional values?

There are talented people within the congregation that are called to serve. The parable of the talents demonstrates how the Lord has entrusted people with different gifts, talents, and opportunities to be used for the Kingdom (Matt 25:14-30). Therefore, when looking for security experts to build your ministry, start within the Kingdom before considering the secular options. Concentrate your search by intentionally seeking believers who understand the Great Commandment and Great Commission and who are experts in security. The Kingdom is filled with people who have been given skills that can be used in a security ministry. Do not let these gifts from God sit on the sidelines!

Be aware that people outside of the Kingdom with gifts that are beneficial for enhancing security may also have tendencies that can be detrimental to the vision of the church. This is why the use of secular elements has to be *strategic*. For example, the SLS Tactical Strategy calls for the use of first responders who are beneficial to the enhancement of the security of the church and provide an opportunity for outreach. James wrote that "every good and perfect gift is from above, coming down from the Father of the heavenly lights, who does not change like shifting shadows" (Jas 1:17). If we can identify the good gifts that have been bestowed to others, we can use them to strengthen the Kingdom. We can benefit from them even if those who have been gifted have yet to recognize the Source of their gifting. Because of this, non-believers can still be used by God as they can provide good gifts from above, but their ability is limited until their hearts are changed. When that occurs, their spiritual gifts and talents can be released. Until then, the "good" that secular first responders provide will enhance the security of the church and through the established relationship with the Safety Team, hopefully they will be led to Christ.

We all have a purpose and mission to complete. We have a mutual responsibility to be good stewards, protect the congregation, and spread the Gospel. I would not be writing this book if I did not believe that I have a stewardship responsibility to share what God has placed on my heart with the church. This is my current mission. What is your assigned role concerning the security ministry at your church? What is your current mission? It is an important question to ask. Whatever role that is, strive to be found faithful in it.

Failure is guaranteed if we do nothing. By ignoring His purpose for us in this current role, we will fail in our stewardship responsibilities to protect the *ninety-nine* and seek the *one*. So, what actions can you take? Since each local church has its own set of unique characteristics that make up that church, no two church's security ministries will look exactly alike. Therefore, what you choose to do will be based upon your calling, the church's size, location, and resources. Your decisions and actions will provide the opportunity to help preserve life and reach lost souls. Action is necessary!

The foundation of stewardship emphasizes the responsibility that comes with your role in the SLS strategy. As important as it is to define that role, you must also embrace it. The SLS strategy has demonstrated that success can be achieved in security without sacrificing the church's mission. You can enhance security while pursuing the lost. Your calling and purpose require a response. What is your response?

To begin, start in prayer, own your role and the stewardship required of it, and stay focused on the mission. Create a Safety Team that goes beyond security and will be a ministry to first responders. Finally, look at the recommendations offered throughout this book on how to establish an Emergency Preparedness Plan. Adopt and adapt them to the needs of your church, its vision, and its place within the Kingdom. Determine your role in the security ministry and take direct action in both the preparation and execution of that role.

Pillar of Action

"Do not merely listen to the word, and so deceive yourselves. Do what it says" James 1:22

"Be always on the watch, and pray that you may be able to escape all that is about to happen." Luke 21:36

The foundation of the SLS biblical basis has two sides: prayer and stewardship. As previously discussed, the prayer side supports the pillars of *controlling fear* and *wisdom*. These pillars offered what we must *acquire* to be successful. On the stewardship side of the foundation arise the pillars of *action* and *vigilance*. These pillars demonstrate what is *required* of us to be successful.

The biblical basis for action and vigilance may be very familiar to some readers. For others, this may be new material. Regardless, it is important (and Scriptural) to review (2 Pet 1:12-13).[39] Even if you are very familiar with the following verses, this may be the first time that you read them through a security-conceptual lens.

The ensuing paragraphs address some biblical examples of security measures used by Jesus and the early church. The pillars of action (to take an active response to a threat) and vigilance (to stand ready before, during, and after an attack) are found throughout the Bible. The application of each of these

---

[39] Peter wrote: "So I will always remind you of these things, even though you know them and are firmly established in the truth you now have. I think that it is right to refresh your memory as long as I live in the tent of this body" (2 Pet 1:12-13).

areas to your life will increase your overall personal security inside and outside of the physical church. Therefore, as you read the following examples take note how Jesus and His disciples remained *situationally-aware* and made *wise* decisions to preserve their lives. They chose to *act* to increase their personal security and the security of the early church.

Acting to *Deter*, *Avoid*, and *Mitigate* threats is essential to the SLS strategy. There was no greater action ever taken than Christ's sacrifice. The Lord acted assuring that His life would be sacrificially given, and that His resurrection was revealed just as He planned (Matt 16:21-28; Mark 8:31-33; Matt 20:17-19; Matt 27:39-54; John 2:19). His plans were not disrupted by the Jewish officials or Roman rulers (Acts 2:23).[40] The crucifixion fulfilled numerous prophecies and served as the ultimate sacrifice for humankind's salvation.

Jesus was born into this world under attack. Just after His birth, Herod set out to kill Him, fulfilling the prophecy of Jeremiah 31:15 (Matt 2:16-18). But, that attempt, like others, would fail because the Lord controlled the fulfillment of His purpose. We can see that during His ministry, the Lord acted to assure His safety and the timely fulfillment of His plan. What is of particular interest are the examples where His life was "threatened" and the actions He took to "escape" the attacks. On each occasion, He acted to preserve His life and the lives of others.

When Jesus boldly proclaimed His Divinity by saying, "I tell you the truth, if anyone keeps my word, he will never see death (John 8:51) . . . before Abraham was born, I am!" (John 8:58), it enraged the Jewish religious leaders. In response they immediately set up to kill Him. But Jesus took action to avoid

---

[40] Everything is under God's control. His plan is not disrupted or altered. The sovereignty of God and the fulfillment of His plan was comforting to those facing persecution and oppression during the time of the early church.

harm. In John 8:59, the Bible tells us that they picked up rocks to stone Him, but Jesus hid Himself, slipping away from the temple grounds. This is an example of when an attack was coming and Jesus took action to avoid being hit. He used tactics to escape and hide in order to preserve life.

Another time when Jesus faced being killed occurred during the Feast of Dedication. On this occasion, Jesus was at the Temple and was surrounded by the religious leaders who questioned His authority. Jesus responded by saying "... you do not believe me because you are not my sheep. My sheep listen to my voice; I know them, and they follow me, I give them eternal life, and they shall never perish; no one can snatch them out of my hand. My Father, who has given them to me, is greater than all; no one can snatch them out of my Father's hand. I and the Father are one" (John 10: 26-30). Upon hearing this, they picked up stones to kill Him (John 10:31). The religious leaders said that they were going to stone Him because He claimed to be God (John 10:33). After Jesus explained that the Father is in Him and that He is in the Father, they tried to seize Him, but He escaped their grasp (John 10: 38-39). Again, Jesus took an active response to avoid the threat. This decisive action provided an avenue of escape.

John 7 provides an example of how Jesus took action to avoid danger. This occurred just prior to the Feast of Tabernacles. At this time, the disciples wanted to go to Judea but Jesus was focused on His mission and had another plan. John records that Jesus did not want to go to Judea and purposely stayed away because the Jewish leaders there were looking for a way to kill Him (John 7:1). Once again, facing danger, He wisely choose to actively avoid the threat.

Following a meeting of the Sanhedrin, the Jewish religious leaders plotted to kill Jesus. Having acknowledged the miraculous signs that Jesus performed, many Jews became followers of Christ. The religious leaders feared that soon everyone would believe in Him (John 11:45-58). Therefore, they plotted to kill Jesus (John 11:45-53). Jesus responded and no longer moved about publicly among the people of Judea. Instead, He withdrew to Ephraim, a village in a wilderness region near the desert where He stayed with His disciples (John 11:54). These examples show how Jesus took action by moving about in secret and relocating to a safer location.

† † †

Just as the previous examples highlight some of the actions taken by Jesus, the Bible also provides examples of how the early church modeled a security mindset. The early church faced great persecution. Disciples often had to relocate and escape danger in order to preserve their lives. For example, Acts 9 records how Jewish leaders were conspiring to kill Saul. In one instance, while the city was locked down with the gates being watched, the disciples strategically used the cover of night to lower Saul in a basket through the walls of the city (Acts 9:24-25). Acts chapter 9 also records how the disciples took action to save his life. Luke wrote: "He debated with some Greek-speaking [Hellenistic] Jews, but they tried to murder him. When the believers heard about this, they took him down to Caesarea and sent him away to Tarsus, his hometown" (Acts 9:29-30 NLT). These examples demonstrate that safety and protection was sought. In these instances, we find evidence of immediate action, operational planning, tactical movement, and managing logistics, in the face of being killed.

Another case of the early church's active response to avoid an attack is seen in Acts 14: 5-7. Here it is recorded that an attempt was made by both the Gentiles and the Jews (along with their leaders) to stone Paul and Barnabas. However, they received intel that the attack was coming and fled to the cities of Lycaonia, Lystra and Derbe, and the surrounding region where they continued with their mission to preach the Gospel. They took action to preserve life, avoided the attack, relocated, and continued with their mission to preach the Gospel.

Acts 20:3 offers another account of how people plotted against Paul. This occasion occurred just as he was about to sail for Syria. Learning of the plot, Paul wisely decided to go back through Macedonia instead. Syria was the danger zone, a hostile area with a planned attack on Paul. Rather than proceeding directly into an attack, Paul avoided it all together. Had he continued to Syria he would have placed himself on the "X" (right in the crosshairs of the attack).

The actions exemplified in the previous examples demonstrate how Jesus and the early church maneuvered to get off the "X." When under attack, the danger zone is called the "X." It simply identifies the designated target area of an attack. The size of the "X" is determined by the type of attack. The "X" could be a large geographical area such as a city. However, more than likely the "X" during an attack is a small area. The "X" could be where you are standing if you are being shot at. But if someone is trying to drive a Vehicle-Borne Improvised Explosive Device (VBIED) into a church building, the church and the immediate area around it are the "X."

Remaining on the "X" while under attack may lead to catastrophic damage. For example, if punches are being thrown at you, you have to move out of the way. If you are in a car that is disabled and being shot at, you have to get out of that bullet magnet. If you are in a building that is on fire, you must maneuver to exit the building. When under attack, you must always get off the "X." Paul and the leaders of churches of Asia who were accompanying him chose to avoid the danger zone. They exhibited wise decision making for self-preservation and took action to avoid an attack. If you find yourself under attack, you must take action. Wisely maneuver to get off the "X." Immediately, relocate to a position of advantage and reassess your situation.

These basic examples of actions that Jesus and the early church took exemplify wise decision making to preserve life. Their actions were taken to save lives and, in each occurrence, the actions led to avoiding a direct attack. The danger and sense of urgency that the early church faced is still lived out today throughout the world. Having spent years as part of a faith-based security organization that trains missionaries in dangerous locations throughout the world, I have seen how the non-western Christian church serves under a threat condition that fluctuates from *high* to *imminent*. The missionaries who are serving to spread the Gospel to unreached people groups in these hostile locations constantly face the threat of imminent death. They truly are on the frontlines facing danger head on. They are courageous.

Fortunately, the local church in the United States has not reached that level of threat. However, the threat we face is very real! The amount of crime and church violence that occurs in the United States presents a clear and present danger nonetheless. A simple internet search of "church shooting" will bring up an astounding list of incidents from across the country. Therefore, in order to protect the *ninety-nine,* we must take *Action* to *Deter, Avoid,* and *Mitigate* attacks.

You cannot afford to become comfortable just because you have not been attacked. That approach relies on luck to avoid becoming a victim. Jesus and the early church were mission-focused, they made wise decisions, and took action to preserve life. We should emulate this position by continuing to seek the lost and remaining vigilant to protect our congregations. As demonstrated, we should train ourselves to overcome fear through prayer and faith. This will place us in a position of peace where we can make wise decisions. But don't just plan how to do this, see that it is completed. Prepare now, before an attack. If you find yourself under attack, get off the "X," move to a position of advantage and reassess your situation. Take action, your life and the lives of others depend on it.

The Biblical Basis

Pillar of Vigilance

"Stay alert! Watch out for your great enemy the devil. He prowls around like a roaring lion looking, for someone to devour." 1 Peter 5:8 NLT

The final pillar rising up from the biblical foundation of prayer and stewardship is *vigilance*. Ask yourself right now, no matter where you are as you read this book, what is your mindset? How do you perceive the world around you? What is your situational awareness? How much of the immediate environment are your currently perceiving? How much of what you are perceiving is an accurate assessment of potential attacks? Are you operating on one extreme that is completely blind to what is going on? Or, are you a member of the other extreme, completely paranoid of everything that could be a threat? Don't just limit yourself to the potential natural attacks; what about the spiritual warfare being waged?

Both of the aforementioned extremes are unacceptable ways to live. They bring with them their own tendencies that can lead to incapacitation. In the following chapter a great deal of attention will be paid to empowering people to live a life in *condition yellow*. This is a relaxed state of vigilance where one has optimal situational awareness.

That fact that you are reading this means that you acknowledge the need for security. The type of security measures you choose to employ will depend on the many variables that make up your church. As stated earlier, each church's size, location, capabilities, and resources are unique. Therefore, the security plan for each church will also be unique. It is important to remember that *you* are called to be a good steward of all the resources God has provided you (Gen 2:15; 1 Pet 4:10; Prov 16:3; Titus 1:7; Luke 14:28; 1 Cor 4:2). This is why we do not base our plans off of what other churches have. Every church within the Kingdom has an exclusive plan for balancing what they decide is too much or too little security.

† † †

Vigilance matters! The 21st century threat on churches in the United States is frighteningly real. Western churches are not isolated from the attacks that occur in other parts of the world. Statistics show that the amount of violence occurring on church facilities continues to rise. In 2017, there were 118 deaths at churches in the United States. Unfortunately, that number represents a record high.[41]

As good stewards who share in the love of God and a love for people, we must remain on guard and keep watch for attacks. Matthew 10:17 cries out for us to be on your guard! 1 Pet 5:8 says: "Be self-controlled and alert. Your enemy the devil prowls around like a roaring lion looking for someone to devour." Just as Christians do not know when Christ will return, neither do we know when attacks will be launched. In both cases, we must stay vigilant and be ready. Mark 13:33 says: "Be on guard! Be alert!" The time of the attack is not going to be given to you ahead of time. Be ready, stay alert, live, love, and remain on guard!

Just as Matthew warns everyone to be on alert for the return of Jesus, Christians should also be attentive to attacks on the church. Jesus instructed His disciples to keep watch, because the day and hour of His return is not known to man. He says, "Understand this: If the owner of the house had known at what time of night the thief was coming, he would have kept watch and would not have let his house be broken into. So, you also must be ready, because the Son of Man will come at an hour when you do not expect Him" (Matt 24:42-44). The church

---

[41] Taken from http://www.carlchinn.com/deadly-force-statistics.html

must be warned and remain vigilant. You have no idea when, where, or by what means an attack will occur. Remain vigilant!

† † †

The preceding paragraphs were focused on the era of the ministry of Jesus and the early church. In addition, there is one Old Testament example that should be looked at when considering the pillars of action and vigilance in the biblical security model. Although, there are many examples throughout the Bible concerning security, action, and vigilance, this segment of the book will focus on Nehemiah Chapter 4. It provides everyone in service of the Lord a biblical example of a security mindset with a heightened situational awareness.

The setting of Nehemiah chapter 4 is tenuous. At that time the Temple had been restored but the walls protecting the city of Jerusalem had not been rebuilt. This left the city vulnerable to attack. As construction of the walls ensued, the threat to Jerusalem increased. Nehemiah records that the work was proceeding successfully: "But when Sanballat, Tobiah, the Arabs, the Ammonites and the people of Ashdod heard that the repairs to Jerusalem's walls had gone ahead and that the gaps were being closed, they were very angry. They all plotted together to come and fight against Jerusalem and stir up trouble against it. But we prayed to our God and posted a guard day and night to meet this threat" (Neh 4:7-9).

From this passage we can see that Nehemiah is a great example of a God-fearing man who took action. First, he prayed and then wisely posted guards. His prayer and faith allowed him to overcome fear. Because of this, Nehemiah faced the threat from a position of peace. He then employed a strategy of vigilant preparation and deterrence.

In fact, not only did his people serve as guards against an attack, they were armed (Neh 4:13-16, 4:17-18, 4:21-22, 4:23). Nehemiah said: "Neither I nor my brothers nor my men nor the guards with me took off our clothes; each had his weapon, even when he went for water" (Neh 4:23). Nehemiah directed his people to be on guard. He stationed people for security details armed with "swords, spears, and bows" (Neh 4:13). As half of the people did work, "the other half were equipped with spears, shields, bows, and armor" (Neh 4:16). Nehemiah continues: "At that time, I also said to the people, 'Have every man and his helper stay inside Jerusalem at night, so they can serve us as guards by night and workmen by day'" (Neh 4:22). Nehemiah took strategic action steps to protect the city from the threats. As they plotted against Jerusalem, he prayed and posted guards (Neh 4:8-9). He was situationally aware as he began his endeavor to build the walls and protect the people of Jerusalem.

This brief glance at Nehemiah 4 and the preceding sections that looked at the events which occurred in Jesus' ministry and the early church, provide biblical examples of how taking action, remaining vigilant, and exhibiting situational awareness can enhance security. The modern church can emulate these examples by taking *Action*, to *Deter*, *Avoid*, and *Mitigate* threats. It begins by starting in prayer and accepting the stewardship responsibility over the security ministry. Then, by controlling fear through faith, establishing a position of peace, and making wise decisions, we can be courageous. The actions that we take in preparation for, or during a critical event, have the ability to save lives and reach lost souls. Like Jesus, the early church, and countless Christians that have come before us, we must take action to pursue the *one* and protect the *ninety-nine*.

Chapter 3

The SLS Strategy for a Security Ministry

"So, do not fear, for I am with you; do not be dismayed, for I am your God. I will strengthen you and help you; I will uphold you with my righteous right hand." Isaiah 41:10

Security Ministry Basic Training

In order to establish your security ministry, you will need to become familiar with the Christian Warrior Mindset and provide training to the Safety Team and Force Multipliers. The Christian Warrior Mindset is an established set of attitudes of a Christian who sees a corrupted world and chooses to actively confront evil on a spiritual and natural level. These attitudes include protecting the innocent (stewardship), seeking the lost (outreach), and growth (discipleship). Training the Safety Team and Force Multipliers on the Christian Warrior Mindset will strengthen the safety and security of the church and foster spiritual growth.

Building upon the SLS biblical basis of prayer and stewardship, the four pillars of wisdom, controlling fear, action, and vigilance, and the commitment to take *Action* to *Deter*, *Avoid*, and *Mitigate* threats, the Christian Warrior Mindset requires mental conditioning for efficient decision making. This mindset is life changing and critical during an emergency situation. This chapter demonstrates how you can achieve this by improving your situational awareness, exploring the cognitive science of decision making, blueprinting for contingency planning and preparation, the OODA loop, and developing a condition yellow mindset.

Many security-minded professionals in the military and law enforcement communities possess a unique mindset. They live their lives in a way which allows them to maintain a higher degree of vigilance than individuals who are not security-conscientious. Although many of these men and women appear to be naturally "wired" this way, they still have to learn how to employ their giftings and talents to their lives. This means, we have to apply this mindset to church security.

Everyone called to be a part of the church security ministry can utilize their giftings and learn the tradecraft. Like the sport of basketball, not everyone who learns how to play the game will be an all-star. But everyone can get into the game at some level with an opportunity to progress. Through training and experience, everyone can find their niche and improve their proficiency.

The easiest and most cost-effective way to enhance the overall security and safety of your church is to empower your people. Provide them with a way of thinking that keys in on safety and security. The size of your church and the number of people that you have serving does not matter. Through education and empowerment, you can immediately enhance the overall security at little to no cost. You just need to get them into the game.

The philosophy is this: When an individual serving on Sunday increases their individual, personal aptitude over security, the church benefits. As that person *looks out* for their personal security, they also provide a limited but effective area where they make an impact on the church. Additionally, as that individual grows in their capacity to create a safe worship environment, the growth is seen exponentially throughout the church. Therefore, a single person that increases their personal security will have an effect on a small part of the safety of the church. Because of this, the church should provide training to everyone that serves to increase its overall security.

In the SLS strategy this is called Security Ministry Basic Training. Security Ministry Basic Training is the foundational instruction that empowers people serving with a focus on the security and safety of the worship environment. For these Force Multipliers, the training focuses on proper observation and communication of suspicious items, people, and activity without creating a disruption to the worship environment. It consists of the information provided in this book excluding the Safety Team Operational Training which is advanced material specific to the function of the Safety Team.

Empowering every ministry will exponentially increase the safety of the church without changing anyone's role or position in their respective ministry. The organized convergence of numerous individuals' security awareness will create a hedge of security around the church. The first step in completing this process is identifying those who are serving in various ministries. Next, train them to apply a security mindset while they serve within that capacity.

You may find that some people in careers that have a greater propensity to danger (military, police, firefighters) have adopted a security mindset. This is not to be confused with the aforementioned Christian Warrior Mindset or a hunter/prey warrior mindset. Rather, this is proclivity to be security conscious. This causes them to increase their personal safety and that of the people around them. You may also find that people who are not facing or are unaware that they are facing imminent danger have no idea what any of these mindsets entail. This means, that the Christian Warrior Mindset may be a foreign concept for many at the church. Do not be discouraged. As you will see throughout this chapter, the road to this mindset is very empowering especially to the least security-conscience person.

You do not need to have a military or law enforcement background to embrace this mindset. All that is needed is being educated on something that rarely gets outside of the military and law enforcement circles. This book provides everything you need to train the people serving at your church. This chapter is fixated on establishing the Christian Warrior Mindset. One thing that my experience has taught me is this: the greatest weapon a warrior possesses is their mind. It is where emotion and spirit collide, faith defeats fear, and the decision to take action is made. All of the other weaponry that a warrior can tangibly possess are just tools to aid in the fight. This chapter welcomes individuals to grow in vigilance, awareness, and conditioning the mind to efficiently respond to threats and emergency situations. By empowering people with the proper mindset, you can achieve immediate enhancements to the safety and security of the church.

The actions that you take before, during, and after an attack have the ability to preserve life. Not just yours, but others as well. Anyone who has faced a life-threatening situation knows that it is not enough to make the right decision. *You have to make the right decision before it's too late.* Unfortunately, trying to determine the proper decision can take excessive time when immediate action is needed. Therefore, if not properly prepared, you may quickly make a decision that is not well thought out. Or you will take too much time deciding what to do and miss the opportunity to effectively act. During a critical event this can be the difference between lives saved or lost. This is why we strive to rapidly make the right decision with as little mental effort being applied as possible.

Both reckless decision making and wasting time planning when action is necessary can lead to catastrophic failures. Therefore, in order to increase your likelihood for success, you must maximize your mental ability. In order to place yourself in the best position to act quickly and correctly, *the mind must be conditioned* for the proper response. The Christian Warrior's goal is to maintain a high degree of situational awareness with little mental effort being applied. This is achieved through training and experience which establishes mental patterns (blueprints) to respond to threats, emergency situations, and critical events.

Critical events often occur in the form of medical emergencies, weather emergencies, and violent attacks. They are found in all environments and effect every segment of society. Critical events happen at home, at school, at work, in public, and at church. No matter where they occur, proper decisions must be made in a rapid manner to be effective. During a critical event, time is of the essence!

Unfortunately, rapid decisions are often hastily made and not well thought out. This presents a problem when a rapid decision is required to address a complex problem since complex problems require time to work through and a rapid decision will not be a well-researched one. Complex decision making requires time to diligently analyze the situation and consider options before deciding to act. But, as stated, critical events present complex problems and provide little time to act. Therefore, outside of chance, an unprepared mind is not capable of making the right decision in a short amount of time.

Professionals, like police, EMS, and medical personnel working in hospitals, encounter emergency situations daily that require lifesaving decisions. How do they effectively make the right decision? The answer is from their mental preparation. They have trained their mind in both skill and mental development. They tactically place themselves in the best position to respond. They are aware of the events occurring around them, and, through training and experience, they have created mental associations that assist them during rapid decision making.

Part of the answer to the previous question rests in how the body and mind function. People who are first responders are not superheroes. As a matter of fact, most feel very uncomfortable when you call them heroic (even when it is well-deserved). Of course, first responders do heroic things, but their mind fundamentally functions the same way as everyone else's. This means everyone has the capacity to be heroic.

Everyone serving must increase their mental capacity specifically in their understanding and ability to grow in four key areas: situational awareness, the autonomic nervous system, operating in condition yellow, and finally, conditioning the two systems of the cognitive mind by blueprinting. Growth in these areas will increase each person's ability (and comprehensively the ability of everyone serving at the church) to create a safer worship environment.

As a matter of stewardship, everyone has a role to play but not everyone is going to acknowledge the threatening world around them. They would rather live in an ignorant bliss than have to address safety concerns. Do you know people like this at the church? They may be against anything that involves "security." So, in order to overcome this opposition, you will have to open their eyes to the need for increased security. If you are willing to grow and can convince others to as well, then the opportunity for an immediate increase in the safety of the church is well on its way.

As established, the SLS biblical basis has a foundation of prayer and stewardship. Two of the pillars arising from it are action and vigilance. Growth in the realm of safety and security will require your action to increase the amount of vigilance that you incorporate in your lifestyle. The first step is to acknowledge the numerous spiritual and natural threats to your safety, the safety of others, and the church. Secondly, you must act against these threats with a vigilant mindset. Admittingly, no one can ever be 100% vigilant 100% of the time. People have to sleep, people get distracted, people are lazy, people constantly ebb and flow between vigilance and obliviousness. However, with the certainty of the threats facing the church, an effort must be made to be as prepared as possible to counter them. Of course, this is done without compromising the vision or mission of the church.

As seen in the previous chapter, the foundation of the SLS strategy comes from prayer and stewardship and the four pillars of wisdom, controlling fear, action, and vigilance. It is through this conceptual lens that a new mindset must be established. No matter what position in the church you occupy, you will benefit from this mindset.

For many, this section of the book is life-changing. It will alter the way you look at the world around you. It is a very comprehensive segment of the book created to be used to empower you to increase the overall safety of the local church and the people in it. It is essential that all Safety Team members and Force Multipliers be well versed in this chapter because the training and tactics throughout the rest of the book are grounded in its philosophy. By the chapter's end, it is my hope that you will have an increased situational awareness, be better prepared for emergency events, intensify your mental conditioning, and share what you have learned with others. The first step in this process is to challenge your perception of the world around you and how people act within it.

Sheep, Wolves, and Sheepdogs

People can be an influential social force. In the context of the local church, this can work in favor of, or against a security ministry. Although large groups can band together to effect change, it only takes a charismatic individual to achieve the same result. The world is filled with complex and unpredictable people. Individuals you think will support a security ministry may end up being your greatest obstacles. Others who appear to have no concern for security whatsoever, may actually be the ones who have been apprehensive about security for a long time. If you are the person who is spearheading security changes in your church, do not feel that you need a large group of followers or a charismatic speaker to create that change. Rather than creating a "revolution" within your church, offer leadership the idea of enhancing the security of the church through the education and empowerment of those already serving. Then, create a security ministry and Safety Team that is focused on protecting the *ninety-nine* and pursuing the *one*. Finally, offer to create an Emergency Preparedness Plan. For people who are opposed to addressing "security," this will break down any misperceptions that they maintain.

To better understand how security is perceived in the church and offer you a stronger position to foster change, this section is going to look at a depiction of society offered by Dave Grossman, a United States Army Ranger, former West Point Psychology Professor, author, and director of the Killology Research Group. In a simple but very effective way, he categorizes people into three unique groups. These groups divide society into the general population, predators, and protectors. Grossman refers to them as sheep, wolves, and sheepdogs.

In, *On Combat: The Psychology and Physiology of Deadly Conflict in War and Peace,* Grossman writes of a conversation that he had with a Vietnam Veteran whom he referred to as an "old retired Colonel." That conversation framed the basic understanding for the three types of people in the world: sheep, wolves, and sheepdogs. Take any given group of people that you find at a shopping center, restaurant, or church, and more than likely they will fit into one of these categories.[42]

The first group that Grossman describes are the sheep. They represent the majority of people living their daily lives as a part of society. They are kind, decent, and highly unlikely to intentionally hurt another person. They live peaceful and productive lives. It would take an extreme provocation or an accident for this type of person to cause harm to another human. The sheep live their lives knowing that evil exists, but are not on the frontline against it. Their situational awareness is very low. Therefore, they rely on others to protect them. There is nothing wrong with being a sheep. We want to be in a society filled with sheep. Unfortunately, terrorists, criminals, and predators also exist. They are the ones who seek to cause harm to the sheep.

The second group of people in society are classified as wolves. These are the vicious predators who prey upon the sheep. Without mercy, they cause destruction and harm (mentally and physically) as they feed upon society. Terrorists, child predators, robbers, and other violent criminals are examples found in the family of wolves. Wolves have no concern for anyone but themselves as they pursue their own selfish, greedy desires. The sheep may not always show concern about the wolf, but they know the wolf *and they fear it*!

Fear can cause the sheep to be left vulnerable. Often, out of fear, the sheep choose to mentally block out the danger. Thus, *they choose to ignore the wolf.* People do this all the time. In the context of the church, it occurs in the mission field and within the walls of our local churches. Why would the sheep ignore the threat? The answer is simple: thinking about the

---

[42] Dave Grossman, *On Combat: The Psychology and Physiology of Deadly Conflict in War and Peace,* (Millstadt, IL: Warrior Science Publications, 2008), 180.

wolf causes discomfort. They don't want to think about the carnage, the violence, the horror, and death that the wolf can cause. Therefore, when the wolf attacks, the sheep are not prepared. If they are lucky, they will frantically flee. If they are not, they will become victims.

The sheep have very few opportunities to protect themselves from the wolf's vicious attack. Their only path to victory is to escape. The sheep are unable to fight to protect themselves. Therefore, if they are attacked, they have no way to defeat the wolf. Just like most of society who live normal peaceful lives, the sheep are in essence either not attacked, or become a defeated target when an attack comes.

Finally, the third animal that represents a segment of society is the sheepdog. If you are reading this book, you are likely a sheepdog. There are many types of sheepdogs but all of them live to protect the flock and confront the wolf. Like the wolf, sheepdogs have the capacity for violence but unlike the wolf they would never use it against the flock. The heart of the sheepdog is its love for the flock. This love is such a strong love they are willing to risk their own lives to protect the sheep.

Grossman identifies that being a sheepdog is both a curse and a blessing. This is something that sheepdogs understand. We are outcasts in that we are fundamentally different from those they live to protect. We are concerned about safety and security in a way that others do not think about. Additionally, whereas the sheep abhor violence, sheepdogs have a capacity for violence that can be used to protect the flock. The ability to use force is essential for the survival of the sheep. The capacity for violence causes some sheep to despise them and others to look upon them in wonder. The sheep just don't understand them. What most sheep fail to fully comprehend is that *sheepdogs have a profound love for the sheep* and are *committed to protect them*. That is what makes them warriors.

The wolf violently preys upon the sheep and despises the sheepdogs. Sheepdogs love the sheep and stand prepared to confront the wolf. Both the sheepdog and wolf share a capacity for violence but the sheepdog's profound love for the flock makes it different from the wolf.[43] The two will inevitably always be in conflict. This foundational difference between sheepdogs and wolves is simply a matter of the heart.

Ironically, the same sheepdog who is protecting the sheep intimidates them. This reinforces how the sheepdog is perceived as an outsider to the flock. The sheepdog, with its constant vigilance is an odd character. Many in church congregations can perceive a security ministry in this way. What compounds the issue is that when the sheep sees a sheepdog, they are reminded of the wolf. Both sheepdogs and wolves have sharp pointed teeth. Since the sheep don't have a need for sharp, pointed teeth they don't understand why anyone, other than the wolf, would have them. When they think of the wolf, those sharp pointed teeth come to mind. So, when they see the sheepdog with its sharp teeth, it reminds them of the wolf.

Because of this, the presence of the sheepdog can raise fear among the sheep. The same sheep that need the sheepdogs for protection ironically have an unmerited fear of them. As you move forward in the establishment of your security ministry, Safety Team, and law enforcement presence to protect the congregation, similar fears among the flock may arise. A security ministry may remind them of the threats that they would rather ignore than prepare for.

Some people prefer to live in an ignorant bliss rather than address the threat. They are not concerned about what may be threatening at church. They know that someone may break into their car. They know that someone may become an active shooter. They know that someone may be trying to get into the kid's ministry to molest or kidnap children. They know that all of these things are possible. However, rather than deal with the

---

[43] Grossman, *On Combat*, 190.

threat, they choose to ignore it. They hope that the odds of an attack occurring are in their favor and that it will not happen.

They choose to ignore the wolf rather than prepare for it. They find comfort and security in their ignorance. Sheepdogs, however, are not able to think this way. Their concern is always to look out for the safety of the flock (whether the flock likes them or not). As virtuous as this way of thinking is, it further alienates sheepdogs from the sheep. This can happen when sheepdogs in the church prepare for the wolf by simply suggesting that "security" be addressed.

When people have an extremely "sheepish" mindset, they want to push the thought of the wolf out of their mind. They fear the wolf so much that even the presence of the sheepdog reminds them of what they are trying to block out. Seeing a protector reminds them of the evil wolf that is searching for its prey. People in this mindset are vulnerable. If they are in leadership positions, they are not being good stewards of the Lord's provision. They have a responsibility to acknowledge the wolf and take action to protect those under their authority.

Within your congregation you will find sheep who want to dismiss the threats altogether. They want to come to church and pretend that it is a safe place where nothing can go wrong. After all, it's "God's house" right? This is not a wise state of mind, it is not biblical, nor is it logical. That mindset has been proven wrong historically time and time again. Attacks can and do occur. For the most part, the church *is relatively a very safe place,* but that does not negate the fact that attacks can ensue at any time. Nor does it mean that we can ignore that the Lord has forewarned the church to remain vigilant, be wise, and be good stewards over the flock. Fortunately, most leaders do not have an extremely "sheepish" mindset. They care about their flock and are concerned about security. They just need to know how to enhance it.

Extremely "sheepish" people will be obstacles to your effort for a security ministry. For example, the mere presence of a police officer will make some people remember the evil that exists and can strike anywhere. Regardless of their opposition, sheepdogs are to love and protect them. For sheepdogs, this is our stewardship responsibility. It is one of the reasons that the SLS Tactical Strategy is set up in a way that creates a high level of deterrence through the use of welcoming, friendly, Force Multipliers and covert surveillance via the Safety Team. This strategy means that the security aspect is hidden from the congregation. It is a strategy that says, "we will serve to protect you without you even knowing that we are doing it." After all, even the most "sheepish" person wants the same thing as the sheepdog, a safe and peaceful worship environment for everyone.

Uneasiness amongst the sheep that is directed towards the sheepdog, relates back to the violent threat that the wolf presents. If you do not have a law enforcement presence at your church and decide to incorporate one, be prepared for the proportionally few but effectively loud people who will not like it. When some people observe a police officer with a firearm, the mere sight of it reminds them that there is an evil out there willing to use firearms to attack innocent people. It reminds them that active shooters use firearms to commit mass shootings. When most people arrive at church, they do not want to be concerned about mass shootings. Fortunately, the vast majority of people will never experience one. Nonetheless, the police officer that is there to protect the sheep still reminds them that the wolf exists. They don't like that and may let you know of their discomfort.

Therefore, if you do choose to start using a uniformed law enforcement presence, get ahead of the questioning by easing the congregation's fears. Advise the them that there *is no specific threat* that prompted the use of hired law enforcement.

Educate the congregation on the state of the world (fallen and currently under attack) and emphasize that the church is taking responsibility to enhance security. Then, ask the congregation to be welcoming to the law enforcement officers. Never forget, *they are to be ministered to*. They are guests at the church and should be treated as such.

For every sheep that does not want the sheepdog present, there comes a point when everything changes. That point is when the wolf comes! The same sheep that were uneasy because of the presence of the sheepdog now frantically look to them for protection. They need the sheepdog even if they do not want to admit it. If the wolf appears and there are no sheepdogs for protection, those sheep will be slaughtered. If they survive, they will be the ones who will charge that you did not have sheepdogs to protect them.

Many people will be uneasy with a security ministry because the presence of the Safety Team will remind them of the wolf. For them, the team represents the teeth that sheep are weary of. Although it is unlikely, it is possible that some people may seek another church based on their feelings concerning security. Those people were probably already looking for an excuse to leave anyway. Your church is more than likely, not the first one that they have walked out of. As a leader in the church you have to address that having a law enforcement officer present to protect the church may disturb some in the flock.

Most people in the congregation will not be resistant to your efforts to protect them. It has been my experience that the vast majority of the congregation will be gracious to the law enforcement presence. They will demonstrate great appreciation as they interact with the law enforcement officers. When kids come up to the law enforcement officers to take pictures with them, you will see how your effort in enhancing the security of the church has affected both the officer and members of the congregation.

As mentioned above, when an emergency situation occurs, the same people worried about the sheepdog's teeth, will be looking for the sheepdogs to arise and save them. This whimsical distrust of the sheepdog and immediate need that arises in an emergency situation is part of the Pastor's Paradox. The lead pastor must balance the amount of security required (stewardship over the flock) without compromising the church's vision and mission to obey the Great Commandment and Great Commission. Therefore, by educating the congregation and staff, most of the resistance that comes out of ignorance and fear will be alleviated.

Finally, the main difference between the wolf and the sheepdog is the condition of the heart. One is a *predator* the other is a *protector*. The sheep often form emotional opinions based on fear rather than wise discernment concerning the condition of the sheepdog's heart. However, if the heart of the sheepdog is sound, then the sheep need not fear its sharp, pointed teeth. By educating and empowering people within the church, you will work against the minor resistance you may experience. In doing so, you will help resolve part of the dilemma that is the Pastor's Paradox. The first step in educating and empowering people to create a safer church environment is to increase their *situational awareness*.

Situational Awareness

Situational awareness is the real time perception of the environment and the events occurring in it. It includes the sub-categories of spatial awareness, self-awareness, and spiritual awareness. Being aware of your location and what is going on around you without being over stimulated is a characteristic of the Christian Warrior Mindset.

The Christian Warrior Mindset is an established set of attitudes of a Christian who sees a corrupted world and chooses to actively confront evil on a spiritual and natural level. These attitudes include protecting the innocent (stewardship), seeking the lost (outreach), and growth (discipleship). Therefore, a Christian Warrior is a sheepdog who seeks to operate in condition yellow knowing that evil is always scheming to steal, kill, and destroy. The Christian Warrior accepts the responsibility of protecting the congregation of the church and being obedient to the commands of the Great Commission and Great Commandment to honor God, love people, and reach the lost. Therefore, the Christian Warrior is concerned for the wellbeing of all of the sheep. As a humbled servant, the Christian Warrior is committed to discipleship which produces growth in relationship with the Lord and with others. This growth comes through a commitment to obedience, prayer, and stewardship. A Christian Warrior is committed to pursuing the *one* while protecting the *ninety-nine*.

If you have never seen the world through this conceptual lens, adopting a mindset such as this may be difficult. Obviously, it goes far beyond any secular concept of a security mindset. It will involve a drastic change in your established way of perceiving the world and a discipline to avoid becoming hypervigilant. It is the mindset required for members of the Safety Team and one recommended for everyone serving in church. The following paragraphs will provide an instructive, eye-opening, way to enhance personal safety regardless of location or circumstance.

Situational Awareness: SLS defines situational awareness as the real time perception of the environment and the events occurring in it. This includes the three subcategories of: spatial awareness, self-awareness, and spiritual awareness.

Spatial Awareness: A subcategory of SLS situational awareness. It refers to the ability to determine your proximity to the threat. For example, if gunshots are heard, how far away are they? If a hurricane is coming towards your home, how far out is it? Spatial awareness requires making an estimate of the distance between you and the threat and the time it takes for that threat to become imminent. You must take into consideration the distance, obstacles, terrain, cover, concealment, and the avenues of approach. Some threats like a hurricane may offer days until it is upon you, but others like tornados may be upon you in less than a minute. Determining the best course of action requires that you be spatially aware.

Threats come in various forms. For example, imagine that you are standing inside the front door of your church at a time when service is not in session. Being situationally aware, you observe a man with a knife standing in the parking lot. Considering spatial awareness, you determine that he has to travel 25 yards to the doors and enter the building in order to harm you. This gives you time to lock the doors, call 911, and possibly even take a photograph of the assailant to assist the police in identifying him. The time it would take him to cover the distance between you and overcoming the obstacle of a locked door has provided you the opportunity to act to avoid an attack.

If, however, the man in the parking lot is armed with a firearm, the spatial calculation changes. Although the proximity of the threat remains constant, his ability to harm you has changed. He is capable of firing rounds at you which almost instantaneously cover the distance between you and penetrate through the door. In this situation, there is no time to do anything but seek cover.

Another aspect of spatial awareness is the direction of the threat. In the cases above, the assailant was attacking you. But, if however, his intended target is in a different direction, you have an increased amount of time to act. The type of action you choose to take is determined by your preparedness, state of mind, ability to calculate the changing variables, and opportunity to act. Therefore, in order to increase your ability to make successful decisions, you must be both situationally and spatially aware of the events going on around you.

Self-Awareness: A subcategory of SLS situational awareness that refers to one's need to have an accurate assessment of their mental and physical condition. This is another important feature that influences decision making. You must determine if you (or a person you encounter) is mentally *in the game*. If not, a rational conversation with a person, or your ability to make quality decisions will not occur. If you are not mentally fit, you will have to yield to someone who is. This is not always the easiest choice to make, but it may be the wise thing to do. If a person you encounter is not mentally functioning, you can only address them at their level.

Critical incidents can be overwhelming mentally. Often the mind is trying to deal with complex problems without adequate time to solve them. It is also being exposed to graphic and painful sights, smells, and sounds which it had not prepared for. A critical event, be it a violent attack, weather event, or medical emergency that results in carnage and injury, can be catastrophic to one's mental aptitude and cause a mental breakdown. If you come across someone who is, for example in mental shock, you will have to make decisions for them until they regain their cognitive abilities.

Another part of self-awareness is determining your physical condition. You have to assess your physical capabilities before, during, and after an emergency situation has occurred. What physical limitations do you have before an event occurs? Do not fool yourself into trying to do something that you are not capable of. Rather, focus on your strengths and prepare to use them while working to improve your weakness.

During an emergency, the physiological component of the human body may redirect your focus away from self-awareness to focus on the threat. This can be a great thing in order to deal with the threat, but it can also blind you to physical injuries you may have sustained. You may be injured and not know it because the body has said, "we are dealing with a threat right now, there is no time to deal with that broken arm or profuse bleeding." Without a doubt, adrenaline can mask pain and allow this to happen. This has happened to me and many others in the military and law enforcement communities. The positive and negative effects of adrenaline must be accounted for. Therefore, you have to conscientiously check yourself for damage.

Spiritual Awareness: A subcategory of SLS situational awareness that refers to one's need to recognize their focus on Christ. Spiritual awareness is the ability to recognize how in tune (or out of tune) one is with the Lord. The distractions of the world can shift our focus off Jesus, especially during a critical event. Just as a critical event can be overwhelming mentally and physically, it can affect you spiritually. An emergency situation may come in the form of a medical issue, violent crime, natural disaster, or spiritual attack. Each type of event has the potential to shift your focus to the severity of the incident and away from the presence of the Lord. Peter had this issue as his faith weakened when he focused on the wind and waves and not on Christ. The result, he began to sink as he cried out to the Lord to save him. Even in his weakened faith, he turned to the Lord who reached out and saved him (Matt 14:27-32).

This passage reinforces how much influence the world has on us. Even in the presence of the Lord, fear can creep in and disrupt our focus. It is in the direst moments that we need the Lord the most. However, the magnitude of a crisis can shift our focus away from the source of hope and to the trouble we are facing. This happens all the time. Therefore, we must monitor ourselves during emergency situations to make sure we have not become spiritually disconnected.

We want to remain focused on Christ, but pride can reveal its destructive nature during critical events. Matthew 26:41 says: "The spirit is willing but the body is weak." Thus, it is common for people to find themselves saying that they don't have time for God because they have a crisis to deal with! For believers this sounds crazy but, when we are overwhelmed by emotion facing tremendous danger, it can happen. Therefore, we must check our spiritual awareness to remain vigilant. Make every effort to be spiritually, mentally, and physically aware of your status as it will place you in the best position to take *Action* to *Deter*, *Avoid*, and *Mitigate* attacks.

† † †

Being situationally aware of the environment and its effects on your physical, mental, and spiritual condition can be a taxing endeavor. It requires effort, continual preparation, and discipline to get out of a state of obliviousness and live a lifestyle of relaxed vigilance. The lazy side of the mind has to be put to work. But over time, with repetition in disciplined situational awareness, it will become easier. Eventually, you will achieve a state of relaxed awareness with optimal situational awareness.

Often emergency situations occur without any warning. Therefore, your response will be made automatically based on pre-established mental patterns. These are memories that come from experiences and training. The mind sees an unexpected emergency situation and associates with pre-established mental patterns to make a rapid decision. These past experiences come from actual events, training, and preparation which includes cognitive blueprinting (making mental patterns that constitute contingency plans).

This means your response to an emergency situation will often be decided without any time to formulate a plan to counter the emergency you are facing. Your default response will be in part based on the preparation you have made to defeat that attack. Many people in emergency situations experience, a fight, flight, or freeze response to a given stimulus. This is often due to the existing mental preparation established through experience, training, and planning. When the preservation of life is on the line, you want to have more options available than just fight, flight, or freeze. Additionally, in every situation it is better to make less of an emotional response and more of a reasoned one. Responding rapidly with the best option will place you in the greatest position to survive and help others.

During a critical event you must remain aware of your emotions as they can fluctuate rapidly. An emotional response based upon fear, pain, or arrogance can lead to a high state of arousal and poor decision making. Decisions that come from over-stimulated or under-stimulated responses to a threat often will be ineffective. Too much arousal to a threat cannot be processed efficiently, prompting an automatic response based upon emotion likely leading to regrettable results. Too little arousal is equally problematic. A decision that comes from a position of lethargy diminishes vigilance and the ability to act quickly.

Part of self-awareness is understanding how your body reacts to stress, particularly that which is presented by life threatening events. The relationship between arousal and performance is affected by: the nature of the skill or task; the complexity of the skill or task; experience in the skill or task; and individual characteristics.[44] Individual characteristics determine what the optimal level of arousal is for each person at each task. Therefore, what is too much for one person may be too little for another.

Knowledge of all of these are characteristics of self-awareness. You must know yourself and your capabilities physically and mentally. Does an emergency situation cause you to overreact, see things far worse than they are, or even misperceive reality? If so, be aware of this in order to increase performance. Does an emergency situation cause you to pause and try to think things through when it is time to act? This is another effect that you must be conscious of and work on to increase performance. Does injury affect your ability and if so, are you cognizant of any detrimental effects?

What is your situational awareness right now? Assess yourself: How aware are you of the world around you? How aware

---

[44] Asken, *Warrior Mindset*, 33.

are you of the people, the key terrain features, and the events occurring in it? What is your perception? What do you see? More importantly, what are you missing? Are there threats? You cannot act upon something if you do not know that it is there. If you sense a threat, how far is it from you? Is your condition one in which you are able to respond to the threat? Are you so focused on the temporal that you are not engaged spiritually? Are you mentally preparing for contingencies?

Fully encompassing situational awareness is complex. It requires a lot of effort to train and condition the mind. Do not be discouraged if this does not happen overnight. Becoming situationally aware and maintaining a relaxed state of mind takes effort but does not have to be an overwhelming endeavor. Remember, in the end it is a way to increase your overall safety and that of others around you.

Take situational awareness and apply it to a church service. What is your mindset regarding church security? Are you oblivious to the threats (active shooters, terrorism, theft, burglaries, attacks on children)? Are you too relaxed to see a possible threat or are you so overly vigilant that you place yourself in a combative mindset? On one extreme you may be so passive that you miss an attack that is coming or even ongoing. On the other extreme, you may perceive everything and everyone as a threat! Neither is an optimal way to operate. A balance is needed in order to achieve the proper mindset. Being situationally aware and conditioning the mind for success will prepare you to efficiently *Act* to *Deter*, *Avoid*, and *Mitigate* attacks.

† † †

A color-coded system commonly associated with situational awareness has been adopted and adapted by many elite law enforcement and military agencies. This code was created to aid shooters in overcoming obstacles to act when deadly force was necessary. It consists of four states of mind that can be used to gauge a person's situational awareness and preparation to react when an emergency situation occurs. These four colors set a foundation which is used to identify different states of mind. It is not a measurement of situational awareness although that is a component of the color-coded system. It does, however, demonstrate the efficiency of different states of mind in human reaction to emergency situations. The color code provides an opportunity to check your awareness and overcome obstacles that prevent you from acting during emergency situations.

John Dean "Jeff" Cooper developed a simple color code that demonstrates what he identified as the four states of the mind. Each state, white, yellow, orange, and red represent a specific mindset. What Copper was trying to accomplish through the color code is the reduction of mental blocks that slow down or block a person from shooting during a deadly force encounter. For a law enforcement officer, those mental blocks can cause hesitation or inaction allowing a suspect to kill the officer or another person. Cooper's color code has generated a great deal of research, refining, and instruction over the past four decades.

SLS uses part of the Cooper Color Code but expands on it to demonstrate different states of mind. Through the SLS approach to the color code, I provide a simple understanding of situational awareness that when combined with preparation (*cognitive blueprinting*) and training the body, mind, and spirit (*conditioning*), it can produce a vigilant mindset where a person is best positioned to act in an emergency situation. *Blueprinting* and *conditioning* the mind will be discussed at length after looking at the Cooper Color Code.

Cooper's color code, or some derivative of it has been adopted by countless military, law enforcement, and combative organizations. It is a simple and sound way of categorizing one's mindset and preparing for optimal performance. NOTE:

The following color code includes condition black, something that was not part of Cooper's original creation.[45]

In the following pages I break down how each color represents the different conditions of an individual's mindset in a way to instruct a church security ministry. As you read what each color represents, consider how it relates to your situational awareness. Determine what are the advantages and pitfalls of each condition. Think also about friends, family, and other people in your life and what condition they generally operate in.

<u>CONDITION WHITE</u>: *A state of mind where one is oblivious to what is occurring in the environment around them.* Imagine a person walking on the sidewalk looking down at their phone and not paying attention to anyone around them. They are wearing headphones and their eyes are locked on the screen. How much of the world are they seeing or hearing? Not much; they are oblivious to the environment around them. Another example of condition white can be demonstrated by the actions of a puppy that is mesmerized by its own tail. All of its intent is calmly focused on its tail. When a person is in condition white, they have no idea if a threat is around or not. A person in this

---

[45] In *On Combat,* Grossman and Christensen study the effects of hormonal or fear induced heart rates. Starting from a normal heart rate of 60-80 bpm and that which exceeds 200 bpm. Expanding from prior research by Grossman and Siddle, they look at the influence of an increased heart rate on performance. Using a color code beginning with white and proceeding through yellow, red, gray, and black as heart rates increase. This author is grateful for their pioneering research which has influenced the countless number of *color codes* utilized in military and law enforcement circles. It has also branched into the sports arena and business realms. Although the color code utilized by the author of this book is concerned with situational awareness and the ability to observe and communicate information in the context of church security, it was inspired by the aforementioned research. This author recommends that the reader read *On Combat,* particularly Chapter Four: Fear, Physiological Arousal, and Performance.

state of mind is useless to help themselves or others. They have set themselves up to be a casualty of an attack.

CONDITION YELLOW: *A relaxed state of vigilance where one has optimal situational awareness.* In condition yellow the mind is primed to identify threats. Imagine that you are at a family barbeque. You and about a dozen family members are in the back yard. Some of the family is together having a conversation, a few members are near the grill, and the kids are playing in the yard. Found among all the activity is the family dog who is sitting upright in the yard. The dog is calm and aware of everything around him. He sees the kids, smells the food, hears the conversation but is also clearly watching the perimeter of the yard. While everyone else is oblivious to what is going on in the woods just past the back yard, the dog is not. He is aware of the animals that may emerge from the wood line. The dog also is familiar with the sounds of car doors closing, unfamiliar voices, and the noise that the gate makes when someone comes into the yard. Everything is on his radar. The beloved family pet is relaxed just like the family members are, but he is alert. The dog in this condition is not focused on any particular threat but his situational awareness radar is on.

CONDITION ORANGE: *A condensed state of situational awareness.* An example of condition orange can be built upon the previous example. Think about that same dog sitting upright in the yard. As soon as something rustles in the bushes, the dog's ears go up and his senses are heightened. Something suspicious has popped up on his radar. Although he is still aware of the world around him, he now has a condensed focus on a potential threat. The dog watches the bushes and may even walk over to the bush to investigate the noise further. He has moved from condition yellow to condition orange.

CONDITION RED: *A state of mind where one is actively engaged in a fight against a specific threat.* Condition red occurs when an attack ensues. It does not matter if you were prepared or not, when you are engaged in a fight, you are in condition red. Using the example of the dog, imagine that someone or something chose to attack the dog or a family member. The dog will not hesitate to fight to protect the family. The dog immediately acts and it engages in battle with a determined focus on winning.

CONDITION BLACK: *A mental state where one is not able to effectively mentally function.* In this state of mind, you are unable to act. This can be explained as being frozen in place. Or, it could be a state of unconsciousness, like being knocked out or passed out due to the influence of alcohol or drugs. Returning to the example of the family pet, a canine found in this state is more like a child's stuffed animal than a protective dog. When it comes to situational awareness and the ability to act upon an attack, condition black is a state of inoperability. Like condition white, people in condition black are rendered useless to help themselves or others.

Taking into consideration these conditions, consider where the mindset is of individuals at your church. How many people are in condition yellow? Are they enjoying the worship service but also aware of their surroundings? More than likely, they are oblivious to the environment around them and will not observe potential threats. Their security concerns probably ended when they locked the doors to their vehicle before walking into the church. For them to see the world in condition yellow, they have to become aware of their vulnerability and willingness to address it. Therefore, they must be educated on the vulnerability that comes with condition white and the necessity of a condition yellow approach.

Although everyone will enhance the security of the church by operating in condition yellow, we all experience times where our focus condenses on a task being performed. If the lead pastor is focused on the sermon, the musicians are focused on worship, the greeters are focused on first time guests, the kid's ministries are focused on songs, snacks, and diapers, who is attentively looking for the threat that may walk into the church?

All of those ministries are vulnerable. If you do not have a designated Safety Team and trained Force Multipliers who are vigilantly on guard, the entire worship environment is vulnerable to an attack.

As the next few chapters will demonstrate, the SLS strategy seeks to cover the church in condition yellow through the use of a Safety Team and Force Multipliers. SLS provides a way to have a Safety Team that operates to enhance the safety and security of the church without creating a distraction to service. The members covertly operate in condition yellow specifically looking for suspicious people, bags, electrical cords that people may trip over, spilled coffee, and other potential threats to the safety of everyone at the church. They operate in a state of relaxed vigilance.

A vigilant mindset positions you to successfully function to help others during an emergency situation. Everyone who seeks to operate in condition yellow must put in the work to condition themselves to be relaxed and alert. It takes discipline to be successful, but when achieved this mindset is life changing.

Condition Yellow is a *relaxed* state of vigilance where one has optimal situational awareness. In condition yellow the mind is primed to identify threats. A person in this state is situationally, spatially, self, and spiritually in tune. Achieving this state of mind takes effort and discipline. Although it is part of the Security Ministry Basic Training that all Safety Team and Force Multipliers should receive, having a condition yellow mindset is not just for them.

Everyone should learn to live within this relaxed state of awareness while at church, at home, on mission trips, living amongst unreached people's groups, or out in public. Over time, through repetition and association, it will become easier and almost natural to live in this relaxed state of awareness. Eventually, being in condition yellow becomes a way of life that takes very little effort. So, how do you get to a condition yellow mindset where you operate in relaxed awareness? You must condition the mind.

Conditioning the Mind

If every member of the Safety Team and those serving at the church can operate in condition yellow, the overall security and safety of the church is greatly enhanced. In essence, the Safety Team and its Force Multipliers are able to *cover the church* in condition yellow. One great benefit from the SLS strategy is that security is enhanced as the church functions normally in a relaxed, warm, welcoming environment. Enhancing security involves empowering each person serving to be aware of their surroundings. This starts with making people situationally aware of what is going on around them and conditioning the mind to act accordingly. This includes identifying threats and executing the proper response. When this occurs, security is enhanced without compromising the church's effort to welcome guests and seek the lost. It is an efficient way to pursue the *one* and protect the *ninety-nine*.

Conditioning the mind means training the mind to function efficiently in condition yellow. Just understanding situational awareness is not enough. You must be able to identify items that are out of place in the world around you and rapidly make the correct decisions to address them. Cognitive science provides insight into how decision-making works. Understanding how the mind makes decisions will allow you to put yourself in a position to make the best decisions rapidly. In an emergency situation these decisions may be life-saving choices.

Cognitive science focuses on how the nervous systems process and transform information. It is the study of the mind and its processes. Everyone has a neural network which consists of over a 100-billion neurons. Neurons are the nerve cells that transport nerve impulses. Each neuron has thousands of synapses. A synapse is the junction between two nerve cells where electrical or chemical signals are passed from one neuron to another. What is astonishing is that synapses are able to change their chemical composition as a person learns. This means that the cognitive system develops and changes through experience allowing people to grow intellectually.

Through experience, training, and preparation new neural networks are created with new recognizable patterns. These patterns are associations, or "mental files," that present recognizable options the mind can access when confronted with an emergency situation. The more experience and use, the stronger the synaptic connections and patterns become. Therefore, by repeating something over and over strong patterns are formed. This is why experience and training (blueprinting) are important in preparation for emergency situations at church. *Cognitive blueprinting* is a mental process that creates patterns that the brain can quickly access and respond to. Each new pattern established is a new concept that a person can use for cognition. When a perceived pattern is found to be valid, the reaction is almost instantaneous. Simply put, when an emergency presents itself, the brain recognizes the previously established pattern, positively associates the emergency situation with it, and finds an acceptable solution to execute. Therefore, time is not wasted contemplating what to do to resolve the emergency. The correct decision is made rapidly due to previously established patterns based on experience, blueprinting, and training.

In *Thinking Fast and Slow*, Daniel Kahneman explains mental life using the metaphor of two systems that produce fast and slow thinking. He refers to these classifications simply as Systems 1 and 2.[46] For illustrative purposes concerning safety and security, SLS describes these two systems of cognitive decision making as two mental *heroes*. Together, they are responsible for the fast and slow judgments and decisions that

---

[46] Daniel Kahneman, *Thinking Fast and Slow* (New York: Farrar, Straus and Giroux, 2011) 13.

you make. Do not be confused, you are not one or the other. You mind is a combination of both types of thinking. You are both Hero 1 and Hero 2.[47]

Unfortunately, neither of these heroes' actions are perfect which partially explains why we make bad choices. Decisions can be made rashly, slowly, inefficiently, and during emergency situations they are often disrupted. Part of inefficient decision making is due to mental laziness. In addition, there are times when bad decision making is the result of the wrong system taking the lead role. When this occurs, often the result will yield less than optimal outcomes. SLS seeks to condition the mind to be situationally aware and operate in condition yellow. Through experience, cognitive blueprinting, and training SLS will prepare the mind to respond better during an emergency situation where decisions must be made in an instant. This will aid you in conditioning your mind to think fast and slow efficiently.

† † †

You have one mind that you use to make decisions. However, it contains two systems. Each system is capable of being the decision maker but one must take the lead. This is similar to having two hands; each is capable of being used to perform a task, but generally the dominant hand takes the lead. For example, I am right handed and can shoot a basketball much more efficiently with my right hand than my left. I *prefer* to shoot the ball with my right hand even if I have the ball in my left hand. This is because it is more efficient for me to switch

---

[47] In psychology, Dual Process Theory has many variants and forms. This author uses very simplified examples concerning the topics of conditioning of the mind, cognitive blueprinting, and understanding situational awareness in a way not presented prior to this book. Kahneman's research is extensive and should be sought by the reader for further understanding.

the ball from my left to my right before shooting. By shooting with my dominant right hand, I increase the chance of making a basket. However, if you create a situation where time matters, for example, if the clock is running down to zero, I may not have time to transfer it to my right hand and get the shot off before the clock expires. Hence, I will have to shoot with my left hand to have a chance to make a basket before time expires. It may not be as effective as shooting with my dominant hand but, at least I am getting the shot off and have a chance to be victorious.

No matter which hand shoots the ball, I am taking the shot. Through training and practice I can increase my left hand's ability to shoot. As proficiency increases it can become a viable option when circumstances like those above require that I shoot with my left hand. I can also improve my ability to transfer the ball from my left to my right more efficiently to get a quicker shot off. I have two systems to shoot the ball, one from my dominant right hand, and the other from my left. Regardless of which I use, it is still "my" shot.

The two systems of the mind provide you with two ways of making a decision. One is used when time is not a factor and the other is used when a decision has to be made without planning. No matter which system comes to a decision, it is *your* decision. Just like in the example above, it doesn't matter which hand I shoot the ball with, it is *my* shot. Additionally, just as you can train your hands to perform better, you can also train your mind through practice and experience. This becomes beneficial when an emergency situation arises because proficiency in mental ability allows you to react quickly without having to think a decision through.

The two systems of the mind operate very differently. To explore this, imagine System 1 as the *Action Hero* and System 2 as the *Intellectual Hero*. System 1 is characterized as the hero who wants to take immediate action. Intuition and impulses are his key traits. System 1 relates to Proverbs 12:24 which states: "The hand of the diligent will rule, while the slothful will be put to forced labor (ESV)." System 1 is decisive and operates automatically. That is, the system operates without using much energy. With little to no effort, it quickly makes decisions with no sense of voluntary control.[48] Unless anomalies are perceived, this system functions using an intuitive decision-making process basing its conclusion on the immediately available information. Therefore, if it is presented with a problem that it has experienced before, it recognizes the previous pattern, associates the new problem with that memory and formulates a decision by applying the current problem to the previously established pattern.

Some examples of the automatic activities of System 1 provided by Kahneman include:

- Determining that one object is closer than another.
- Finishing the phrase "bread and . . ."
- Perceiving hostility in a person's voice
- Solving 2 + 2 =?
- Comprehending basic sentences.[49]

System 2 is very different than System 1, although it too is a hero. The hero of System 2 is the *intellectual* who is more deliberate in its decision-making process. Because the process is more deliberate, System 2 allocates relatively more resources to the effortful mental activities that need the system's attention than that of System 1.[50] System 2 is a planner. This intellectual hero finds comfort in Proverbs 21:5: "The plans of the diligent lead to profit as surely as haste leads to poverty." System 2

---

[48] Kahneman, *Thinking Fast and Slow,* 20.

[49] Kahneman, *Thinking Fast and Slow,* 21. This is an abridged version of the examples provided by Kahneman.

[50] Kahneman, *Thinking Fast and Slow,* 20, 21.

thrives on planning. That is why System 2 is perfect for complex computations where concentration is needed. Because the complex computations take additional effort, they also need additional time to assess the situation and consider multiple options. Since vital tasks are worked out in System 2, greater effort and self-control are required than that found in System 1.

Some examples of the highly diverse operations of system 2 that require deliberate attention (and are disrupted when attention is taken from them) that Kahneman provides include:

- Isolating the voice of a specific person in a jam-packed, noisy room.
- Being aware of the appropriateness of your behavior when around others.
- Counting how many times the letter W appears in a text page.
- Completing tax documents.
- Verifying the accuracy of multifaceted arguments.[51]

The automatic operations of System 1, the *action hero*, can generate complex patterns of ideas. However, only the slower, deliberate, analytical *intellectual hero* of System 2 can construct thoughts in an orderly series of steps. Whereas System 1 operates automatically, System 2 remains controlled and conscious. The mind generally relies on the effortless function of System 1. It constantly associates memories to construct a coherent interpretation of perceived reality. It then generates impulses about how to respond to environmental changes.[52]

---

[51] Kahneman, *Thinking Fast and Slow*, 22. This is an abridged version of the examples provided by Kahneman.

[52] Christina McRorie, "Rethinking Moral Agency in Markets: A Book Discussion on Behavioral Economics," *Journal of Religious Ethics* 44, no. 1 (March 2016): 198.

The control of attention to a stimulus is shared by both systems; System 1 automatically and System 2 when needed. For example, when a loud sound is heard, orienting yourself to it is generally an involuntary operation of System 1. The *action hero* reacts without much thought or effort and says, "What was that?" This immediately mobilizes the voluntary attention of the *intellectual hero* who begins working on analytics.[53] System 2 deliberately starts trying to figure out options to respond to the noise.

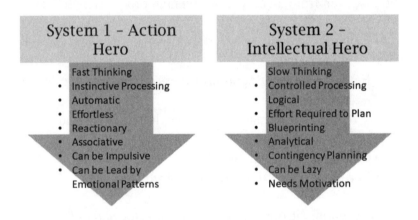

Characteristics Systems 1 and 2.

Imagine that the following scenario occurs while you are at church. It will demonstrate how the two systems work and how *cognitive blueprinting* (a form of mental preparation) can prime you to make the best response. In this scenario, you are serving as an usher inside of the sanctuary during a Sunday service. A very loud noise is heard from outside of the sanctuary. The noise is so loud that it interrupts the pastor's sermon causing him to momentarily pause. Some people in the congregation turn around and focus their attention towards the origin of the sound. A couple of other ushers do as well. Two people stand,

---

[53] Kahneman, *Thinking Fast and Slow*, 21, 22.

but within seconds the pastor continues with his message right where he left off. Seeking guidance and following the lead of the pastor, the majority of the congregation turns its attention back to the pastor.

The loud noise causes your System 1 to react. You immediately look towards the sound of the noise "without thinking." It was loud and not recognizable but the *action hero* of System 1 reacts. But there is no previously established mental pattern or plan for a loud noise that interrupts church service. This causes a pause in action with an urgency to act. Therefore, any action taken will be based upon limited information. Those circumstances can lead to a less than optimal decision. So, rather than acting, you freeze. The *intellectual hero* says: "I'm working on the solution" and you begin to focus on the problem, identification, options, evaluations, and discerning what the best course of action is. But this takes time and in a critical event that is a problem. You have one mind with two systems trying to formulate a plan and decision. But due to the lack of experience, cognitive blueprinting, and training it is not developing well.

The *intellectual hero* of System 2 is working diligently to weigh options. He is taking time to work through the process of observation of the stimulus, orientation, and weighing out decisions that will lead to action.[54]

Before you work your way through all the options and formulate a plan, a person bursts through the doors at the back of the sanctuary and yells "someone was just shot!" The *action* and *intellectual heroes* each receive this new information. The new information has disrupted the problem that the System 2 hero was trying to work through and presented a new problem. This causes System 1 to take over decision making. The urgency of the situation has caused the System 1 *action hero* to react.

The new information that a person was just shot presents an imminent danger to your child. Your mind is aware of this

---

[54] The OODA loop will be discussed in detail later in this chapter.

and System 1 is now in control. It relies on the only default pattern established in your memory which is, *if something bad happens immediately get to your child*. Therefore, you instantly find yourself running to the children's ministry to check on the safety of your child. Unfortunately, every other parent is doing the same thing!

The doors to the children's ministry become jammed with people as everyone is trying to push through the sea of parents. Some people are even being trampled over. The crowd has crammed the doorway, people are acting chaotically, and some are getting hurt. The injured now create additional problems for the mind to deal with. Each new obstacle presents a new problem that must be worked through, but there is no time for the *intellectual hero* of System 2 to contemplate solutions. New problems keep presenting themselves and the only planning that the *action hero* of System 1 has access to is, "*get to the child.*" System 1 therefore focuses on getting to the childcare area of the church. It does this by making choices based on little information.

An off-duty police officer and his wife are also in attendance when the loud noise is heard. As professional law enforcement officers, they operate with a vigilant mindset. They live their lives in condition yellow. Therefore, they have already *blueprinted* what to do in a critical event. They have repeatedly trained their minds to prepare for emergency situations by blueprinting scenarios for the mind to quickly access. They calmly live in condition yellow and have a pre-established contingency plan that is ready to be executed for a scenario like this.

Long before the emergency situation occurred, they took the time to have a "System 2 meeting." Their vigilant mindset recognized that they need to have *blueprints* on file for the *action hero* of System 1 to access if a critical event occurs. At a time when there was no urgency to come up with a plan, they *blueprinted* what to do if an emergency situation presented itself. They also decided what each of their roles would be if an incident occurs. This "System 2 meeting" is a training session that caused the System 2 *intellectual hero* to do what it is best at: diligent planning for efficient decision making. Well before those incidents occurred, it created plans to assist System 1 if an emergency like this occurs.

When the loud noise was heard by the couple, they each oriented themselves to it and perceived it as suspected gunfire. The System 1 *action hero* quickly searched for a pattern to apply to the problem. Fortunately, it found blueprinted plans filed away in its memory that the System 2 *intellectual hero* previously created. System 1 *action hero* associates the current situation with the blueprinted option and acts based on the acceptable association. That plan calls for him to move towards the sound of the noise while she moves to get their daughter. They are out of their seats and moving while the other people in the congregation are still trying to process the initial noise that they heard. They are the first through the doors on their way to get their daughter and deal with the threat. They blueprinted a contingency plan and properly executed it which allowed them to quickly take the best course of action to mitigate the attack.

Failure to properly plan is planning to fail. Everyone serving at the church should be operating in condition yellow. This includes blueprinting for emergency scenarios which create files that the System 1 *action hero* can access if a critical event occurs. The *intellectual hero* in System 2 must deliberately create these plans based upon analysis of potential situations and the options that you will have during a critical event. The time to do this is *now*, when there is no sense of urgency and when selections can be scrutinized to determine the best option. Once the contingency plan is created, it is filed where the System 1 *action hero* can access and implement it in an emergency situation. The only obstacle to achieving this is the laziness of System 2. It takes effort to create those blueprints and it takes discipline to reinforce them as part of your daily life.

The System 2 *intellectual hero* generally enters into the decision-making process because the System 1 *action hero* identified a red flag. But you should not wait for an emergency situation to get to work. System 2 has the ability to influence and change the way that System 1 works. This is done by programming the normally automatic functions of attention and memory.[55] Use System 2 to blueprint what to do if you have to evacuate the church, get to your loved ones, evade an active shooter, render medical aid to yourself or others, and *Act* to *Deter*, *Avoid*, and *Mitigate* attacks.

As previously discussed, one of the subcomponents of situational awareness is self-awareness. Are you training yourself to be in condition yellow? Checking your self-awareness will make sure that you are being situationally aware by paying attention to your surroundings, and controlling where you focus your attention. To be successful in the rapid decision-making process, you must first fill your memory with files based on experiences that includes training and *blueprinting*. If you find that you are not doing this, a check of your self-awareness will get you back on track.

Cognitive Blueprinting

Cognitive Blueprinting is a technique used to prepare the mind to act efficiently by continually creating contingency plans of action for unexpected situations. It encompasses awareness, imagination, and discipline. General blueprinting (master plans) occurs in condition yellow and specific blueprinting (addendums and attachments) occurs in condition orange. Cognitive blueprinting is taking preemptive action to

---

[55] Kahneman, *Thinking Fast and Slow*, 23.

increase performance and reduce the effort of Systems 1 and 2 during a critical event.

In condition yellow, blueprints are for general emergencies such as a violent attack at church, an active shooter, a weather or fire incident, or a medical emergency. Things change when a suspicious person walks into the sanctuary, sits front row and center, is fidgeting, and sweating profusely. Now, a potential target has appeared on your condition yellow radar. You transition into condition orange as you give specific attention to a possible threat.

The System 1 *action hero* tells the System 2 *intellectual hero,* "we need contingency plans specific to this potential threat." Plans are needed because if this person initiates a violent attack, the time to prepare will have passed. These mental blueprints created in condition yellow and the specific ones created in condition orange are linked. If the specific threat becomes an active shooter, the System 1 mind will associate the problem to the blueprints and execute the plan rapidly. Very little effort is placed on System 2 to create these blueprints in condition yellow, but increased effort is needed to formulate plans in condition orange. Operating for prolonged periods of time in condition orange can cause mental and physical fatigue and lapses in judgement. This is why you must become proficient in operation the relaxed state of awareness found in condition yellow and focus your blueprinting effort there.

Think of cognitive blueprinting as creating a mental plan for the "what if" scenarios. For example, what if you are sitting at a coffee shop typing on your computer when a fire breaks out causing an evacuation. If you did not have a mental file that is a blueprint reminding you where the exits are, you would have to take time to locate them. During the chaos of the employees yelling at everyone to get out and people reacting in panic, it may be difficult to locate an exit. Your System 1 *action hero* will make a decision based on the limited information it has. Without a blueprint, the only pattern that System 1 recognizes is the way you entered in the building. That may be the optimal choice. But it also may be blocked by fire or by people who are trying to get out.

If you had walked in and had System 2 familiarized itself with the location of the exits, it would have created a blueprint and assigned it to the previously established plan for evacuation. The general master plan for all restaurants says grab your valuables and walk towards the nearest exit. This file for evacuation now has an attachment specific to this coffee shop including the location of the exits. Therefore, when an emergency occurs the System 1 *action hero* will find established patterns for evacuation and the specific locations of exits. Thus, action can be taken immediately without having to look to System 2 for a plan. This saves time and thus lives. Blueprinting must be a part of a condition yellow state of mind. It is an *action* you can take before an emergency occurs to *deter*, *avoid*, and *mitigate* threats.

Let's look at the blueprinted master plan and blueprinted attachment again. In the chaotic frenzy following the initiation of an emergency, people may flock to the known exit and trample upon each other. The general master plan says: "in an emergency situation, grab your valuables and take the best avenue to get out." Your valuables may include your family, your wallet/purse, phone, and keys. That's your master plan for all locations which is repetitively updated every time you enter a new place. This is the blueprinted attachment to that master mental file. It is an addendum for each new location you visit and subsequent situation. It creates a specific contingency plan based upon the latest intel for that situation. With little effort this information is fashioned by System 2 while in condition yellow for use by System 1 if an emergency situation transpires. Since System 2 does take effort and can be lazy, cognitive blueprinting does not come naturally. It is necessary, therefore, to be disciplined and force System 2 to get to work and blueprint contingency plans.

We strive to have System 1 running automatically in condition yellow with System 2 constantly blueprinting contingency plans. System 1 continues to make the majority of decisions while System 2 is in a planning mode. A problem can occur when System 1 runs into difficulty and calls on System 2 for support, but there is not enough time for System 2 to deliberately look at all the options. Generally, this occurs in one of two scenarios. The first is when you are in condition red and fully engaged in a fight. The other occurs during the transition from condition orange to red as a potential threat becomes an active threat. In this second scenario, if System 2 has not finished its contingency planning, the system becomes frustrated because it gets cut off in the middle of planning. The result is that System 1 is forced to act with incomplete contingencies. Now, even though this occurs, the mind does not shut down. System 1 has previously established blueprints, including master plans to access. Therefore, even in the worst-case scenario, efficient decision making is made and a mental freeze or shut down is avoided.

Blueprinting brings out the most efficient use of each system and thus is a salient part of a Christian Warrior Mindset. When it comes to reacting to emergency situations inside or outside the church, you are in the best position to be successful if you have this mindset, are situationally aware, operating in condition yellow, and directing System 2 to create mental blueprints. Cognitive blueprinting is taking preemptive action to increase performance and reduce the effort of Systems 1 and 2 during a critical event.

The experience that you gain through the repetition of training and blueprinting will condition the mind to act more efficiently. The more skilled you get at the task, it's demand for energy will decrease. As skill and talent increases, less effort is needed to complete the tasks. Therefore, the more you blueprint, the safer you will be concerning numerous types of emergencies.

When you train yourself, it will start out with general blueprinting of master plans including the exits of locations you find yourself in. This training will grow in complexity as your mind creates more files and patterns to utilize. These mental files continue to produce associations that will create additional recognizable patterns for System 1 to utilize. General blueprints for emergencies mature into blueprints for active shooters, specific weather events, and medical emergencies. The mind continually grows more efficient in preparing System 1 to make rapid and correct decisions. By disciplining System 2 to blueprint, you are empowering System 1 when it is time for action.

Every unexpected emergency situation presents itself with an initial stimulus. A loud noise, a person screaming, a car accident, a child crying, the smell of smoke, or by any other type of indicator that something may be terribly wrong. From the onset of the stimulus until you act takes time. The quicker you can move from the stimulus to correct action, the greater the likelihood that you can react in a positive way. By blueprinting you are effectively utilizing Systems 1 and 2 to make a rapid and correct decision.

When you blueprint and begin to efficiently use both Systems appropriately, you have overcome fear with faith, are operating from a position of peace, are exercising condition yellow situational awareness, and efficiently making wise decisions to take action. Action, as stated earlier in the book is a requirement of the SLS strategy. What do you blueprint? The possibilities are endless. Blueprint a response to a person who has a medical emergency, a person who comes to the church under the influence of drugs or alcohol, a person who is disruptive during service, a passive protest, knife attack, active shooter, fire, vehicle burglary in progress, a person entering into a restricted area, tornado, a person who gets sick and throws up; blueprint your actions and those of others, and on and on and on. Once you have reached the point where you have blueprinted for a blimp attack, I think that you are good!

The OODA Loop: Observation, Orientation, Decision, Action

The OODA loop describes a mental cycle that people go through following the observation of a stimulus. Created by John Boyd (1927-1997) a former U.S. Air Force pilot and instructor who is credited with shifting the air combat focus from gunnery (how to shoot) to tactics (how to prevail).[56] This was a foundational change in aerial combat. The philosophical focus on prevailing tactically has been adopted by elite military and law enforcement special operations and SWAT units. Tactical fluidity and the ability to be more mentally proficient than your adversary is a salient characteristic of all military special operations units, SWAT teams and tactical operators.

The start of the OODA loop is the observation of a stimulus in a fluid situation. This observation may initially be detected by any of the five senses. For example, you may see a person enter a church building with a firearm. Or, the first thing you observe is hearing a gunshot. Regardless, you observe the stimulus and begin a process towards executing your action.

Once you have observed the stimulus, you then must orient yourself to it. This must be done quickly because the situation is fluid and there are always additional unfolding circumstances. Therefore, it is essential that you quickly orient yourself to the stimulus. You must determine which direction the threat is in, which direction is it moving, and what your options are. Then, after orienting yourself to the threat, you have to decide what action to take. Do you evade, hide, or fight? A decision must be made before a new stimulus is observed because that new stimulus will begin the OODA loop process again. Thus, you

---

[56] Daniel Ford, *A Vision So Noble* (Durham, New Hampshire: Warbird Books, 2010), 8.

not only have to reach the point of action as quickly as possible, you must follow through and act!

The OODA loop

- Observe:
  - Identify the event/situation/attack.
  - Observations are made through multiple senses.
  - DO NOT DENY what you are observing.
  - DO NOT LET EMOTIONS make you *wish* it is not occurring.

- Orient:
  - Focus on the stimulus.
  - Gather information as it relates to you.
  - Make predictions, create options, and strategize optimal outcomes.

- Decide:
  - Make a decision based upon your observation and orientation.
  - Training, experience, and blueprinting will increase efficiency.
  - Commit to the decision prior to another stimulus.

- Act:
  - Respond to the stimulus through action.
  - Execute the plan.

OODA loop description.

The more efficiently you move through this decision-making process, the greater the likelihood of your survival. If you have mentally blueprinted scenarios, you will decrease the time it takes to move from the onset of the stimulus to action. Unfortunately, no emergency situation will be limited to a single decision that has to be made. In fact, the chaos of the incident will cause continuous breaks in your OODA loop as you try to get from observation to action when presented with multiple stimuli. You must fight through the chaos and overcome the obstacles.

The goal is to increase the capacity for independent action. Individuals join with others to cooperate and compete towards the achievement of an objective. However, since resources are finite, a struggle begins that actually never ends. From Boyd we learn that action and decision become critically important and therefore must be able to form mental concepts based on observation and change these concepts as observed reality changes.[57] As you begin the OODA loop in response to a stimulus, the correct action needs to be taken quickly in order to succeed.

The fluidity of the situation means that new variables (new stimuli) may be introduced at any time. Each time a new stimulus appears, that new information has to be processed and the loop begins again. The more chaotic the scenario the more variables that will be introduced. This increase means the ability to achieve a quick and accurate action is far more difficult in an emergency situation than an orderly one. When the System 2 intellectual hero has little to no time to formulate plans, the System 1 action hero is rapidly trying to make decisions while being bombarded with new stimuli and no previously established patterns for association.

Failure to properly plan is planning to fail. Therefore, you must prepare yourself to efficiently work through the OODA loop during a critical event at the church. Since observation is increased through an enhanced situational awareness, a controlled vigilance allows you to avoid being blindsided by an attack. If you are operating in *condition yellow,* then you are more likely to observe a threat early on. Because of this early detection, you are able to orient yourself faster and thus move through the OODA loop at a more efficient pace.

When it comes to deciding what action to take, your mind is going to be heavily influenced by the *blueprinted* patterns that have been established by System 2 and filed in the patterns that System 1 references. The System 1 mind quickly accesses the preestablished plans and immediately acts upon them. If you are not in condition yellow, have no blueprinted options, and

---

[57] Ford, *A Vision So Noble,* 17.

are not able to take action, you will be unable to move through the OODA loop. In essence, you will be defeated.

This is not the state that Boyd wanted his fighter pilots to be in. He focused on the ongoing process and the ability to move through the loop faster than his opponent. In *A Vision So Noble*, Ford discusses how the warrior's object is to create chaos and disorder that your opponent cannot overcome as you sweep out the debris. If you can operate in a world of chaos that continually overwhelms your opponent with stimuli, you win. Boyd taught that individuals must get an image or picture in their head that orients them to what they observed. That leads to decision and implementation (action). Next, the resulting action, plus new observation creates new data and a new cycle. According to Boyd, orientation isn't just a state, it's a process. The object is to operate fluidly in this process while your opponent fails to keep up.[58]

Every time there is a new stimulus, there is additional orientation. Therefore, it is important to move through the loop as efficiently as possible. Racing through to action is not enough. The decision you make and action you take must be the correct ones. Remember, the System 1 mind will act impulsively based on the patterns that have been pre-established. Therefore, if there are no blueprints or pre-established patterns, the decision made may be the wrong one. Blueprinting is essential to prepare the System 1 mind to make the right choice rapidly.

Critical events are fluid and chaotic as they continually introduce new stimuli. If, for example, you observe a shooter enter the church that is the first stimulus that you observe. Before you are able to move through the OODA loop and act, he begins firing from a position located at the primary exit point. This is the second stimulus you observe before being able to act. Quickly, you orient yourself to the shooter and decide to move to the alternative exit that you blueprinted when

---

[58] Ford, *A Vision So Noble*, 29.

The SLS Strategy for a Security Ministry

you first sat in the sanctuary. However, before you are able to act, another shooter *enters in through that exit.* You keep trying to complete the OODA process and *act* but new stimuli keep resetting that cycle. All of this occurs in a matter of a couple of seconds.

At this point, you have observed two shooters, oriented yourself to them, and deicide you are going to get low and make as small a target as possible while moving towards cover and concealment. Then you move. Finally, you have been able to *act* and start the loop again. The OODA loop decision making process never stops unless you decide to do nothing but curl up in the fetal position and hope to survive. Unfortunately, many victims of mass shootings have reacted this way. It was the last decision they made before being killed. The Christian Warrior Mindset does not allow for this. You will never give up, you will always take some form of *Action* to *Deter*, *Avoid*, or *Mitigate* and attack.

- The OODA loop occurs between the onset of a stimulus and the onset of an action to counter that stimulus.

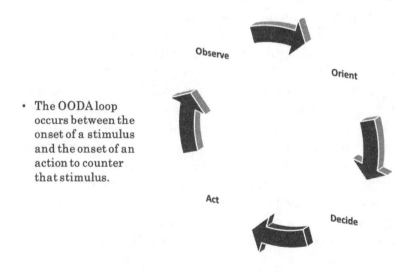

The OODA loop cycle.

It is desirable to complete the OODA loop as quickly as possible, but everyone is limited by many variables as to how quickly they can react. Asken indicates that the loop can require a faster response than a person is able to provide. An example is when excessive negative emotional arousal paralyzes cognition, which can cause a loss of situational awareness.[59] Think of a person who appears lost in the moment, they are gazing off into the distance oblivious to your presence. This person has lost all situational awareness. They are not able to process or remember events.

When caught in this position, a person is unable to complete the OODA loop and is susceptible to being defeated. They are in essence in condition black. These individuals must get back into the game. The sooner they acknowledge what is occurring around them, the sooner they become situationally aware, the sooner they can complete the loop and survive an attack. It is not just people you encounter who can be caught in this position. You too are susceptible to it. Remember that part of situational awareness is self-awareness. Therefore, prepare yourself to recognize it and get through it.

One final thought on the OODA loop is the advantage it gives you when you identify that your adversary is not efficiently working through it. Like a football quarterback who did not recognize a shift in the defense and is being overwhelmed by a blitz, your adversary may not be able to efficiently move through the OODA loop when something overwhelms him. That something could be any number of variables, a weapon jamming, fumbling though reloading, an unexpected phone call in the middle of their attack, or having to deal with people fighting back. All of these have occurred in real life scenarios and presented opportunities to mitigate the damage of the attack. If, for example an active shooter is attacking and gets caught in a position where they are not able to process through

---

[59] Asken, *Warrior Mindset,* 130.

the OODA loop, *that is your opportunity to act.* Their inability to act gives you the opportunity to take advantage by escaping or attacking them. Therefore, you can be victorious by efficiently moving through the OODA loop and taking advantage of the enemy when they are not able to process through it.

Conditioning the Body

In addition to the mental obstacles that emergency situations present, we must overcome the detrimental psychological and physiological effects that the body experiences. As a part of self-awareness it is important to understand the physiological and psychological responses that can accompany a critical event. This begins with looking at the Autonomic, Sympathetic, and Parasympathetic Nervous Systems

The Autonomic Nervous System (ANS) is part of the peripheral nervous system that regulates subconscious control of visceral organs. It is split into two anatomically distinct subsystems known as the Sympathetic Nervous System and Parasympathetic Nervous Systems. The Sympathetic Nervous System (SNS) and Parasympathetic Nervous System (PNS) are divisions of the ANS that exert subconscious control on a variety of instinctive functions.

During a critical incident where the body has perceived that a life-threatening event is occurring, the SNS may produce numerous unusual effects on the body. For example, the pupils of the eyes may dilate. They open wide to take in as much information as possible. Pupils can be indicators of mental effort. Research indicates that the increased dilation occurs when difficult problems are presented like multiplying multi-digit numbers.[60] This produces the "Oh my God" look on a person's face when a life-threatening critical event occurs. When this transpires, it becomes difficult for the person experiencing it to

---

[60] Kahneman, *Thinking Fast and Slow*, 32.

have a condensed focus. Therefore, knowing this, you should anticipate it happening. By blueprinting this scenario, you can counter the negative effect of not being able to focus as your System 1 mind attempts to respond to this physiological effect to life threatening stress. This physiological effect may affect you and others that you encounter during a critical event.

Another example a person in a life-threatening situation may experience is vasoconstriction. This is a constriction of the blood vessels that causes an increase in blood pressure that can inhibit secretion. The result is a reduction in the use of motor skills which can even effect how one bleeds.[61] The sweat glands however, do the opposite. They increase secretion producing profuse sweating. Vasoconstriction is promoted to enhance/preload the heart which causes a shift of priority from peripheral areas to the heart. These responses to the stimuli *cannot be controlled*. However, recognizing that they occur better prepares you to function as you directly deal with the root cause and repercussions of the effect.

Another physiological effect is that the gastrointestinal system will increase peristalsis. In essence, this means that the body may cut loose the control over the bowels. Logically,

---

[61] Note: Dave Grossman and Bruce Siddle offer an enormous amount of research and experience into the physiological effects of what they call combat stress. See *On Combat* and *Warrior Mindset* for additional research and explanation. I have experienced many of these effects during high risk operations. These effects can have a significant, negative impact on task performance including what you hear (auditory exclusion), see (tunnel vision, and loss of near vision), think (irrational behavior), and what you do (loss of motor control). In shootings that I was a part of, I, as well as witnesses, experienced some or all of these effects. Admittingly, this process can never be completely overcome, but properly prepared individuals will be able to anticipate and identify these responses in themselves and others. First, one must understand how and why the effects occurred. People who are familiar with these effects are also able to initiate some countermeasures to limit or control the effects of combat stress on task performance.

the body is responding to a perceived threat to its life and has moved into a lifesaving mode. Rather than waste energy on retaining urine and feces, it uses that energy to aid in life-saving measures. If you were to experience massive hemorrhaging, acute damage to an organ, or even extreme fear, this can naturally result.

Another effect is an increased heart rate. Experiencing a sudden and rapid increase in heart rate and respiration produces a feeling of panic. It can make you think that you are out of breath. Controlling this will mitigate the damage and place you in a better position to survive a life-threatening event.

All of these responses by the body can make it difficult to take the proper action to preserve life even if you have made the best decision to act. If the effect is detrimental, you must fight through it. For example, the inability to have a condensed focus can lead to difficulty to perform tasks such as applying a tourniquet, operating a cell phone, or listening to a person who is mentally overwhelmed. Additionally, the body's response can create a reduction in fine motor skills such as use of the fingers. This further makes the aforementioned tasks difficult to perform. The physiological effects can also reduce the function of gross motor skills. A person experiencing the loss of gross motor skills may become unable to walk, communicate, or even understand where they are. Every human being is susceptible to these adverse effects that the body takes to survive. Understanding them and being able to overcome them places you in the best position to survive an attack. Knowing this, it is important that you mentally blueprint how to handle these situations and condition your body to function at its best during these extreme emergency situations.

Conditioning the body also involves maintaining good health and proper use of your body. Maintaining good health will place you in the best position to be successful when an emergency situation occurs. During a critical event, the Sympathetic Nervous System (SNS) may produce numerous unusual effects on the body including an inability for condensed focus, vasoconstriction reducing control of motor skills, loss of control over the bowels, and an increased heart rate causing additional respiration and a feeling of panic. Many of the negative effects of the SNS response can be lessened or controlled when the person experiencing them is physically fit and in a good state of health.

Conditioning the body includes taking practical steps to place yourself in a more advantageous position. For example, as was discussed earlier, if you find yourself under attack, you must get off the "X" and move to a better position. But even if you are not on the "X," you should take steps to avoid danger. For example, being spatially aware, you can link (a form of maintaining physical contact with loved ones to avoid being separated) as you tactically move during an emergency situation. Advantageous positioning also includes moving yourself and people to points of cover, concealment, and always keeping your eyes open as you scan for *red flags* or signs of threats. *Red flags* are indicators of suspicious activity. They highlight anything that appears out of the norm. This includes items that seem out of place and actions that appear out of character.

Here is another example of a type of advantageous positioning that you can take. Imagine that you go to a restaurant for dinner. Choose a seat that gives you the greatest vantage point of the restaurant and the primary entrance/exit. This allows you to increase your situational awareness and observe the majority of the people who come and go. If a threat presents itself, you are able to condense your focus on the threat sooner (moving from condition yellow to orange) and more efficiently work thorough the OODA loop. Continually being in an advantageous position further conditions the mind as you blueprint additional contingencies. You should do this wherever you find yourself, be it serving at church, at school, work, or out in public at a restaurant, bank, or sporting event.

The Christian Warrior Mindset

Of the three types of people mentioned earlier (sheep, sheepdogs, and wolves), Christian Warriors are the sheepdogs. They live to protect the flock that they love. They are obedient to their shepherd and pursue the lost. They operate in condition yellow. This means that they strive to continually conduct cognitive blueprinting to prepare the System 1 and System 2 minds for action, understand how to use the OODA loop, condition their body, and advantageously position themselves for victory. It takes discipline and continual effort. Although 100% vigilance 100% of the time is not attainable (or sustainable for that matter), condition yellow is pursued.

In that pursuit, warriors serving at church remain relaxed while being vigilant of the potential spiritual attacks, active shooters, burglaries, theft, abuse, and safety hazards that can occur. When serving in the church, they remain in *condition yellow*. This allows Christian Warriors to encourage and uplift others while also mentally blueprinting in preparation for an emergency situation. They do this without creating a distraction to the service and operate within the framework of the vision of the church. People who function this way maintain a Christian Warrior Mindset.

The Christian Warrior Mindset is an established set of attitudes of a Christian who sees a corrupted world and chooses to actively confront evil on a spiritual and natural level. These attitudes include protecting the innocent (stewardship), seeking the lost (outreach), and growth (discipleship). Therefore, a Christian Warrior is a sheepdog who seeks to operate in condition yellow knowing that evil is always scheming to steal, kill, and destroy (John 10:10). The Christian Warrior accepts the responsibility of protecting the innocent which includes the congregation of the church and being obedient to the commands of the Great Commission and Great Commandment to honor God, love people, and reach the lost (Matt 22, 28).

Therefore, the Christian Warrior is concerned for the wellbeing of all of the sheep. As a humbled servant, the Christian Warrior is committed to discipleship which produces growth in relationship with the Lord and with others. This growth comes through a commitment to obedience, prayer, and stewardship. A Christian Warrior is committed to pursuing the *one* while protecting the *ninety-nine*.

Chapter 4

Target Hardening

"Afterward, the prophet came to the king of Israel and said, 'Strengthen your position and see what must be done, because next spring the king of Aram will attack you again.'"
1 Kings 20:22

Making Your Church a Hard Target

The difference between a hard target and a soft target is the degree of effort an adversary must apply to successfully commit an attack. That could be breaking into vehicles during service, entering into an area of the church they should not be in such as the children's ministry, or perpetrating a violent attack such as is the case with an active shooter. Hard targets must present numerous obstacles for assailants to overcome. In general, most security actions are taken to discourage or hinder access but do not go much further than that.

The objective of target hardening is to create circumstances where the assailant deems it too difficult to commit the attack, burglary, robbery, abduction etc. This can cause people to move on to a location where they haven't taken measures to make their church secure.[62] Hard targets not only attempt to deter an attack, they also contain mitigation strategies that counter the effects of an attack. The SLS strategy for enhancing the security of the church contains layers of security where individuals must take *Action* to *Deter*, *Avoid*, and *Mitigate* threats by making the church a hard target.

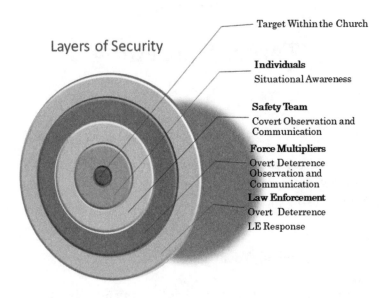

Everyone is involved in security creating multiple layers of defense.

There are many practical actions that can be taken to effectively enhance your church's security. In the SLS strategy one of the primary actions include the creation and proper use of a Safety Team, exploiting every ministry as a Force Multiplier, and having a law enforcement presence. In addition to this core element of the SLS strategy the church can increase its overall safety by taking simple but effective measures to harden its fortification. These include:

---

[62] Welch, *serving by Safeguarding Your Church*, 22.

- Maintaining Access Control
- Providing Highly Visible and Identifiable People Serving
- Utilizing Overt Video Surveillance
- Increasing Lighting and Signage
- Incorporating Functional Design and Placement of Assets
- Obtaining External Training from Government and Private Sector Entities

The church must maintain the integrity of the campus by maintaining access control to all areas of the building(s). Safeguarding access should never be taken lightly. Although this must be done from a security standpoint, it also provides for the efficient function of a church service. For example, people not permitted to access the church offices should not be there unless escorted by someone with access. This not only deters crime, it prevents the *perception* of someone being where they should not be. That misperception can lead to complaints or accusations of wrongdoing that are unfounded. Avoid these headaches by maintaining access control to areas such as the church office.

Additionally, doors should not be propped open to circumvent them from locking. If a door is meant to be closed and locked after someone passes through it, it must function with integrity. Anyone who circumvents the locking system of an access point should be made aware of the security vulnerability that they have created. Propped open doors create a red flag that the Safety Team will see and address. It is easy to see the benefits of maintaining access control and easy to create guidelines for people to follow. However, it takes more than just creating procedures to prevent breaches, people must be held accountable in order for the process to work. If not, the system collapses.

Another way to *harden* the church is to make sure that the people serving are wearing recognizable church identification. Utilizing proper identification creates a welcoming atmosphere to guests and serves as a deterrent against nefarious activity. All staff, leaders, and others serving should have a recognizable and current form of church identification. This is in addition to their own personal identification (for example a driver's license). With the sole exception of the Safety Team, the church identification should be visible at all times. This creates a "we are here to help you" atmosphere for guests and provides a "we have eyes everywhere" feeling for those with malicious intent.

Additional ways of deterring criminal activity include using video surveillance and properly illuminating vulnerable locations. Effective lighting around all access points of the building and throughout the parking lot should be maintained regardless if the facility is closed or open. This must also include illuminating areas that people could use to conceal themselves such as garbage, storage, kid's play grounds etc. In addition, the use of video cameras will assist in the surveillance and documentation of suspicious activity. By using highly visible cameras and signs that indicate that the church is conducting video surveillance, you create an effective form of deterrence. Signs should also clearly indicate restrictions such as "no trespassing" or "no public access" or "no church activities beyond this point." Finally, taking steps to improve illumination and conduct video surveillance demonstrate actions of due diligence by the church to provide for a safe worship environment. Therefore, they should be documented.

Target hardening demonstrates that the church is making an effort to increase safety. If your church has dumpsters, a children's play area, or other areas that may entice people (attractive nuisances) you must make an effort to secure them. For example, a play area may attract children to enter it even if it is secured by a locked fence. If a child gets hurt playing on the playground it will attract lawyers seeking damages from the church. They may charge that you did not do enough to prevent the child from entering. I am not saying they are right. I am only providing a warning that lawyers are naturally looking for opportunities to litigate. Therefore, make sure you take diligent steps to prevent being a victim of a frivolous lawsuit by securing these areas and having highly visible signs to deter people from trespassing.

Inevitably, you will come across people who will try to gain access to restricted areas. Although this may be the result of criminal intent, more often than not, it will involve children. In order to reduce the temptation to access restricted areas and deter crime, take action to limit access to areas that are not for general use and those that present themselves as attractive places for people to go. You also must educate the people serving as to what is restricted and what is not. For example, if a play area has a safety concern (a broken slide) and is deemed to be off limits to children, you must let your people serving know this. If not, they will observe children there and think nothing of it. If everyone serving is striving to have a condition yellow mindset, they must be aware of the restricted areas in order to function properly. Part of their responsibility as a Force Multiplier is to be looking for suspicious activity and when observed, they will know what the notification process is to address it. If a someone gets injured in an area they were not supposed to be, but a person serving who saw them there did not know it was restricted, and thus permitted them to remain there, lawyers will come.[63]

Effective communication is a salient characteristic of the security ministry. The Safety Team and Force Multipliers must embrace the responsibility to observe and communicate suspicious activity during church activities. It behooves the ministry to be efficient in observation and communication to avoid

---

[63] Training Force Multipliers and Safety Team operational procedures will be covered in the following chapters.

potentially catastrophic events such as a child who gets injured in an area that should be restricted. A security ministry will create the opportunity to avoid or mitigate damage.

If a child wanders into a place that s/he should not be and becomes injured, the parents will be asking questions concerning the church's supervision over that area. If it is not clearly marked off limits, then a reasonable person would assume that the child was free to go in and play. Furthermore, lawyers may argue that it was reasonable to assume that the area was maintained and monitored by the church to ensure safety. This could lead to the church becoming the target of a lawsuit. Therefore, to effectively avoid negative litigation, place highly visible signs in vital areas indicting *no trespassing* or *no church activities beyond this point* and train the security ministry to monitor access to those restricted areas.

There are additional practical ways that your church can set itself up to mitigate damages if an emergency event occurs. The paragraphs above demonstrated how signage can be used as a deterrent. Signs can also be used as a means to mitigate damage. Signs not only direct first-time guests where to go when visiting a church, they provide direction to first responders. This is extremely important because in an emergency situation time management is crucial. The sooner a first responders gets to a victim, the greater the likelihood of their survival. In many cases, seconds may be the difference between life and death.

Imagine that there is an emergency at your church and you have called 911. Once the first responders are dispatched, they will rush to the church driving on roads they are familiar with. However, once they arrive at the church they may not know where to go. Figuring out where they are and where they need to get to takes time. That is why clear signage indicating building numbers and rooms within the buildings is essential to mitigate the emergency situation. It doesn't matter if that emergency is a heart attack that occurred to a member of the congregation during service or an active shooter. You must do your best to help the first responders get to the emergency quickly by having clear signage. Because the SLS strategy entails your Safety Team to interact with first responders regularly, they should be providing them with current floor plans that map out the locations of the buildings and the rooms within them. All of these steps to harden the church should be documented in the Emergency Preparedness Plan. Finally, part of the outreach responsibility of the Safety Team includes inviting first responders to assess the church and provide training to the church. This interaction is part of the relationship building and outreach that the Safety Team should conduct with the first responder community throughout the year.

The preceding paragraphs focused on ways to reduce risk and make your church a hard target. In addition to promoting *Action* to *Deter*, *Avoid*, and *Mitigate* attacks, the SLS strategy seeks to deter, avoid, and mitigate *litigation*. Litigation is simply the process of taking a legal action. Ideally, the church does not want to be in the position of taking or receiving a legal action. If the church has to take action, that means that something went wrong and the church was the victim. If the church is on the receiving end, that means someone is accusing the church of being at fault for a wrong that occurred. This can come in the form of criminal charges or civil litigation such as a liability lawsuit. Essentially, a liability lawsuit comes as a formal accusation that the church has committed a wrongful act leading to civil liability (tort). If found at fault, the church could be ordered to pay a financial penalty and award to the victim. To avoid this, the church must act to reduce the possibility of being on the receiving end of a lawsuit.

There are basically four elements to tort law: duty, breach of duty, causation, and injury. In order for an accuser to claim damages, there must be a breach in the duty of the church towards the plaintiff, which results in an injury. The three main types of torts are negligence, strict liability (product liability), and intentional torts.[64] The church could face litigation concerning the negligence over those it supervises (staff and those volunteering/serving) as well as not addressing a known dangerous condition.

As an entity, the church has a role and degree of responsibility over its property and the people on it. The church also has an obligation to oversee those serving as volunteers in addition to the paid staff. It also has a responsibility to address known conditions that present danger such as unsafe areas that people walk through (for example: pot holes, electrical cords, and other obstacles that can cause a person to trip, slip, or fall). Fortunately, the Safety Team acts not only to enhance security, they actively pursue the overall safety of the church by looking to address all safety concerns. This includes training the other ministries (Force Multipliers) to observe and address any and all safety concerns.

In order to avoid litigation, the church should take diligent steps to avoid incidents and lawsuits. Every church has room to improve concerning risk management. Therefore, look at these basic areas where your church can better address risk:

- Take immediate and reasonable steps to make the church a hard target and provide a safer environment.
- Document actions, policies, procedures, training provided to staff and volunteers, and all incidents.
- Maintain high standards of employees and volunteers to include conducting background checks.
- Create a Safety Team with Force Multipliers.
- Create an Emergency Preparedness Plan.

---

[64] General information from https://tort.laws.com/tort-law

The creation of the Safety Team is key in performing your due diligence, but it must be documented. By creating a functioning Safety Team and outlining strategy, procedures, and responsibilities in an Emergency Preparedness Plan, the church's actions are documented in a simple and efficient way.

Establishing an Emergency Preparedness Plan

"Commit your work to the LORD, and your plans will be established." Proverbs 16:3 ESV

An Emergency Preparedness Plan (EPP) is a standalone document that provides an overview of the measures taken to enhance the security and safety of the church, guidance and accountability for maintaining standards, and effort made to reduce hazard. It is designed to take *Action* to *Deter*, *Avoid*, and *Mitigate* risks. The EPP provides direction on how to prepare for potential emergency situations. Although it can never be all inclusive, it takes affirmative steps towards mitigating risk stemming from weather, medical, and manmade emergencies. This includes, but is not limited to: preparation for active shooters, disruptive individuals, medical/health emergencies, direct threats towards church attendees and staff, internal investigations, background investigations, interviewing, collection of evidence, and referring criminal matters to law enforcement.

The EPP also outlines the structure and responsibilities of the Safety Team. This includes standard operation procedures for the members of the team and conducting ongoing training of team members and staff. It is highly recommended that before creating your EPP, you consult with your legal advisor and insurance provider for advice concerning the laws in your state and your specific insurance policy. Because your plan will be reviewed by each entity anyway, why not get ahead of the game and seek their guidance? This can save you from having to make additional changes and revisions that could have been avoided at the beginning of the planning process. This also affords you opportunity to read the *fine print* material that may be in your insurance policy that is often overlooked when it comes to having security procedures. Finally, it allows you to tailor your plan to be within the confines of the laws that govern the area your church is located.

Once you obtain the aforementioned guidance, the next step in creating the EPP is to determine where you stand. Have an *assessment* conducted on your facility. In most cases, local law enforcement will provide one free of charge. This is not only a great way to start your EPP, but develops a relationship between your Safety Team leader(s) and local law enforcement. Remember, SLS consistently pursues outreach to first responders while enhancing the security of the church.

Do not limit yourself to law enforcement. Contact your local fire department and EMS and request their assistance in creating your plan. Specifically ask for suggestions that would enhance their response to a medical emergency. Just as the case with local law enforcement, this is an opportunity to continue developing relationships and future outreach ministry to first responders.

Once you have obtained the free professional information available from your local government agencies, conduct your own assessment. Focus particularly in the areas that are not covered by law enforcement and fire department/EMS recommendations. There are two things to remember when doing this additional step. First, no one knows and understands what the flow of your church looks like before, during, and after service better than you. Your expertise is essential to creating a functional plan. Therefore, it is imperative to take the information you receive and adapt it to your church. Second, the information provided by secular entities may offer recommendations that hinder your church's mission to fulfill the Great Commandment and Great Commission. These recommendations obviously will not be adopted. Therefore, all security recommendations

Target Hardening

must be filtered through a Christian-conceptual lens. Some suggestions by secular entities may have to be disregarded because they do not fit within the vision and mission of your church. After completing the assessment phase, it is time to design your plan. Create a mission statement that is the purpose for your plan. For example, here is one recommendation: *The purpose of the EPP is to enhance the safety of the church, its members, guests, and staff through preparation, response, and cooperation with local law enforcement, the fire department, and EMS.*

Next, break the plan into sections. Each and every church is unique in its size, location, and numerous other variables that affect how your plan will look. Therefore, consider which of the following examples are important for your church to include in its plan:

- Identify the person who is responsible for the plan and annual accountability.
- Create a list of emergency contacts that includes the local police (emergency and non-emergency), fire/EMS, poison control, victim services, the church insurance contact and the church's legal counsel.
- Create a Preventative Maintenance Log: This is to be used to ensure accountability and reliability of items such as First Aid Kits, AED Units, Fire Extinguishers, Evacuation Maps, Severe Trauma Kits, etc. The Preventative Maintenance Log should identify the person(s) responsible for maintaining the log and each piece of equipment.
- Concerning Emergencies: In all emergency situations, it is imperative that the first call be to 911. This ensures that an effort is made to get professional help to the location as quickly as possible.
- Concerning Non-Emergency situations: Not all incidents are emergencies requiring 911. Therefore, one section of your EPP needs to outline who to call in

non-emergency situations. That requires having the local law enforcement agency's non-emergency number, as well as numbers for child protective services, local government victims' advocates, pregnancy centers, addiction hotlines, crime lines (to provide tips to law enforcement), homeless shelters, inclement weather shelters, animal hospitals, veterinarians, and animal shelters. The size and structure of your church, as well as your geographic area, will impact who is called for what type of issue. If there is ever a question if the situation is an emergency or non-emergency, call 911. If there is any debate over the mere perception that the situation is an emergency, call 911 immediately.

- Create Procedural Sections for: Medical Emergencies, Threatening Weather, Fires, Bomb Threats, Suspicious Devices, Suspicious Persons, Violent Persons, Bomb and Weapons Threats (in person, via phone, or email), Evacuations, and Shelter in Place scenarios.
- Provide a section that declares that you will have a Safety Team and outline its purpose and the scope of responsibility of the members serving on the team based upon position such as Team Leader, Assistant Team Leader(s), and team members. Make sure the plan has a current architectural floorplan of the building(s). Have fire escape routes located on maps in the plan and make them highly visible in each building/room in the church.
- Include a media sheet that has a general statement about the church, its mission, and focus. If an incident occurs this will be your starting point in giving a statement. It will be followed by the limited event specific information that you want to give.
- Finally, have a general closing statement that you can make. Having this preplanned beginning to and end of the statement will assure that you can provide the

proper message when a critical event occurs. If not, you may have to address the media in an emotional condition that is not conducive to creating an accurate and professional statement. Remember, your initial statement will be eternalized by the media, get it right.
- Have an established way to communicate to the entire church (via audio and video in conjunction with the Safety Team and Force Multipliers) information regarding emergency situations and what they need to do.
- Finally, the plan should include current photographs and information on all staff members. This includes emergency contacts, family members, addresses, and phone numbers for each.

The EPP should contain comprehensive information concerning the enhancement of the security and overall safety of the church. Any specific information that the church decides to omit from the EPP should still be documented and maintained separately with other standard operating procedures. Your church may choose an approach that has a comprehensive plan that is maintained at the church and a synopsized plan to be submitted to the insurance company. However, this consideration should be addressed with legal counsel and the insurance provider to get guidance on what information should be submitted and what should be omitted.

It is recommended that the EPP contain general guidelines including: actions in deterrence, target hardening, critical event preparation and response, and the establishment of the Safety Team. Concerning the Safety Team, the plan should include outlined standards, scope of responsibility, tactics, and training. Each section should also provide the potential benefits (both in safety and in outreach), implementation, objectives and oversight.

The SLS team has created recommendation reports for EPP's and understands that each recommendation is unique to the local church it was designed for. Although the plan will have a lot of similarity in content, a boiler plate plan that can be applied to any church does not exist. Due to the differing size, location, personnel, and needs, no two churches can have the same plan. For example, a church with a 100-person congregation will have a structured EPP that is similar to a church with 1700 members, however, the content will be drastically different. Finally, because each local church creates a plan designed by its architects (pastor, Safety Team leader, staff, legal counsel, insurance advisor), it will be a uniquely completed work. This is an efficient and comprehensive way of making sure that the plan implemented is agreed to by all parties and within the legal guidelines, church vision, and insurance policy.

† † †

There are many supplementary ways to harden your church against an attack during service. These are considered additional resources to be used in conjunction with the Safety Team. Each additional resource requires added attention and funding. Hence, you must determine if they are needed and will be a good investment. These resources may be very beneficial or prove to be a wasteful purchase. Determining what to add to the Safety Team's effort to enhance the security of the church is completely dependent upon the specific characteristics of your church. Therefore, a cost benefit analysis must be made to decide what will benefit your strategy and what is not a good investment.

This consideration is a stewardship issue as it concerns protecting the congregation and managing finances. So, do not discount using supplementary resources, but at the same time, avoid making hasty purchases. It is best to take the time to make informed decisions about the tools and resources you consider purchasing. The SLS strategy offers you the opportunity to immediately transform your security status by focusing on the people that the Lord has placed in your sphere before purchasing resources. Therefore, begin by creating a Safety Team and empowering Force Multipliers already serving at the church. This is an immediate, no cost adjustment you can make. Remember, the SLS strategy is people-focused and centers around the Safety Team. Therefore, any additional resources must enhance the Safety Team's role in securing the church while supporting the lead pastor's vision for the church. It is best to get your team together before you spend money on resources. Rather than blindly purchasing items, the team will be able to offer functional feedback as to what is needed and what will not work. This can save the church from making wasteful purchases.

Cameras and Radios

Many technological tools offer ways to be more efficient in surveilling the church and communicating the observations of those who are serving. Cameras and radios are the most commonly purchased resources. Cameras provide a way for one person to monitor multiple areas of the church at one time. This can free up manpower and provide recorded evidence of crimes or suspicious activity. They also create a visible presence that serves as a deterrent against criminal activity. Installing cameras (with a video recording system that retains quality images for at a *minimum* of one week) may be an advantageous option for your church. Coordinate with your Safety Team leader and evaluate the cost and benefits of adding video surveillance to your security ministry.

Additionally, radios provide a way to instantaneously communicate information from one person to a team. However, anyone utilizing a radio must be considered an overt presence.

Safety Team members utilizing radios *will not* be able to surveille suspicious people effectively. If the radio is visible (or the wires, earpiece, transmitter, case, or any other indicator that a person is utilizing a radio) that person is not able to function in a covert, low visibility mode. Their ability becomes extremely limited on surveillance. Also, the visibility of a radio, and even an earpiece, can become a distraction to the congregation and service. Therefore, radios have a limited function in the security ministry and cannot be the primary means of communication for the Safety Team.

Although the detrimental effects of the covert church Safety Team using radios can be very problematic, there are limited positive uses that can be incorporated if you have substantial personnel. Radios can serve to relay information to people who are overtly serving in other ministries including parking lot details, ushers, and a person designated to monitor cameras. The strategic use of radios will be discussed further in the section outlining strategy and tactics during service. For now, the main point about radios (and other technology) is to recognize that they have limitations, initial costs, and reoccurring maintenance costs. They may or may not be a wise investment for your church.

We must not haphazardly purchase resources. If you are advocating the use of radios, make sure you can justify why and how you will utilize them to benefit the church and its vision. Without testing them, you may come to realize that they don't function well during worship when the noise level is too loud to transmit, or the radios signal is so strong that it interrupts the signal that the production team is using during service. If you do decide to integrate radios into your plan (as there are very good uses for them), make sure you test them before employing them during an actual service. The last thing you want to do is spend money on radios and put them into use on Sunday only to watch them interfere with the service.

If you choose to operate radios, cameras, or other forms of technology, make sure you train everyone on their proper use. Training will help to prevent the equipment creating a distraction to the worship environment. Additionally, all training should be documented in the Emergency Preparedness Plan. Proper documentation chronicles the steps you are taking to enhance security and safety. These records will be beneficial if any accusations are made claiming that the church has not taken reasonable steps to safeguard the church.

Functional Design

Another way to strengthen the church and make it a hard target is through the use of functional design to deter crime. This is the strategic use of obstacles, decorations, furniture, walls, signs, and other features to enhance security. For example, utilizing decorative bollards and foliage outside of church buildings as obstacles may prevent vehicular attacks where a driver purposefully runs down bystanders or rams a vehicle into the entryway.

These decorative obstacles aid in deterrence, avoidance, and mitigation as well as guiding guests to the route you want them to take as they enter the premises. Inside of the church, the placement of tables, signs, and even people serving can function as obstacles to the avenues of approach a criminal may take to encroach the children's ministry, the church offices, or the collection room. Their placement can also provide clear fields of observation for people serving as a Force Multiplier and Safety Team member during a service or a special event.

The placement of the people serving in regular ministries during service should always be considered. They should be advantageously positioned to foster a welcoming environment and enhance the area that can be observed for suspicious activity. Ushers who have assigned positions must be able to scan the congregation for suspicious activity without having signs or decorations that block their view. People serving in the children's ministry should be able to have a clear view of the access points in and out of their area. Finally, greeters should have an unobstructed view that allows them to see people *before* they get to the doors of the church or into the area they are serving in. As seen in the information on conditioning the mind, being able to observe something suspicious early on creates additional reaction time. This in turn also allows for better decision making.

Advantageous positioning of people will enhance the security of the church and create a more efficiently functioning ministry. This simple adjustment of personnel will allow them to observe threats as soon as possible while also making a great first impression on guests. As with the technology mentioned above, the advantageous use of design is an action step you are taking to increase the safety of the church. It should be documented as it demonstrates the due diligence you have made to enhance security and safety throughout the church. Like many aspects of the SLS strategy, advantageous positioning has no cost to it.

If you are situationally away and operating in condition yellow, advantageous positioning will come naturally. It will become part of the blueprinting you do to condition your mind to act. When you do this, the System 2 mind is preparing the System 1 mind to efficiently and quickly act. As important as this is, remember that other people may have purposefully placed items in locations that benefit their ministry. They may not have been considering security when they positioned it there. Nonetheless, when you start moving tables, banners, flags, chairs, or anything that someone has placed in a specific location, you affect their vision of how it should function. So, before you move a plant or table, consult with the people who placed it there and educate them as to why it is important for you to move it. This will help avoid conflict as you can find a location for that item that serves both a security need and its ministry purpose.

Advanced Training from External Sources

Making the church a hard target may require advanced training from external sources. It is a way to further reduce risk and enhance the overall safety of the church. There are many entities who provide various types of training for churches ranging from first aid to various types of martial arts. Everything along that spectrum can be very beneficial to the security ministry. If you are going to hire them, make sure that their goals line up with yours. Seek first people from within the Kingdom who are as concerned for the lost as they are for the congregation.

Also, take advantage of any free training provided by your local law enforcement, fire departments, and emergency medical personnel. Remember, when emergencies occur, litigation may follow. That is why it is important not only to have training but also document it. Good training should empower those who received it and encourage them to teach it to others who were not able to attend. So, take advantage of free training, document it, and empower people.

Training on Internal Investigations

The local church is not immune from internal problems, disputes, or other actions that require an investigation. Target hardening of the church includes training on internal investigations. Churches generally do not have a separate investigative body that comes in and looks at the problem. Often, pastors are thrust into the role of investigator which is a position that they have not been trained on. Thus, criminals have a soft path to take to defeat the church's effort to investigate suspicious activity. Therefore, an area where the church can benefit from additional training is how to conduct investigations. This includes how to interview, interrogate, collect evidence, and refer criminal activity to law enforcement.

Although the focus of this book in centered on enhancing the safety and security of the church during service, conducting investigations is a proper part of hardening the church against attack. Because of this, conducting interviews and interrogations must be addressed. Some law enforcement agencies will provide free training on these techniques and many private entities will do so for a cost. This section will discuss interviewing/interrogations and the collection of evidence to highlight the importance of each. Your church may choose to get additional training in either area. However, like any supplementary resource that the church considers, a cost benefit analysis must be made to determine how much funding should be delegated to it.

Interviewing is a method used to obtain truthful information through conversation. It involves analysis of verbal and non-verbal information provided by the person being interviewed. Often, interviews are conducted in a cordial and non-threatening manner but can move from an interview to an interrogation at any point during the process. *Interrogation* is also a technique used to obtain truthful information. However, interrogations are conducted on people who are suspected to be concealing truthful information. An interrogation may start out accusatory or strategically develop into accusatory questioning over time. In both techniques, the purpose of the interview/interrogation is to obtain truthful information. Deciphering what is truthful and what is not is the job of the interviewer(s). The person conducting the interview/interrogation is constantly monitoring the subject for indicators of truthfulness, deception, and evasiveness.

Being skilled at conducting interviews can *Act* to *Deter*, *Avoid*, and *Mitigate* threats. An interview before a planned attack, whether it is a theft, active shooter, or abduction, can serve to deter that person from committing the offense. It can also provide information that can cause the church or person who is on the "X" of an attack to avoid being directly hit. Finally, the information obtained through skilled interviewing has the potential to mitigate the damage that has occurred. Therefore, your church may seek to have certain people trained in these techniques. As your team grows, you may discover members who are willing and able to provide training on interviewing and interrogations and not have to seek outside resources.

Training on the collection of potential evidence can also benefit the church when internal investigations lead to civil or criminal litigation. Proper collection is important in order to preserve the physical evidence. If an incident occurs at the church and there is a crime scene, the evidence will be collected by the responding law enforcement agency. However, concerning internal matters that do not involve law enforcement, it should still be carefully handled. The reason is something that does not initially look like a criminal act may end up being determined as a criminal matter once sufficient information is obtained. At that time, local law enforcement should be called to initiate a criminal investigation.

For example, assume that a member of the Safety Team observes two young adults consoling a young girl who is crying. That Safety Team member observes that she is in distress and clearly trying to hide her face. The upset girl avoids making eye contact with the team member and says that she does not want to talk about what is bothering her. The Safety Team member remains with the girl while her parents are located.

While waiting for her parents to arrive, one of the youths comforting the girl hands the Safety Team member a white baseball hat. She says that she does not know who it belongs to. The young lady says that she found it on the floor immediately around the corner from where the disturbed girl was crying. Rather than tell the girl to place it in the church's lost and found, the Safety Team member holds on to it.

The girl's parents arrive and immediately begin talking to their daughter who clearly does not want to look at them. She exhibits numerous non-verbal cues of emotional pain. People offer her a bottle of water, but she exclaims that she just wants to go home. The young girl latches onto her mother clearly hiding the side of her face that is visibly swollen. Her father notices the swelling and asks "what happened?" Immediately the girl starts to cry loudly.

The family is taken to a private area and the Safety Team member asks the father if he would like EMS to respond. Looking at his crying daughters face and swollen eye he says "yes" and immediately asks "what happened" and "who did this?" The girl, who is overcome with pain and fear, says that she just wants to go home. She lets on that a "guy" hit her.

The young girl eventually says it was not a guy from the church and that she had never seen him before. Obtaining this information from the girl takes time. Eventually, she described him as wearing a white hat. She advises that the guy talked to her in the hallway and then grabbed her in an attempt to take her out a side door. As she screamed, he punched her in the face and ran off.

The church has no video surveillance and at that moment, the only known link to the assailant is the hat. Obviously, a criminal investigation will take place involving the local police. Numerous interviews will be conducted. The hat is now clearly evidence and must be preserved. Therefore, before the police arrive, it is placed into a bag by the Safety Team member. That member is going to preserve the chain of custody by remaining with the hat until the police take seize it.

The Safety Team member is able to articulate where the hat came from (the youth who gave it to him) and that he has maintained control of it since then. As a piece of evidence, it is essential that it not be contaminated or go missing. It may be the only link to the person who attacked this girl. Also, it is potentially a clue that can lead to other victims and other crimes. The man may have no prior criminal history or, quite possibly, he may be part of a human trafficking organization. Identifying him will lead to additional information and the hat plays a key role in that process.

What if a canvass of the local gas stations yields a video of him as he stopped there before going to the church? That hat could be the connection that shows the assailant on video footage at the gas station wearing that hat. The victim may identify him from that photo. Also, the video may show other people he was with and the license plate of the vehicle. The hat itself may also contain DNA evidence that will identify him. What was initially just a hat found on the ground can turn into a valuable piece of evidence. Therefore, it is important to properly handle anything that is potentially evidence.

Even without obtaining advanced training in evidence collection, the Safety Team can be taught the importance of handling potential evidence. In this illustration, what started out as a girl crying turned into a matter that gets referred to the police. When the Safety Team member received the white hat, he did not haphazardly handle it. Rather, he preserved the hat until its value was determined. Once it was determined that the hat was evidence, it was processed and provided to law enforcement in a way that retained its integrity.

This incident, like all others, must be documented. As I have stressed, part of hardening the church against attack includes attacks in the form of litigation. In Chapter 6, you will find recommendations on how to document incidents. I have included examples of an Intel Report and After Action Report as well as instruction on how to implement their use. Properly documenting emergencies not only helps law enforcement in their effort to solve the crime, it reduces the church's liability risk.

† † †

Hard targets *Act* to *Deter*, *Avoid*, and *Mitigate* threats. When something appears to be an emergency, do not hesitate to call 911. Here are two examples as to why that is important. One involves criminal activity and the other an emergency situation at the church involving a child. Remember, after critical events occur, your preparation, action, and inaction will be scrutinized. This underscores the importance of preemptively taking *Action* to *Deter*, *Avoid*, and *Mitigate* threats.

Scenario 1 – A couple is seen shouting at each other in the parking lot. The man is yelling in the woman's face and grabs her. He doesn't hit her, he doesn't shake her, but he is holding her against her will (a crime) as he verbally scolds her. She is yelling too and they both perceive that people are watching. They stop yelling, but tension is still visibly high. The man (while still holding her tightly) walks her to the passenger door of the car. She opens it and gets in. It is not until she is in the car that he lets go of his grasp. The man then walks around to the driver's side, enters the car, starts the engine and drives off.

If this is observed occurring at you church, 911 should be called immediately. The person making the call should be prepared to describe the physical characteristics of the people involved, the vehicle, the license plate, the direction of travel, and what just occurred. You cannot dismiss this as being a volatile situation that calmed down and then left the church premises. You do not know what is going on nor are you trained to determine if any laws have been broken. Therefore, out of concern for everyone involved, you should call the professionals who can look into the matter. Maybe the couple calms down and resolves the matter, or maybe not. What if it got worse and you did nothing? Maybe, once out of sight of the church he pulls the car over and begins physically beating the woman. You don't know what is going to happen but you do know what you observed. That is why it is important that you contact the police and let them deal with the situation. You also must document the incident using the aforementioned Intel Report and After Action Report.

Scenario 2- A Safety Team member overhears a person serving in the children's ministry yelling for help. He immediately walks in and observes another person (a church children's ministry worker) performing first aid on a choking infant. Because the woman serving in the nursery was trained, she knew the proper technique for a choking child and administered it effectively. Before the Safety Team member is able to assist, the child coughs up the toy. The baby is crying but is breathing. Everyone is relieved and the people serving in the childcare ministry contact the parents. By the time the parents arrive, the child's color has returned to normal, he is no longer crying, and is joyfully playing with a plush toy. This was a victory, the training that the childcare worker had was executed properly.

By the time that the parents arrive, the child appeared to be fine. During this critical event should 911 have been called? Absolutely! If the call was not initiated immediately, it still should be made even after the child coughed up the toy. Are you willing to say that the person serving at the church has the training and ability to determine that a child, who nearly died is now ok? Call the professionals who will respond and assess the baby. There is a plethora of injuries that the child could have sustained that are not immediately recognizable. If that baby is in need of additional care and you sent him home stating that he was fine, you may be found liable for damage that occurs. Never forget to be diligent in your concern and actions to be a good steward over safety. When a life-threatening event occurs, always call 911 and get the assistance of professionals.

† † †

There are numerous ways to make the church a hard target. For the SLS strategy, the establishment of a Safety Team and an Emergency Preparedness Plan are a must. Other tools can be implemented to assist the team including cameras, radios, external training, and advantageously designing and positioning of assets. What you choose to implement at your church will depend on the numerous variables that are unique to it. One church may not invest in radios where another will find a great need for them. The same can be said for cameras and other resources. Every local church, however, should at a minimum establish a functioning Safety Team with Force Multipliers, create an Emergency Preparedness Plan, and take advantage of the free training that can be provided by your local first responders. Never forget, your interaction with them is not just about security, it is about establishing relationships that foster outreach. Always remember the *one* that you are pursuing while you are protecting the *ninety-nine*.

One final thought on first responders. When an emergency situation occurs and there is reason to believe that a crime has been committed, or a life was in danger, it is time to call them for assistance. This should be notated in your Emergency Preparedness Plan and all staff and leaders should be trained to make sure someone calls 911 in an emergency situation. If you have a law enforcement officer serving at the church and an immediate emergency occurs, notify both the law enforcement officer and 911.

Why notify both? Because 911 is a lifeline. What if there is an active shooter at the church and the only notification is to the law enforcement officer who gets killed before s/he can get the information relayed to dispatch? What if during the chaos the officer's radio does not function properly allowing a transmission? Sometimes radios don't work well or get ripped away from the officer during a fight. If no one knows to respond, time is being wasted that may cost lives. You must notify 911 of all emergency situations as soon as they occur. It is the best way to get emergency care to the church and *mitigate* the damage that is occurring. Finally, document all incidents, trainings, and actions taken to harden the church. This will create a safer worship environment and demonstrate the due diligence of the church if lawyers, litigation, or lawsuits appear.

Chapter 5

Creating a Safety Team

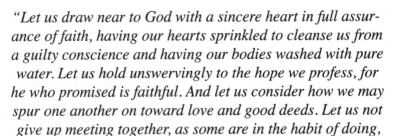

"Let us draw near to God with a sincere heart in full assurance of faith, having our hearts sprinkled to cleanse us from a guilty conscience and having our bodies washed with pure water. Let us hold unswervingly to the hope we profess, for he who promised is faithful. And let us consider how we may spur one another on toward love and good deeds. Let us not give up meeting together, as some are in the habit of doing, but let us encourage one another and all the more as you see the Day approaching." Hebrews 10:22-25

Establishing a Safety Team

Creating a Safety Team starts with the pastor's vision for the church. Therefore, the first step is to know what that vision is to assure that the team will be aligned with it. Next, begin looking for potential members and obtaining free advice from local first responders. Concerning potential team members, the SLS strategy recommends that the Safety Team be comprised of members called to the ministry who are strictly vetted. A member of the team is someone discovered, has been vetted, and been acknowledged as a team member following the competition of a quarterly training session. Up until that point, they are considered a probationary member. A successful team comes from discovering people and empowering them in their gifting rather than recruiting people to fill spots on a roster.

Within your congregation you may have individuals primed to be a part of the team. For example, those who are current or former first responders are ideal candidates. Their professional expertise will help establish the team and are natural points of contact with the local police and fire departments. These men and women will facilitate the church obtaining free services provided by their agencies. Finally, the creation of the Safety Team will involve the development of team leaders. These individuals will begin to take ownership over the creation and development of the team and ensure that the team is committed to its natural and spiritual mission. It is the objective of this chapter to assist you in each of these areas.

Vision and a Team Name

Every ministry serving as part of the church must fit within its vision. It is the church's vision that articulates its role within the Kingdom and in the local community. Therefore, the formation of the Safety Team begins with identifying the vision of your church. That vision cannot be compromised by the creation of a security ministry or Safety Team. Once you have recognized your church's vision, visualize how the Safety Team will support it.

Your team is going to need a name. Some may say that the team name is inconsequential especially because it is a team within the security ministry. However, choosing a team name should not be taken lightly and must be approved by the lead pastor. This may not sound like a big deal but, it is an important one. A poorly chosen team name can be detrimental to the team's success. That is why you must identify the church's vision first as the team name should support that vision. As has been well established throughout this book, SLS recommends using *Safety Team* as the team name. It provides a simple description of the ministry and is not offensive. Of course, you can call your team whatever you desire, but choose wisely. Safety Team implies teamwork focused on safety. It also identifies that the team's purpose goes beyond security and has an emphasis on safety. Therefore, *Safety Team appropriately describes a team of individuals dedicated to providing a safe worship experience for everyone.*

As you consider options for your team name, be global in your thoughts and diligent in your approach. By global, I mean consider what other people will perceive when they hear the team name. Take into account the point of view of other ministries, first time guests, and lawyers. An abrasive name can work against the vision of your church. Therefore, make sure your team name is consistent with pursuing the *one* and protecting the *ninety-nine*.

For example, if your church's mission is to be a sanctuary to all, to love the lost, and provide for the needy, then, having a team named *Gladiators* does not reinforce that vision. In addition, try to avoid a team name that draws undesired attention. If your team is involved in a critical incident, *Gladiators* does not convey the image of Christ or the pursuit of a safe worship environment. A team name such as *Gladiators* paints a picture of a security ministry that is about might and power. To avoid this perception, choose a name that reinforces a missional Spirit Led Security Safety Team not an attack team. Zechariah 4:6 says: "This is the word of the Lord to Zerubbabel: 'Not by might nor by power, but by my Spirit,' says the LORD Almighty." Begin searching for the team name by starting in prayer and the leading of the Holy Spirit. Finally, keep in mind that the action of creating a team name should be strategic as you are attempting to deter, avoid, and mitigate those who have an agenda against the team.

The team name should be functional, conducive to outreach, and risk aversive. From an outreach standpoint, the team name carries significance as it is a representation of the church to the lost. *Gladiators* creates an adversarial image that hinders the ability to reach the lost. From a litigation standpoint an abrasive name such as this will create the perception of an overzealous militant group seeking to discipline anyone who is out of line. If you choose to be creative and have a specific name for the team, consider less confrontational titles such as: Watchmen, Guardians, Emissaries, Ambassadors, Messengers, or use a particular Bible verse such a Nehemiah 4:9.

Think globally. The way a person interprets a title or description is significant because it is their reality. For example, the word *security* itself can create numerous misperceptions. When people think of security, often what comes to mind are weapons, intimidation, power, force, and violence. Therefore, if you name your team *Security*, some people will wrongly associate those characteristics with a team that is in fact a ministry. Although this imagery may be part of some types of security, they are not its salient attributes. For many reasons, it is important to avoid being misperceived in the eyes of the congregation, guests, media, or in a court of law. This is why it is beneficial to select a name that is not abrasive or one that requires an explanation.

So, what is security anyway? Security is an attempt to be free from danger, harm, threats, and tragedy. In the fallen state of the world, it is an unattainable goal. *Actions* can be taken, to *Deter*, *Avoid*, and *Mitigate* the destruction caused by natural threats (weather or medical emergencies), man-caused threats (criminal and/or terrorist attacks), and the persistent spiritual warfare launched at the church. By establishing a Safety Team, educating everyone serving at church, fostering the proper mindset, and using sound tactics you *will* enhance the overall safety of the church.

Security in the context of the local church is very broad. It involves everyone serving whether designated in a security role or not. Therefore, security should not be an intimidating word. People take responsibility over their own personal security every day whether at church, at home, or in public. They attempt to avoid touching things that will poke, prick, or cut them. People lock doors to their homes and vehicles to secure them. They go inside when a thunderstorm approaches and avoid other dangers that present themselves.

If people are already taking these measures to enhance their personal security, they can be trained and utilized to enhance the overall security of the church. This means that they have a stewardship obligation over the safety and security of the ministry that they have been entrusted with. However, this does not mean that they should be part of the Safety Team. The Safety Team should be comprised of select individuals discovered to be part of the ministry. For this reason, and the perception issues presented above, SLS distinguishes between the security ministry in which everyone is involved and the Safety Team that consists of vetted team members.

The enhancement of the security of the church should be a priority, but it often is an overlooked ministry that only gets attention following a tragic event. Each time there is a heartbreaking event that occurs in the mission field or on church grounds, many local churches consider readdressing their vulnerabilities but effectually do nothing. This is an "after the fact" or "after the tragedy" approach. Although, it is normal to focus on security after a tragic event, you should be preparing before tragedy prompts action. The lessons learned from past catastrophic events must be used to formulate plans of *Action* to *Deter*, *Avoid*, and *Mitigate* potential attacks. Having a designated Safety Team ensures that this is being addressed.

With the problem of increasing threats against local churches, each must weigh its options and develop a plan. Providing "security" in and of itself is not the solution. It does nothing to address the dilemma of the Pastor's Paradox. However, enhancing the *security* of the church through applying the SLS strategy does. By establishing a security ministry that has a designated Safety Team, Force Multipliers, and sound tactics to deter, avoid, and mitigate threats, your church's security will immediately be enhanced.

Creating a Safety Team involves planning and growth. Planning includes identifying individuals called to the team, gathering information from local sources, and raising up leaders. It also includes obtaining guidance from the church legal counsel and a review the parameters of the insurance policy. This must be done to make sure that members operate within the established guidelines. Do this before you get the team established so you do not have to make changes after it is created. Once you have determined the laws and guidelines that affect your church, you can begin formulating what enhancing the security of the church will look like. By this point you will have a general idea of how the team will operate within the church's Kingdom focused vision.

Once you have identified the vision, created the team name, and have found a core group of individuals to build the team upon, you can consult with security experts. These can come from members within the church, government entities, and individuals in the private sector. The SLS strategy acknowledges that each element offers positive attributes that can be utilized when properly assessed. As always, use only what is consistent with the vision of your church and the commands of the Great Commandment and Great Commission. As you consult with security experts, look at their philosophy concerning security and see if its objectives are congruent with the vision of you church. Always consider if implementing their advice will enhance or hinder your church's ministry in the community.

Consulting Security Experts

There are far more secular security options than ones that are Kingdom-focused. The Safety Team embraces the Christian Warrior Mindset and has a mission that exceeds securing people and property. It is a Spirit-led, Kingdom-focused ministry that takes on the stewardship responsibility of enhancing the security of the church while following the Great Commandment and Great Commission. Although this is a fundamental difference between secular security and SLS, it does not prohibit you from strategically using secular options. Actually, they (for example first responders) play a prominent role in the overall strategy and are the prime target for outreach by the team.

Local churches are in the unique position of having to overcome the Pastor's Paradox. They are responsible for watching over and following the Great Commandment and Great Commission. Churches are inherently vulnerable to attack and must maintain vigilance without compromising their vision. When it comes to tactics, most churches do not know where to start so they often contact secular entities and security experts. But not all options are right for the church. Be wise and avoid immediately engaging into a contract with anyone. Take the time to determine the quality of their expertise and the condition of their heart.

Experts in security come with numerous biases, agendas, and financial costs. Some are outright frauds seeking to profit from the trustworthiness of the church. Be wise to discern who you receive counsel from. Verify their credentials, especially when a cost is associated with their advice. Make sure that they are qualified and experienced in what they teach. Beware of anyone trying to *sell* themselves as a "security expert."

Listening to the advice of an unqualified person is a waste of time and resources and will set the team up for failure or undesired litigation.

Vetting security consultants exceeds qualifying their skill; the person's character matters as well. I have had a lot of salesmen try to sell me everything from advanced weapon systems to knives that never go dull. Each believed in their product, but each also had the goal of making a sale. They had no concern if the product actually benefited me. Their bottom line was closing the sale and not my best interest.

Beware of secular security experts who may be doing the same thing to you. Because this is the nature of business, vet all *salesman*. Also process all advice through a Christian-conceptual lens. Are they concerned with the Kingdom and your local church's role in it? Or, are they trying to convince you to buy their product? Finally, scrutinize advice that comes with a financial cost attached to it. As a leader in the church you must determine both the quality of their expertise and the condition of their heart. Look to the Lord for wisdom as you vet "security experts" before entering into an agreement with them. Do not be deceived.

After the fall of Jericho and Ai, fear caused the Gibeonites to create a well-orchestrated ruse that tricked Joshua (Jos 9:3-13). The deception exhibited by the Gibeonites led to a treatise being ratified which created complications as Joshua had to stay true to his oath, even if it was a mistake. Joshua did not consult God and did not follow His command not to create a treaty with the inhabitants of Canaan (Exo 23:32, 34:12; Num 33:55; Deut 7:2, 20;17,18; Jos 9:14). When consulting with experts, seek God first. Then if their bread seems moldy, find out why it appears that way before paying for their expertise.[65]

---

[65] The Gibeonites used a clever ruse to make it appear that they had been traveling for days and thus, provided "evidence" that they were from a distant land. This included their donkeys carrying worn out sacks and

Security experts generally come from two sectors: the government and private entities. Government security is found in the form of federal, state, and local law enforcement agencies. As government organizations, they offer advice that can be free but generally is not tailored to the church. Government sector initiatives come from the perspective of a public entity focused on protecting institutions within their jurisdiction. Often, their strategies are no different than what is applied to commercial businesses. Furthermore, they tend to lump all "religions" together and use phrases such as "security for places of worship" in order to avoid offending anyone. These descriptions should serve as a warning of how broad their advice will be.

This does not mean that the advice they offer is ineffectual. More than likely, it will contain positive points that you may want to incorporate into your strategy. However, their plans will be generic and not structured specifically for the local church. Governmental entities do not give advice from a Christian perspective and therefore cannot adequately address the Pastor's Paradox. Therefore, the instruction you receive may not be specific to your church, let alone the Kingdom-focused body of Christ.

Despite these limitations, government organizations have a role to play in the SLS strategy. They can provide some assistance and may do so free of charge. If they are willing to provide free training on building evacuations, emergency preparations, active shooters, medical care, or any other area that they have an expertise in, take advantage of it. Then adopt and adapt what they have offered to enhance the safety of your church. If an expert is offering free advice, it would be unwise not to take it.

---

old wineskins, patched sandals, and old clothes. The bread they carried was dry and moldy. All of this was to make it appear that they had come from a distant country (Jos 9:3-6).

Since part of the SLS strategy is missional, seeking the consultation offered by government agencies creates interaction between the church and first responders. Hopefully these relationships grow into leading the lost to Christ. The development of good relationships with government entities (specifically first responders), is essential to enhancing the security of the church and pursuing the lost. They play a key role as a partner in the church's security plan and are the recipient of the outreach ministry.

Government agencies are one type of potential security consultant, the other comes from the private sector. Most private sector companies do not have the political constraints that government agencies have. However, with the exception of missional non-governmental organizations, private security experts are often "secularly consumed." Their perspective is not focused on advancing the Kingdom. Thus, the Great Commission and Great Commandments are not a foundational part of their security plan. Some organizations not only ignore the commandments, *they oppose them*. They may have an expertise in security, but lack Jesus. Therefore, their advice will be limited in scope but their need for outreach is high.

† † †

Both government and private security experts can be beneficial to the establishment of your church's security plan. However, godly wisdom must be sought when considering their advice. You have to ask yourself: Does their vision align with yours? Will their advice align with that vision? Do they understand the importance of the Great Commandment and Great Commission? If not, you have to measure the value of their advice. Will the security they provide hinder your efforts to honor God, worship Him, and spread the Gospel to the lost world? If so, maybe their advice is more tailored to protecting corporations and businesses than a church.

The Pastor's Paradox shows that leaders in the church have to walk the tight rope of balancing between too much and too little security. As you seek counsel, pray that the Holy Spirit connects you with people who understand that *wisdom comes from God*. Remember what Paul wrote in 1 Corinthians 1:18: "For the message of the cross is foolishness to those who are perishing, but to us who are being saved it is the power of God. For it is written: 'I will destroy the wisdom of the wise; the intelligence of the intelligent I will frustrate'" (Isa 29:14). We must be wise in our stewardship to secure the church. We have a responsibility to manage security without sacrificing our mission to share the Gospel. This is why balancing outreach and security requires godly wisdom.

The Safety Team focuses on Jesus, stewardship over His provision, and enhancing the security of the local church. Knowing Him means that you know where to go for wisdom. 1 Cor 1:30 states that "it is because of Him that you are in Christ Jesus, who has become for us wisdom from God--that is, our righteousness, holiness and redemption." If this means nothing to the security consultant offering advice, you must weigh that into your value of their advice. May God give to you the Spirit of wisdom and of revelation in the enhancement of the security of your church (Eph 1:17). When someone offers advice, pause to examine the level of their skill and the condition of their heart and discern what will support the vision for your church.

Once you have identified the vision of your local church, acknowledged the legal and insurance parameters you have to operate within, and sought advice from qualified experts, you know the general direction that you will be taking the team. This has to be done before you fill a roster because if you don't know where you are going, how can you lead anyone? Now that you have this, it is time to create your team. Ideally you want to solidify a leader as soon as possible and may have already identified one who has been assisting in the planning up to this point. The same can be said for a couple of team members, but now it is time to fill the ranks by identifying members called to this ministry. Starting a team creates an immediate need for members, but you must be patient not to sign up the wrong people. The next section of this book will cover the difference in *recruiting* and *discovering* the people who will make up the Safety Team.

Recruiting or Discovering Team Members

"Select capable men from all the people – men who fear God, trustworthy men who hate dishonest gain – and appoint them as officials over thousands, hundreds, fifties, and tens."
Exodus 18:21

"Brothers, choose seven men from among you who are known to be full of the Spirit and wisdom. We will turn this responsibility over to them and will give our attention to prayer and the ministry of the word." Acts 6:3-4

The Safety Team is the heart of the Spirit-led, Kingdom-focused security ministry. *Stewardship*, *outreach*, and *discipleship* are in its DNA. Members of the team should embrace the responsibility to protect the congregation, seek the lost, and grow in Christ. The components include internal and external ministries which ensure that the team remains focused, accountable, and active in outreach while serving to maintain a safe worship environment.

Internally, the members of the Safety Team must be focused on discipleship. The team should function as a unit of like-minded individuals that have a concern to secure the church and a desire to grow together in Christ. Members will bond together as a *small group* where they are able to engage in sincere fellowship. The internal discipleship will allow team members to sharpen one another and encourage each other to grow deeper in their relationships with Christ.

Externally, the Safety Team functions as an outreach ministry to the local community. It accomplishes this by maintaining contact with first responders. This contact fosters relationships which lead to a *sustained* outreach ministry to firefighters, EMS, and law enforcement. Thus, securing the church is a partnership between the church Safety Team and the first responders.[66]

Who are the people on the team? They are a group of like-minded individuals walking together as disciples of Christ with a calling to watch over the congregation and reach the lost. They are men and women who have a unique mindset and are willing to act to foster a safe worship environment. They are leaders who interact with others serving in various ministries throughout the church to train and equip them to cover the church with an increased situational awareness. They possess the Christian Warrior Mindset and are willing to serve in the ministry that they are called to.

Today, most corporate entities, schools, law enforcement, and event coordinators (concerts, sports games, etc.) have secular security teams that focus on having an awareness of the world in order to defend their interests (persons, property, and reputation) from harm. They have a secular security mindset. The SLS mindset views security through a biblical conceptual lens. *Security* is therefore addressed as a ministry that honors God and serves people.

By focusing on *stewardship*, *outreach*, and *discipleship*, the team pursues the lost *one* while protecting the *ninety-nine*. The Safety Team operates by observing and communicating information relating to threats, providing aid in emergency situations, and functioning as an outreach ministry to first responders. Because of the complexity of this ministry, the team must be organized and structured to be effective.

---

[66] The process of establishing a sustained outreach to first responders is covered in chapter nine.

There are three basic types of organizational structures found in Scripture. They are: the one-person show, no designated leader, and the delegated structure.[67] The "one-person show" approach is what Jethro saw with regard to Moses (Exodus 18). Jethro warned Moses that he would burn himself out attempting to do all the work. The "one man show" is a prideful, overbearing structure that does not foster encouragement to raise up leaders. The micromanagement of people in this structure will destroy morale and crush potential leaders and thus must be avoided.

The second type of organizational structure is the one that has an absence of leadership. This collegial structure gives a sense that everyone is equal. Welch points out that in 1 Corinthians 14:40 that this type of structure is rejected by Paul. It is called to be confusing. Paul notes that God's work is to be orderly and appropriately accomplished.[68] A structure that is nebulous inhibits leadership. It also complicates individual motivation to take ownership of the roles they are called to.

The third type of structure is organized and hierarchical. This organized structure with delegated responsibility consists of a team led by an individual. Jethro suggested that Moses choose capable men and make them leaders over people. This is an empowering move to raise up leaders. I believe that Jethro understood that micromanaging not only would burn Moses out, it would crush potential leaders and efficiency.

---

[67] Welch, *Serving by Safeguarding Your Church*, 36.

[68] Ibid.

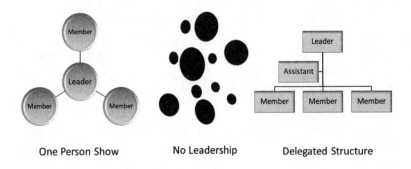

A Depiction of the 3 Organizational Types.

Micromanagement of capable men will hold back potential rather than encouraging giftings. A delegated organizational structure is needed to bring out the potential in each person who is operating in their gifting. For Moses, this structure became a hierarchical system where leaders served as officials over thousands, hundreds, fifties, and tens (Exo. 18:25). Jethro advised Moses to delegate the lesser tasks to others, so he could focus on the issues that needed his attention. These actions create an efficient system providing opportunity to empower people to grow into leaders. This is the type of system in which the Safety Team should operate.

In the New Testament, a similar organization is found within the early church. The apostles appear to be organized into three groups under Peter, Philip, and James son of Alphaeus (Matt. 10:2-4; Mark 3:16-19; Luke 6:14-16; and Acts 1:13).[69] After the post-resurrection 40 days that the Lord spent with His disciples, He was taken up to heaven. The disciples returned to Jerusalem and gathered in the room where they were staying with many men and women (a group numbering about 120). The text appears to be indicative of groups lead by Peter, Philip, and James (Acts 1:7-15). This type of delegation of leadership

---

[69] Welch, *Serving by Safeguarding Your Church,* 36.

increased effectiveness and growth. It is consistent with the ordered nature of God's work.

The SLS strategy calls for a Safety Team that is part of the organized leadership within the local church. The graphic below presents an outline of the basic organization of a team.

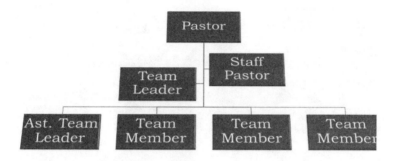

A basic SLS Safety Team hierarchy.

The larger a church is the greater the number of teams it will need to operate during a service or church event. Their structure will reflect the inclusion of multiple teams as depicted in the following graphic. In this picture, the Safety Team is operating multiple units. The first is a large unit led by an assistant team leader, the other two units are smaller, each being led by its own assistant team leader. All three units fall under the Safety Team leader. For efficient communication and identification, each unit will require its own identifier. Examples of how to identify multiple units within the Safety Team include: Labeling each by zone; giving each unit a specific name; using a number; or assigning a phonetic description such as alpha, bravo, or charlie.

Church Security and Outreach

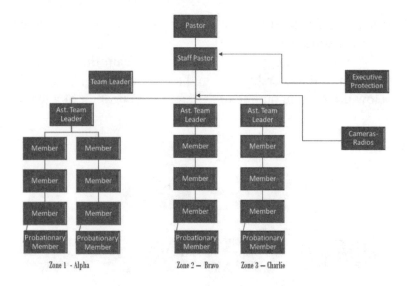

An expanded SLS Safety Team hierarchy.

The positions within these structures will be discussed at greater length later. For now, let's stay focused on *discovering* the members of the team who will fill these roles.

When creating your team, *discover members, do not recruit them.* There is a keen distinction between discovering people called and recruiting people to serve. Recruiting members involves getting people to agree to serve. Sometimes, people will agree to serve but do so reluctantly. At other times, recruited people will prove to be a bad fit for the position, as they were not called to it. Discovering people called to this ministry is far more important than recruiting people because the Safety Team does not have the luxury of being a testing ground for service. The team has a very important role to play in safeguarding the church.

Surely, you will need people to create a team and the simple answer to building one is to get "anybody" who can serve. Building a team, filling a schedule, and having enough assets to cover a service is difficult when you do not have ample personnel. I have been there and created Safety Teams from the beginning when the need is great but the volunteers are few. I know the temptation to get anybody available over finding somebody called.

Rather than recruiting, the SLS strategy focuses on discovering the people that the Lord has strategically placed to be ministers of security. Once discovered, focus on encouraging and empowering them. These men and women will make up your church's Safety Team. They have a calling, a desire, and discipline to serve in that capacity. The likelihood of them serving successfully is greater as they will take ownership over their role on the team. They are far more likely to be successful than plugging random people into a ministry that requires specific gifts and talents. Do not recruit members, discover them!

Who is the person that comes to mind when you think about a Safety Team? Pray that the Lord reveals them to you. Ask for people who have a calling to protect the flock and reach the lost not just those attracted to the security ministry. Not everyone will be an all-star immediately, but if their heart is right, they can become one. Just remember, every ministry needs people and you have to avoid using "warm bodies" to fill those needs. Discover the people called to serve in those capacities and empower them.

Members of the Safety Team need to be vetted. Because they operate throughout the church, they need to be able to access sensitive locations. This includes places such as the children's ministry, the location where the offering is collected, and areas that are reserved for staff. This access will be rare and be made available to Safety Team members even if that means being escorted by a staff member. Because of this, the vetting process of potential team members is crucial. Team members must be held to the highest standard for people serving at the church. Therefore, anyone who is prohibited from serving around children must be excluded from the team. This is non-negotiable. Additionally, Safety Team members will hold a position that requires a high degree of integrity and little recognition. Therefore, members with a humble demeanor will serve well on the team.

Safety Team members must be extremely trustworthy and recognizable to the church staff. Consider these requirements for potential team members:

- Professed Christian over the age of 18
- Member of the church having met all the requirements to serve on a ministry team
- Vetted to be able to access sensitive areas such as the children's ministry, church office, and assist with securing the collection
- Passed a background investigation
- Be personally recommended by a member of the church staff or current team member
- Be approved by the team leader and a designated church pastor
- Have a specified interest and willingness to serve in the ministry

The recommendations above provide a good starting point. You may want to utilize some or all of them in the requirements to serve on your Safety Team. In addition, you may want to add requirements such as length of time that a person has been a member of the church. The important point is that you are utilizing a vetting process and creating standards for team members. This is crucial when considering the legal implications. As always, due diligence needs to be documented. This can easily be done by including the specific requirements for membership in the Emergency Preparedness Plan.

Great Commission Worshippers

The vetting of prospective candidates must include examining the condition of their hearts. The goal is to fill the ranks of the team with the right people and not just warm bodies. The focus should be on people who have a calling to the security ministry, with a heart for the Kingdom, and a desire to protect it. Team members can learn the tradecraft and thus do not need to have experience in security, be a first responder, or have served in the military. Although, it is natural for people with these backgrounds to be attracted to this type of ministry, it is not a pre-requisite. If you discover team members with these backgrounds, they will bring knowledge, skills, and abilities that can be taught to the rest of the team. But these are not the only backgrounds that bring life. A diverse group of team members with various experiences will prove to be highly beneficial.

Your congregation may have numerous members that are prime targets for team membership. It is up to you to discover them. Do not be surprised when you find that some people may have reservations about serving in this capacity *even though they are called to it!* They need help finding freedom from the issues that are holding them back. For example, many security-minded individuals without backgrounds in security may think their lack of experience disqualifies them. They are wrong. In fact, they are prime candidates for the team. Also, there may be people in your congregation who have professional experience in security in the private sector, law enforcement, or the military, but, they feel that their Christian walk is not mature enough to serve on a security ministry. They too are wrong. In each case, *doubt* is being used to keep them from fulfilling their purpose. Help them find the freedom that comes from Christ and seek the purpose that He has for them.

Evil comes to steal, kill, and destroy and self-doubt is one of its primary weapons. In the examples above, members of the Safety Team have the opportunity to serve with others.

Together they can experience growth in tradecraft and in discipleship. Like iron sharpening iron, each team member sharpens the other making the team stronger.

The Safety Team functions as servants of Christ under the shepherding of the lead pastor. The Safety Team must have an allegiance to the Kingdom-focused mission and vision of the lead pastor. Although enhancing security is a functional purpose of the team, service in His Kingdom and the vision for the church must never be sacrificed. Therefore, the standards for the team must be high. This includes the condition of the team member's heart. The easiest way to avoid the peril of placing security ahead of the mission and vision of your church is to seek committed members of the Safety Team that are growing to be Great Commission Worshippers.

In *The Great Commission to Worship: Biblical Principles for Worship-Based Evangelism,* David Wheeler and Vernon Whaley identify Great Commission Worshippers as having a foundation that is balanced between the Great Commission and the Great Commandment. The authors define a Great Commission Worshipper as a person so in love with, committed to worship, and devoted to the obedience of Jesus that they simply cannot restrain from telling others about their incredible relationship with the Son of God. Being a Great Commission Worshipper is not a requisite for the team but desiring to be one should be.

This is the position that all believers strive to achieve and a goal the members of the Safety Team should pursue. For most, this is far from their starting point. Rather, it is an objective that those serving pursue. Success in this endeavor is measured by progress, not attaining perfection.

Great Commission Worshippers are servants committed to the fulfillment of the Great Commandment to worship and the Great Commission of evangelism. There is never a time when a division is made between the two.[70] The same can be said about service on the Safety Team. Never is there a time when we place the security ministry ahead of our commitment to serving God. We are always apologists, evangelists, and stewards. The worshipper never takes off one hat and places on another.[71] We are consistently operating in the security ministry while engaged in worship and evangelism. This combination produces Commanded and Commissioned Warriors.

Commanded and Commissioned Warriors

Not all believers with a heart to be a Great Commission Worshipper are called to serve in a security capacity. The people *wired* for the security ministry are set apart. As stated earlier, the attack on the church is occurring in both the spiritual and natural realms and thus, must be combatted in both. The men and women with a heart to be a Great Commission Worshipper and a calling to fight this battle have the Christian Warrior Mindset. These men and women are the ones called to be a part of the Safety Team. In order to establish your team, you must discover the people with this calling and help them use their gifts and talents for the Kingdom.

In almost any context, "warrior," is a strong word that some do not like to hear. Like "security," for some it conjures up thoughts of violence, battle, conflict, injury, and possibly death. In *On Combat,* Grossman addresses the terms "warrior" and "warriorhood" directly. The image of a warrior may make you think of a historic combatant such as a Zulu warrior, an Apache warrior, a U.S. Marine or any other model that comes

---

[70] David Wheeler and Vernon M. Whaley, *The Great Commission to Worship: Biblical Principles for Worship-Based Evangelism* (Nashville: B&H Publishing Group, 2011), 4.

[71] James K. Beilby, *Thinking About Christian Apologetics: What It Is and Why We Do It.* (Downers Grove, IL: interVarsity Press, 2011), 32.

to mind. Grossman uses the term warrior to mean an individual who has accepted their sacrifice to defend others. They are the people who move toward the sound of the guns as they continue in the face of adversity. They do what needs to be done.[72] Warriors seek to protect others. When you combine the attributes of the warrior Grossman describes with a desire to obey the Great Commission and the Great Commandment, you have a Commanded and Commissioned Warrior.

A Commanded and Commissioned Warrior is one who possesses the Christian Warrior Mindset. These men and women are in pursuit of the *one* and *Act* to *Deter*, *Avoid*, and *Mitigate* attacks against the *ninety-nine*. They do not seek battle, rather they spiritually, mentally, and physically prepare for it. Although they hope that an attack will not come, they know that they have been called to stand their ground between the threat and the flock. Therefore, they operate in condition yellow, and if the enemy attacks, they will engage in battle with a commitment to win.

The men and women in the security ministry have chosen to engage in spiritual and temporal warfare. Spiritual warfare is underway, and the attacks are constantly coming against the church. Temporal threats exist and on any given day these threats can become direct attacks. Therefore, those involved in the security ministry *Act* to help the church *Deter*, *Avoid*, and *Mitigate* spiritual and temporal attacks. As you build your team, you will find people that understand these principles and are seeking a place where they can use them for the Kingdom.

There are people in the church who clearly do not have a calling to the security ministry or the Safety Team. Just as we discover those called to the ministry, we also acknowledge those who are not. Ministry has many roles, most of which we are not called to. The list of ministry positions that I am not called to is long and for good reason. I am not called to be part

---

[72] Grossman, *On Combat*, 176.

of the worship team. Plugging me into a spot just because the church needs a male singer is not good for anybody. Sure, the spot would be filled but I would cause dysfunction on the team and uneasiness for those hearing me sing. Just as the worship team discovers people called to serve there, so too must other ministries including the Safety Team. People not called to be a part of the Safety Team must not be recruited just to fill a vacancy. Rather than using people to plug holes, discover those called to that ministry.

As you discover these individuals it will be evident that they generally will fall into one of two categories. The first group embraces the opportunity to serve. They sense the calling and look forward to the ministry. They have an eager attitude and are highly motivated. They seek the lost and are willing to confront the threats against the church. They actively take ownership of the ministry. The second group is less excited about the calling but willing to step up and do the job. They are called to serve and do so out of a sense of duty. They know that they have a gifting from the Lord and want to use it. They are looking to be part of the team but not necessarily becoming a leader.

Both groups have a calling, a purpose, and opportunity to grow. The circumstances that affect how they are balancing the business of life often forces many people into the second category. At times, they want to do more but just are not able to. There is no value of one group over the other. But, in order to be a good steward of the team you must be able to identify which group the members fall into.

Everyone serving on the Safety Team needs Security Ministry Basic Training. Each one should be encouraged, trained, equipped, and ministered to. They have a like-mindedness and gifting that needs to be exposed. So, when you establish your team, discover them rather than recruit "warm bodies" to fill positions. Identify people who have a calling to serve and a heart to be a Commanded and Commissioned

Warrior. Finally, as you are vetting and discovering team members, set apart those who are prospective leaders. This is your opportunity to shepherd them along to where they are called to be. Your Safety Team will need a team leader, assistant team leader(s), and members to train other ministries to enhance the safety and security of the church. If a person is called to one of these roles, empower them to fulfill their calling and purpose.

† † †

Although enhancing the security of the church is a salient attribute of the Safety Team, the primary focus of the people serving should be growth in their personal relationship God. Within the church we know that this is a priority in all ministries. The security ministry is not an exception to that rule. The upward worship of God influences their ability to fully serve on the Safety Team. It maintains their focus on Christ and enables them to serve Him fully. As a leader, you must know the condition of your flock.[73] Are the people under your authority growing in their relationship with God? This is a question that the Safety Team leader must constantly consider because a God-focused team will be a successful ministry.

The Safety Team member's mindset has to be centered on God. If not, pride, title, position, and power will influence how they serve. Earlier it was shown how self-doubt can be used to keep people off of a team they are called to be a part of. That example was only one weapon used to prevent members from fulfilling their purpose. Another weapon is pride. Satan will use pride to destroy marriages, ministry, and minds. And when it comes to the security of the church, Satan will use it to destroy the Safety Team. Pride will cause members to lose their focus

---

[73] Leaders are challenged to know the condition of those under their authority and protection. Proverbs 27:23 says: "Be sure you know the condition of your flocks, give careful attention to your herds."

on Christ and shift it to a secular security mindset. This is why it is important to continue to encourage one another to remain focused in growing as safeguards of the church and disciples of Christ.

† † †

The Christian Warrior Mindset is an established set of attitudes of a Christian who sees a corrupted world and chooses to actively confront evil on a spiritual and natural level. These attitudes include protecting the innocent (stewardship), seeking the lost (outreach), and growth (discipleship). Therefore, a Christian Warrior is a sheepdog who seeks to operate in condition yellow knowing that evil is always scheming to steal, kill, and destroy (John 10:10). The Christian Warrior accepts the responsibility of protecting the innocent (which includes the congregation of the church) and being obedient to the commands of the Great Commission and Great Commandment to honor God, love people, and reach the lost. Therefore, the Christian Warrior is concerned for the wellbeing of all of the sheep. As a humbled servant, the Christian Warrior is committed to discipleship which produces growth in relationship with the Lord and with others. This growth comes through a commitment to obedience, prayer, and stewardship. A Christian Warrior is committed to pursuing the *one* while protecting the *ninety-nine*.

I am concluding this section with a great source of inspiration that you can share with your Safety Team on how to remain centered on Christ while serving in a dangerous world. It is found in the twenty-two principles provided by Desiderius Erasmus in 1503. Erasmus, a Dutch theologian wrote *Enchridion Militis Chrsitiani* (translated: The Manual of a Christian Knight), in which he outlined twenty-two virtuous principles for the Christian warrior.[74] These twenty-two rules are as follows:

1-Increase your faith in God.
2-Take action by walking out your faith.
3-Control fear.
4-Make virtue a goal of your life.
5-Reject temporal materialism.
6-Condition your mind to discern good and evil.
7-Pray that God raises you out of difficulties.
8-Do not worry about temptation. Seek God who shall not forsake you but will strengthen you.
9-Be vigilant and prepared for an attack.
10-Attack straight away with prayer and Scripture.
11-Through Christ you can defeat pride and giving up.
12-Know your weaknesses, humble yourself, and take on virtue and strength to defeat the enemy.
13-Hope for victory and perpetual peace but always remain vigilant.
14-Do not deceive yourself. Virtue does not allow you to keep a few vices.
15-Actions have consequences. Seek victory and peace.
16-When wounded, be strong in spirit and emerge wiser than before.
17-Defeat mental attacks by focusing on Christ.
18-Seek wisdom and good counsel. Bad decisions will lead to your fall.
19-Remember the benefits of goodness and the damage of evil.
20-Virtue provides peace of mind and eternal blessings. Vice leads to a guilty conscience and damnation.

---

[74] Desiderius Erasmus of Rotterdam, *The Manual of the Christian Knight* (London: Aeterna Press, 2014) i-iii. Originally composed in 1503, this edition was first published in 1905.

21-Life is short and death awaits. A life without Christ is a great peril leading to eternal damnation.

22-It is easy to fall into the pit of sin and difficult to climb your way out. Avoid, repent, and seek God's hand to pull you out.

Security: Gifts and Talents

In this chapter, I have emphasized the importance of discovering Kingdom-focused people with a warrior's affinity for security. These believers have the gifting and the talent to serve to enhance the security of the church and reach the lost. With that being stated, it cannot be overlooked that God has graciously gifted everyone with abilities and talents to include non-believers. Obviously, this is different than the spiritual gifts believers receive as described in 1 Corinthians 12:4-11.[75] Rather, concerning non-believers, I am referring to the talents that God has graciously provided them. Some of those talents and abilities can be used to enhance your security ministry.

This is not to discount the fact that the Bible warns against the influence of others on believers (1 Cor 15:33). Additionally, 2 Cor 2:14 states, "Do not be yoked together with unbelievers. For what do righteousness and wickedness have in common? Or what fellowship can light have with darkness?" These texts are valuable warnings of how believers can be affected by negative influences. Without a doubt, it can weaken their position, commitment, and testimony. However, we have to interact with the lost in order to share the Gospel. While doing this, we can work with those who have natural talents that can help secure the church without compromising our character. Our role is to

---

[75] There are different kinds of spiritual gifts but all of the same Spirit. They are to be used for the common good and are the work of the Spirit. He gives them to each one as He determines.

influence them while we work together to enhance the security of the church.

In the aforementioned verses, Paul was warning about entering into strong relationships with non-believers. He did not say that we must be in isolation from non-believers (1 Cor 5:9-10). We know that the devil has blinded them. Non-believers are ignorant of what the Gospel offers. Paul wrote: "The god of this age has blinded the minds of unbelievers, so that they cannot see the light of the Gospel of the glory of Christ, who is the image of God" (2 Cor 4:4). Paul doesn't stop there, he directs believers to preach Christ as His servants. "For we do not preach ourselves, but Jesus Christ as Lord, and ourselves as your servants for Jesus' sake. For God, who said, 'Let light shine out of darkness,' made his light shine in our hearts to give us the light of the knowledge of the glory of God in the face of Christ" (2 Cor 4:5-6). If Christians are to disassociate themselves with unbelievers, they would have to leave this world (1 Cor 5:10). Doing so would also mean that Christians would not be reaching out to the lost. That is why Paul tells believers to preach Christ and Christ alone with the light that is within them. From this, SLS concludes that using first responders at your church is as much about enhancing the security of the church as it is about providing outreach to them, their families, friends, and the agency they work for.

James wrote that "every good and perfect gift is from above, coming down from the Father of the heavenly lights" (Jas 1:17). If all of His gracious gifts are good, then we can still learn good things from those who are not believers because what is good in them is from God. Many non-believers have received a gift of grace from God and perhaps have become subject matter experts in a particular area that is beneficial to the Kingdom. Although we cannot overlook that their secular vision will not coincide with the vision of the church, we can partner with them in the areas that are for the benefit of His Kingdom.

We know that secular actors are not concerned with the fulfillment of the Greatest Commandments and the Great Commission. It is not part of their security model. Their gifts, therefore, need to be scrutinized through a biblical conceptual lens and used accordingly. While doing this, we should maximize our opportunity to establish relationships, enhance the security of the church, and bring the importance of the Greatest Commandments and Great Commission to them.

† † †

Let's look at this practically by focusing on the use of law enforcement officers during service to enhance the safety of the congregation. The officer or deputy sheriff that works the detail may or may not have an established relationship with Christ. Either way their skills are used as part of the SLS Tactical Strategy. Their presence provides an overt deterrence by a trained professional who can immediately respond to an emergency situation. Upon arrival at the church, they immediately enhance the security of the church.

This is good but we must go further than merely enhancing the security of the church. The Safety Team's interaction with officers and the relationships established will be influential on the law enforcement officer who is working that detail. The officer's presence will place him/her in a position to interact with a congregation and observe the worship service. This includes hearing God's Word as it is preached. Therefore, the compounding effect on the law enforcement officer not only influences their understanding but also creates numerous opportunities for them to ask questions about Christ. While their talents are being used to enhance security, they are, at the same time being directed towards Jesus.

Not all law enforcement officers are functioning on natural talent alone. Many are believers! For those who are believers, they have a special gifting that should be used to glorify God and benefit others. These officers are recipients of spiritual gifts that have been provided by the Holy Spirit (1 Cor 12). They have been set apart to use their gifting for the Kingdom.

Just as there are two types of law enforcement officers (believers and non-believers), there are also two types of subject matter experts. Believers are Kingdom-focused stewards who use their gifts and talents in safety and security for His glory. Non-believers work from a position that is limited to the natural world. Tim Keller said it this way: "The Bible speaks of spiritual gifts (Eph 4, Rom 12, and 1 Cor 12-14) that are abilities to minister to others in Jesus' name. As people created in God's image, Christians have natural talents, and as people regenerated by the Holy Spirit, they also have spiritual gifts that equip them for ministry in and through the church."[76] First responders who are equipped with natural talents and spiritual gifts such as these are the epitome of Commanded and Commissioned Warriors. They will be your church's partner in establishing a team, training, and enhancing the security of the church. Equally important, they will be your partners in bringing the Gospel to their co-workers.

As your Safety Team develops, you will see how its members will generate a spiritually gifted ministry. Leadership is one of those giftings. Leaders on the team will take a path that naturally leads to becoming instructors. Some members on the team will train new members on the mission and vision of the church and the purpose and operation of the Safety Team. This progression and discipleship will ensure that the team will grow in number and in strength. The Safety Team should strive to be the most gifted and talented ministry at the church. Not from a position of pride, but from a dedication to service.

---

[76] Tim Keller: Vocation: Discerning Your Calling www.churchLeaders.com/pastors/pastor-articles/176526-tim-keller-discerning-your-calling.html/2

Developing Leaders

The Safety Team at your church will have members who are called to be leaders. Here are a couple of important points to consider when you discover leaders. First, their character, calling, and ability will determine when they will take on a leadership role. Second, they need to be ready in an area before being thrust into leading it. Therefore, you must be educating them and preparing them as you move them into their purpose. Finally, you must also recognize that not everyone on the Safety Team will be ready to be a team leader. For example, their life schedule may not be able to afford it. Therefore, they may have leadership potential but it must be congruent with the proper timing.

Everyone on the team is there because they want to serve. But they can only serve within their capacity at that time. Time is finite and they may have obligations that limit the amount that they can give. This means that they may be primed to be a team leader but will have to wait until their life schedule allows for it. Never forget that people have control over where they serve. They can volunteer their time to serve the Lord anywhere. As you build a team, stay humble and always remember that they are serving Him, not you. Whether they serve in one ministry or another (or at one church or another) is a choice that they get to make. Aside from a calling to a specific ministry and location, they have the autonomy to choose where and how they serve the Lord. Therefore, you must respect their decisions while encouraging their calling. If someone is not able to be a team leader at the present time, let them serve as a team member until they are ready to lead.

As a leader who identifies someone as being called to the ministry, you must prepare them to operate in that calling. You identified them and thus have a stewardship responsibility to set them up for success. Therefore, if you do not provide them the tools, training, education, and oversight, they will falter because of your failure to raise them up. Provide the people you identify as potential team members and team leaders with the opportunity and the means to be successful. If you withhold either of those, then you have assured their failure. Do not force them into a role that they are not ready for. Help move them into leadership by equipping them not only for the position that they are moving towards, but also how to manage how that position will affect their life. It is crucial that you don't just identify *potential leaders,* you must follow through as you set them up to be *effective leaders.*

In *Warrior Mindset,* an effective leader is described as one who has "the ability to handle crisis because they possess the necessary skills to remain calm and functional when others are rendered confused or overwhelmed by difficult circumstances."[77] These traits describe the men and women found in the law enforcement and military special operations community. Their leadership traits can be successfully applied to ministry. Search to discover a team leader whose character traits will provide you the greatest foundation for your Safety Team regardless of their past experience in leading a team. The best foundation you can create for your Safety Team is to find and develop leaders. When you find and develop them, they will take ownership of the team. You may even find one who is already equipped to establish the team, discover members, and maintain the vision of your church.

The Safety Team is comprised of special men and women with a distinct calling and desire to serve. To lead these men and women requires a leader with a guarded heart. Proverbs 4:23 says: "Above all else, guard your heart, for it is the wellspring of life." This is the type of leader the team needs, one who is a wellspring of life for the team. If you discover that a person has a calling to lead others, provide them the opportunity to lead and prepare them for that role. You must teach and

---

[77] Asken, *Warrior Mindset,* i.

disciple them, so they can be successful in teaching and discipling the rest of the team.

† † †

From the moment your church decides to create a Safety Team, there should be a focus on identifying and developing leaders. Leaders are more than logistical facilitators. They serve to grow the team and replicate the ministry. God has gifted them to lead and you have the ability to help them find and fulfill their purpose.

If *you* are going to be a Safety Team leader, embrace the role that God has called you to. This will help you remain strong and stand before and after the spiritual and temporal battles (Eph 6). Leadership requires a person of good character who is emotionally strong. These traits are needed to remain in control during times of increased stress. Emotionally out of control people will prove to be unreliable in leadership roles. They will find it difficult to lead during times of increased stress and will not be able to function during situations. The leader of the Safety Team should reflect an attitude of God being in control, faith over fear, and confident commitment to the service of His Kingdom.

Part of being an emotionally strong leader is the ability to own your mistakes. This means that you acknowledge them, identify where you went wrong, and prescribe a way to do it right the next time. Mistakes cannot be undone but they can serve as an opportunity to learn, grow, and teach from. Once you own a mistake you must release it. Do not let a mistake create a stronghold on you. If you do, you are letting a mistake from the past continue to have influence over you.

Successful Christian leaders rely on godly wisdom and faith to bring peace. Having a peaceful demeanor will set the stage for you to control your emotions. Faith, coupled with godly wisdom, generates an inner peace that will allow you to control your emotions and focus on the mission. Wisdom gives us the opportunity to control our emotions in areas where the Lord has provided us understanding. While presenting at a conference on church leadership, Dr. Gerald Brooks said: "If you use wisdom in life, there are a lot of things you will not need faith for."[78] If we possess wisdom, then our imaginations are less likely to allow our emotions to direct our actions. If we lack wisdom, our imaginations often step in and create a false reality. The mind will imagine all types of thoughts of worry, fear, and doubt. This imagination is an evil attack that must be defeated. If not, you will process the malevolent thoughts emotionally and increase the amount of doubt and fear you are experiencing.

Wisdom and faith can defeat the paralyzing effects that our imaginations create. They are weapons used to overcome the attacks which prevent people from their calling. If that calling is to lead, but you are not doing it, you are failing to fulfill your purpose. Embrace your role and use your giftings to honor God and help others. If you are called to be a member of the Safety Team or a team leader, assume that role with confidence.

Act to *Deter*, *Avoid*, or *Mitigate* the threats against the church. Stop imagining all the reasons why something cannot be done. Our imaginations can be our worst enemy. When we don't know how to do something, our imaginations begin to assume failure. When we do not have an understanding, our minds come up with an unwarranted explanation. *Where information lacks, imagination fills the void!* Unfortunately, when our imaginations fill the void it is often with fear and doubt. Successful leaders are wise; they take a lack of information and fill it with godly wisdom.

---

[78] Leadership Conference – East Coast Believers Church, Oviedo, Florida – February 12th 2018: 12.

Chapter 6

SLS Tactical Strategy

"But if the watchman sees the enemy coming and doesn't sound the alarm to warn the people, he is responsible for their captivity. They will die in their sins, but I will hold the watchman responsible for their deaths." Ezekiel 33:6

Strategy and Tactics: The *Who* and the *How*

The goal of the SLS Tactical Strategy is to maintain a welcoming worship environment while enhancing the overall safety of everyone at the church. This is achieved through the strategic use three elements: an overt *law enforcement officer(s)*, a covert *Safety Team*, and overt *Force Multipliers*. These three elements are the *who* of the Tactical Strategy; the techniques they utilize are the *how*. By operating in their specified overt and covert capacities to observe and communicate suspicious activity, these three elements *Act* to *Deter, Avoid,* and *Mitigate* threats. The purpose of this chapter is to discuss the tactical use of law enforcement officers, Force Multipliers (staff and non-staff), and the Safety Team.

The three physical layers of security in the SLS system are: Force Multipliers (Overt), Safety Team (Covert), and Law Enforcement (Overt).

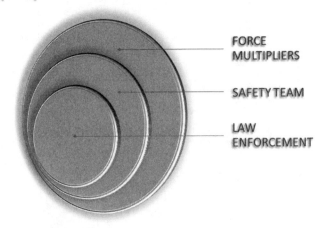

A relative comparison of the amount of area each element physically covers in condition yellow.

Hired Law Enforcement

Of the three *who* elements of the SLS strategy, the only one that comes from outside of the church is the use of local law enforcement. Proportionally it is the least manpower intensive element and the only one with a cost associated with it. The use of local law enforcement is twofold, to *enhance security* and foster relationships for *outreach*. Therefore, having a partnership with local law enforcement is a salient part of the SLS solution to the Pastor's Paradox.

Law enforcement officers take on duties (often referred to as extra or off duty details) that are in addition to their regularly scheduled shifts. The cost of hiring an officer for a church *security detail* is generally determined by a wage set by the employing law enforcement agency. Commonly, this will be the local agency with jurisdiction over the area in which the church is located. In addition to the set wage, there usually is a requirement that the law enforcement officer work a minimum number of hours on the detail.

Most law enforcement agencies have pre-established policies and standardized contracts for these details. Hence, you will not have to reinvent the wheel to begin using law enforcement officers at your service or during special events. The paperwork is often no more than two pages. It will require that you provide basic information such as the location, time, and duties that the church requires the officers to perform. This is a low-cost way of immediately increasing the security of your church and an important part of the SLS strategy.

There are many benefits of having a highly visible law enforcement presence during service. First, they serve as an overt deterrent. Therefore, it is important that the officer(s) are in full uniform and utilize a marked police vehicle. The officer's presence in and of itself is a deterrent to criminal activity. Prospective criminals will see the uniformed officer and recognize that if they come to the church to commit a crime, they will encounter a warrior prepared to stand against them. Not every criminal is going to be dissuaded, but many will. The mere sight of a uniformed, armed law enforcement officer (or the marked patrol car) acts to deter a potential attacker from committing a crime. This alone is well worth the cost but the law enforcement presence brings additional benefits to the church.

The law enforcement officer provides a general sense of security. This creates an atmosphere where people at the church will feel more relaxed knowing that they can attend service where a law enforcement officer is present to deal with threats. In addition, their interaction with the Safety Team, staff, and congregation fosters relationships that will provide the potential for sustained outreach. Finally, the law enforcement officer(s) is there to protect and serve the congregation; they provide immediate support during a critical event. Their expertise and capabilities are crucial to de-escalate and deal directly with emergency situations.

During critical events, every minute is crucial and can be the difference between life and death. It takes time for a person to call 911, speak with dispatch, advise them of the situation, get a law enforcement officer *en route*, have that the first responder drive to the church, and upon arrival determine where to go. The time that all of the actions take may be too long for some victims. However, having a law enforcement officer at the church will expedite the process and mitigate the damage. For example, by simply pressing one button on their radio the officer transmits a distress signal that is received by a dispatcher. This prompts an accelerated response of additional resources. Having a law enforcement officer present during service can be the difference between life and death for victims of medical, weather, or violent attacks.

Additionally, the officer brings professional training and specialized equipment (including medical gear) that can aide in various critical events. By having a law enforcement presence, you are diligently taking A*ction* to *Deter*, *Avoid*, and *Mitigate* threats. Officers are highly trained in conflict de-escalation, use of force, and how to deal with a plethora of emergencies ranging from heart attacks to active shooters. By simply hiring a law enforcement officer, you have taken a responsible measure to safeguard your congregation.

Something that is often overlooked when considering hiring off duty law enforcement officers is that they are trained professionals *acting in a law enforcement capacity*. This means that they are not acting as an employee of the church. This crucial distinction between the actions taken by a member of the church staff (or a volunteer who is serving under the direction of the church) and the actions of a law enforcement officer operating in an official capacity is tremendous. This distinction directly affects the fiduciary liability and responsibilities of the church. Whereas a ministry team member is acting under the umbrella of the church, the law enforcement officer is acting under the umbrella of the law enforcement agency. As mentioned earlier, critical events and emergency situations bring lawyers, litigation, and lawsuits. Therefore, it is wise to have a law enforcement officer present as it demonstrates the due diligence taken by the church and presents a trained professional that can deter, avoid, and mitigate threats.

As previously stated, there is a monetary cost to hiring law enforcement and that amount is determined by the sheriff's office or police department that maintains jurisdiction over the location of the church. Depending on the specific needs of your church, you may have to employ multiple law enforcement officers to provide adequate coverage. Hiring a law enforcement officer to be present during service is a cost-effective way to provide high-visibility security, immediate emergency response, and avoid possible negative litigation.

When an officer or deputy is hired by the church and serves during a service or event, the members of the Safety Team should introduce themselves to the officer. During that initial conversation, the members of the Safety Team should exchange cell phone numbers with the officer. This provides everyone a way to directly communicate in the event that an incident occurs. It also develops a relationship between the officer and Safety Team members. Establishing these relationships will grow the partnership that fosters a sustained outreach ministry.

Never have a myopic view of the role of the law enforcement officer serving. They provide an opportunity for establishing relationships. For the church, and specifically the Safety Team, these officers are partners in protecting the congregation and opportunities for outreach. Get to know them, their families, and appreciate what they are doing. The uniforms that they wear and the marked patrol cars they drive are "billboards" announcing *shoot me first!*

Everyday law enforcement officers risk their lives simply by going to work. Criminals and terrorists take advantage of knowing who the law enforcement officers are during attacks. Despite these high risk and high stress careers, many of them do not know Christ. That is why the SLS strategy recognizes that every law enforcement officer who helps protect the *ninety-nine* is potentially the *one* the church is pursuing.

Force Multipliers

There are three tactical considerations for you to consider at your church. First, a tactical strategy with an emphasis solely on covert, low-visibility personnel and tactics. Second, a strictly high-visibility approach where the tactical strategy is firmly planted in deterrence. Or, third, an effective strategy that utilizes both. The first two options are greatly limited. Neither can adequately function without the other. The SLS Tactical Strategy falls into the third category. It relies heavily on covert tactics to *avoid* and *mitigate* attacks while utilizing overt elements such as police and Force Multipliers to *deter* attacks.

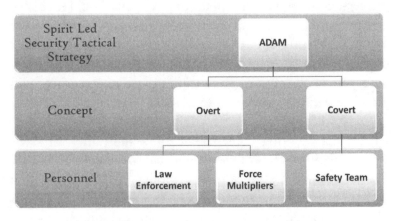

The Spirit Led Security Tactical Strategy.

SLS Tactical Strategy

The SLS Tactical Strategy is the most comprehensive, cost effective, and least disruptive way to enhance the safety and security of the church during services. It utilizes the aforementioned law enforcement presence and empowers every ministry to be a steward over security. The people serving in these ministries become *Force Multipliers* who are trained to *observe* and *communicate* suspicious activity. They are the second *who* of the SLS Tactical Strategy.

Your church has the capability to greatly enhance its security just by providing basic training to the people already serving. Look at every ministry as a potential Force Multiplier. Wherever they serve presents an opportunity to have people who can assist in deterring all types of attacks by observing and communicating suspicious activity. Force Multipliers are the men and women who are serving in their ministry but also enhancing security without the appearance of being "security." Think of a member of the hospitality team who is performing their role to provide for guests while also having a condition yellow mindset. Force Multipliers along with the Safety Team are a *no cost* Kingdom-focused unit that takes *Actions* to *Deter*, *Avoid*, and *Mitigate* attacks.

To be clear, Force Multipliers are not members of the Safety Team; they function as auxiliary support. Force Multipliers consist of people already serving in various capacities at church. For example, they are greeters, the parking team, ushers, bookstore attendants, the coffee team, and all the other personnel serving (including staff) who are managing their responsibilities while at the same time enhancing security. Since the Safety Team operates in a covert role to *avoid* and *mitigate* attacks, the overall security of the church is enhanced through the *deterrence* provided by the law enforcement officer and the Force Multipliers. They provide an additional set of eyes and ears in an attempt to increase the area of the church covered in *condition yellow*. Once they are trained to observe and communicate suspicious activity, these highly visible ministry members enhance security without having to change their ministerial role. During a church service, Force Multipliers provide friendliness while serving in their designated positions. However, they are empowered with a heightened situational awareness and ability to relay any suspicious activity observed to the Safety Team.

Force Multipliers continue to function in their roles as pastors, coffee team members, greeters, or bookstore attendants. Because they are already serving throughout the church they are strategically pre-positioned to watch for suspicious activity. Think about it, the church has people serving spread throughout its facilities during every worship service or event. The assets for deterrence, observation, and communication are already in place. Therefore, once trained they immediately increase the area that is covered in *condition yellow*. The Safety Team cannot be everywhere all the time. Therefore, Force Multipliers play a key role in the enhancement of the overall security and safety of the church.

Existing ministries can only function as Force Multipliers if they are trained on what to look for and how to communicate the suspicious activity they observe. Tony Dungy, in *The Mentor Leader* said: "To succeed in any endeavor, we have to know what we're doing and why we're doing it. That doesn't mean we have to have all the answers, but it does mean we must have a solid foundation of skill, ability, and knowledge."[79] By providing Security Ministry Basic Training to Force Multipliers the church is acting to enhance the safety of the church. If the church has a functioning Safety Team, they are the ones who will train the Force Multipliers. By establishing your Safety Team and enabling them to train the other ministries, you are giving away ministry to competent individuals who can take ownership of it.

---

[79] Tony Dungy, *The Mentor Leader* (Carol Stream, IL: Tyndale House Publishers, Inc. 2010), 72.

By simply empowering your existing teams, you will greatly enhance the overall security without any cost or need for additional resources. These assets are waiting to be empowered. In most churches, they are being held back due to lack of basic training on situational awareness and knowledge of their role in the overall security of the church. Remember, everyone can benefit from Security Ministry Basic Training. It will enhance one's safety and security at church, in the mission field, at home, at work, and out in public.

The following are examples of how Force Multipliers can enhance the safety and security of the church. All you have to do is empower them.

Ushers: Ushers play a key role in your Emergency Preparedness Plan. Their overt presence identifies them as people serving the church. Therefore, they act as a visible deterrent to crime. Each usher is an additional set of eyes looking for suspicious activity (especially within the sanctuary). Ushers have the unique ability to move about and watch people within the sanctuary without appearing out of place. They also can be advantageously positioned in key areas to provide deterrence and protection for the pastor. Finally, they are able to interact with guests which provides them the opportunity to get close up and talk with anyone exhibiting suspicious behavior. Ushers predominantly operate in the sanctuary. In the SLS strategy, the Safety Team operates in the sanctuary to provide an undercover element that assists the ushers. Therefore, the Safety Team must work in concert with the ushers in relaying suspicious observations and in the coordination of responses.

Proper means of communication must be established between the ushers, Safety Team, staff, and law enforcement officer. This includes the use of radios, phones, and direct communication via face to face conversations or covert hand signals. The unique characteristics of your church may allow you to utilize all or just some of these forms of communication. In most churches, the ushers are the ministry that is most closely associated with the Safety Team. Because they commonly work together, SLS recommends that select ushers and Safety Team members be *cross-trained*. This means training them in both roles, so they have interoperability and foster better understanding of each group's service in the enhancement of the security of the church.

Parking Team: At most churches the parking team offers the first layer of observation. The members of this team have an essential part to play in enhancing the security of the church. They welcome people and are observant of suspicious activity. Members of the parking team have the unique ability to see into cars and move about the parking area freely without appearing out of place. This gives the members of the parking team the opportunity to see if someone suspiciously remains in a car as well as observe people who may be loitering, looking to break into cars. In addition to observing suspicious behavior, the parking lot team is in a prime position to look out for safety hazards. They watch out for obstacles, items, and locations that may pose a heightened safety risk as guests arrive at the church.

Children's Ministry: The children's ministry is generally a welcoming and loving place. The people serving there are gifted with a sense of love and patience which allows them to serve in an area that many will not tread. Despite their loving nature, the people serving in the children's ministry are some of the most situationally aware people you will find in the church.

Servants in the children's ministry have a heightened safety awareness that naturally comes with overseeing children. They are constantly keeping their heads on a swivel to keep track of the children and they instinctively condense their focus on people who appear out of place. Additionally, they are the only men and women serving who have an acute knowledge of the identities of the parents and guardians of the kids. This is important information which can aide in the prevention of abductions. It is also crucial intelligence when facilitating the reunion of parents and children during an emergency situation.

It is crucial that the children's ministry brief the Safety Team of any known safety concerns. The ability to affectively share information is essential if the Safety Team is to be prepared to thwart threats towards children. For example, if there is a parent who does not have the right to take a child out of the children's ministry (perhaps due to domestic legal issues), the Safety Team should be aware of the potential threat and relay that information to law enforcement if feasible. Also, the Safety Team should be aware if there are children who frequently attempt to run away from the children's ministry. Some kids just look for the opportunity to run out of an open door every chance that they get. Although they have no mal-intent, they present a safety hazard that the Safety Team can assist in resolving. These are just a couple of examples of how the Safety Team and Force Multipliers in the children's ministry can aid in preventing accidents from occurring. When you establish a Safety Team that trains the Force Multipliers, specific concerns for your church will be discussed and the teams will be able to create feasible solutions to specific problems. Specific issues and concerns that arise and are planned for should be documented in your Emergency Preparedness Plan.

Worship Team: The Worship Team is in a unique and advantageous position to observe suspicious activity. While the vast majority of people in the sanctuary are facing towards the pulpit, the worship team is facing the congregation. In most cases, they are the only people (other than the pastor or someone who is speaking) who can face the congregation and not appear out of place.

The members of the worship team can scan the crowd without creating a disruption to service. If they observe something suspicious that does not require immediate attention, they can inform a member of the Safety Team when they are not leading worship. However, if they want to get the attention of an usher or Safety Team member while on stage, all they have to do is continue to lead worship while staring directly at that team member. It is as if the worship team member is singing directly to that Safety Team member or usher. This is a use of non-verbal communication to avoid creating a distraction to the worship environment. Once the worship team member makes eye contact with the usher, Safety Team member, or staff member being stared at, s/he will understand that something needs to be addressed. This only works if the Safety Team members, ushers, staff, etc. are situationally aware and watching the worship team members for this non-verbal cue.

Once communication is established, the worship team member can use additional non-verbal directions to communicate the location of the suspicious person. One example is to point with your eyes. This is a technique where one person stares at the person you are trying to communicate with until they acknowledge you. Then the person who started the communication shifts the focus of attention to the direction of the suspicious activity. For example, a worship team member who is singing in the middle of a song sees a suspicious person seated alone and clenching his fists. The suspicious person is not participating in worship and appears distressed. The worship team member looks directly at the nearest usher as he continues to sing. The usher notices that the worship team member is not making random eye contact but is staring at him. The usher nods his head and immediately the worship team member stares down to the left. This directs the usher's attention to the person seated in the middle of the front row clinching his fists. The Force Multiplier on the worship team has now observed the suspicious activity and relayed that information to the nearest usher. That usher then communicates it to the other ushers and Safety Team. Since the Safety Team members are able to blend into the congregation, they can be in close proximity to the suspicious person without being detected. This allows them to further investigate why the subject is acting suspiciously. All of this is done without creating a distraction to service.

Worship team members are creative artist who can use a multitude of ways to direct the attention to a particular area. This includes, using instruments, hand gestures, or other non-verbal communication that appears to be part of the song they are singing. Once they are trained by the Safety Team, they become situationally aware and empowered to enhance the security of the church in a way that is unique to their position. Because they face the congregation, they are able to project a *condition yellow* situational awareness away from the direction that everyone else is looking.

Greeters (this includes anyone who serves welcoming guests): Greeters are one of the best examples of an untapped resource to cover the church in *condition yellow*. In most churches, greeters are generally the first people to interact with guests. Their position often means that they will observe people before they enter the building, establish eye contact with them, make physical contact through handshakes and hugs, and verbally welcome them. All of these interactions are key to screening people for suspicious activity.

Observing people early on allows greeters to look for anything that appears out of place. Greeters immediately should take note if a person appears to be concealing something. They should assess if a person is uncharacteristically carrying a bag, back pack, satchel, tube, or other item. Greeters should look for bulges under peoples clothing that is possibly an item being purposely concealed. They should also pay attention to the clothing to see if it is consistent with the weather. Some indicators of red flags include a person wearing a heavy jacket when it is hot out and a person arriving at an evening service wearing sunglasses when it is dark. These alone are not indicators of a person being an attacker, but they are red flags that raise suspicion and need to be addressed.

When a greeter is approached, they should pay attention if a person purposefully avoids eye contact, appears hyper-focused, or lost. As they make contact with people, greeters should mentally note when people try to avoid a hand shake. When people do shake hands, greeters should notice if their hand is uncharacteristically sweaty or they are shaking. Both of these are indicators of nervousness. Greeters should observe every person with attention given to that individual's degree of nervousness and how they respond when they are welcomed to the church. Any of these characteristics can be normal and explainable. However, they present red flags. Individuals acting suspiciously need to be addressed by the Safety Team.

Greeters are screeners. They just need to be trained on what to look for and how to communicate it to the Safety Team. Greeters are already intent on searching for people who look out of place. For example, every greeter is looking for that person who comes into the church and appears lost. They are watching for the person who enters the building but seems like they do not know where to go. Greeters are already trained to identify and speak with these individuals. Not because they are suspicious, but because they appear to be first time guests! Greeters are an important part of the Force Multiplier element of the SLS security strategy. Greeters need to be trained on how to develop their gifts and talents to welcome and screen guest to be used for enhancing the security of the church.

Church Staff: There are two important points concerning the role of church staff in the SLS strategy. First, church staff members have designated roles and responsibilities leading up to, during, and after service. Managing security should not be one of these roles. It must be delegated from the pastors and staff to those who can give it undivided attention. That is the Safety Team, Force Multipliers, and law enforcement.

Church staff is extremely busy on days when service is being held. They are often busy serving, meeting guests, and putting out all the "fires" that occur. This can range from locating lost keys, production problems, filling gaps were volunteers are absent, and directly interacting with the congregation. Therefore, ministry must be delegated to competent leaders. They can effectively oversee trained and reliable people serving in the various ministries.

The second point regarding the staff in the SLS strategy is that they should only be made aware of a suspicious person *if it has elevated to a point requiring their attention*. If a Force Multiplier sees a suspicious person, they do not need to directly inform the pastor. Rather, they should relay that observation to the Safety Team. Once the Safety Team gets involved, they will assess the person and look for additional red flags. As the number of red flags and degree of suspicion increases, the Safety Team will involve more people (Force Multipliers, staff, law enforcement, etc.) as that situation requires.

The Safety Team takes the lead in observing and communicating the actions of a suspicious person. On one extreme, they may immediately determine that the initial red flag that caused suspicion is explainable. Thus, eliminating the need to observe the person any further. On the other extreme the team may determine that the suspicious person presents an imminent threat to which everyone must be warned. An example of this would be an active shooter.

Most suspicious people observed by the Safety Team and Force Multipliers will be handled within the ministry. They will not even require staff involvement. By far, the majority of cases of unexplained suspicious persons or items will only involve the Safety Team. This is ideal as it does not raise any alarm that would distract the ongoing service. The Safety Team operates independently and generally functions without having to involve people outside of the team. The more people that get involved, the greater the chance that there will be a disruption to the service.

It is essential that the Safety Team members be responsible stewards over the safety and security of the congregation. The more competent that they are, the less likely the staff will have to be concerned with *security*. A team that takes ownership over the ministry is a team that allows the pastor and staff to operate without being bogged down into any one ministry.

Note to the church staff: Help yourself by helping the Safety Team! The church staff must empower the Safety Team and Force Multipliers so they (the staff) can be free to serve in their roles on days when service is being held. This includes when the staff observes something suspicious. Like all others ministries serving during a church service, the staff should communicate any observations of suspicious activity to the Safety Team. If you have empowered your Safety Team, they can handle it and you can resume your responsibilities. Don't think that just because you are on staff you have to micromanage everything. If you have a competent leader and a trained member of that ministry, they will be supporting the lead pastor's vision for the church.

It is important that the staff of the church bridge the information gap created between them and the people serving on the Safety Team. This gap is greatest during the week when the two entities are not interacting. The structure of the Safety Team creates a hierarchy in which information should flow. This includes a team leader, assistant team leader(s), current team members, and probationary members. Since most, if not all of the Safety Team members will be volunteers, there is no seat at the table during staff meetings for the Safety Team to *relay* or *receive* information. They are at their own jobs, disconnected from any discussion and decisions made by the staff. To overcome this obstacle, the church must have a designated staff member who serves as a conduit between the team and the entire church staff. If not, vital communication can be lost.

It is crucial that the designated person from the church staff has regular contact with the Safety Team leader. This will aide in logistical planning, assuring the team maintains the vision of the lead pastor and give the Safety Team a voice at the table during staff meetings. If not, the team can easily become disconnected from leadership. That disconnection will create confusion and lead to chaos. In order to maintain a connection from the lead pastor to the team member serving on Sunday, communication must flow up and down a hierarchical chain of command.

This direct flow of information is essential to prevent the breakdown in messaging that often plagues organizations. Since the church is an organization that relies heavily on volunteers serving, the likelihood for a breakdown in communication is significantly high. Therefore, it is mutually beneficial to the church staff and Safety Team to have a designated person to bridge the gap between the two entities. Doing so will ensure that the needs on both ends of the spectrum are relayed effectively.

The team leader may have many important concerns, reports, and issues to bring to the attention of the church, but this will only happen if the team leader has a direct line of communication to the staff. Additionally, the church may institute changes that affect the team, but since the team is only there during church services those changes may not be communicated efficiently. This will cause a disconnect that negatively affects the function of the team and the flow of the service. Usually this type of problem is uncovered on Sunday when everyone is together serving. Sunday is the worst time to deal with a problem! It is when the focus should be on the worship service and those attending, not the problems that arise due to a lack of communication.

Most staff meetings occur during the week and as previously mentioned, the Safety Team leader will likely be at work. Thus, information the team leader needs to convey to the staff will not occur unless a designated staff member presents it. That person functions not only as the voice of the team at staff meetings, but *also the voice of the staff to the team.* Having a person successfully fulfilling this role will assure the team's concerns are being heard. Also, it assures that the team remains in line with the mission and vision of the church and any procedural changes that occur.

Off Duty First Responders in the Congregation: Off duty first responders in the congregation refers to the police officers, sheriff's deputies, state and federal agents, firefighters and other first responders who are attending service. Although they are not serving on a ministry team or hired to be at the church, it behooves the church to know who they are. If you have first responders in the congregation, you must anticipate that they are going to react in an emergency situation. During service, they will naturally have a higher rate of situational awareness than other people in the congregation due to their professional training and a greater propensity to act.

If the Safety Team knows who these people are, they should introduce themselves to them. Not only will the introduction be beneficial during an emergency situation, it will provide an opportunity to initiate a relationship. It is possible that many of the first responders in the congregation will not know about the Safety Team. Therefore, this provides an opportunity to connect and discover new members and an occasion for outreach to the first responder community.

One final note concerning Force Multipliers. The aforementioned examples are just a few of the many ministries that have been effectively serving to enhance the security and safety of many churches. Every ministry is a potential Force Multiplier that should be empowered to observe and communicate suspicious activity. Production teams, coffee teams, outreach ministries, facility teams, and so on all have an equally important role to play as a Force Multiplier. Their specific responsibilities and positioning allow them to utilize their skills to enhance the overall safety of the church.

The Safety Team

The final *who* of the SLS Tactical Strategy is the Safety Team. The Safety Team functions *tactically* to enhance the safety and security of the entire church without creating a distraction to service. It *observes* and *communicates* suspicious activity in order to *Act* to *Deter*, *Avoid*, and M*itigate* threats to the safety of the church. This includes, but is not limited to, threats created by weather emergencies, criminal activity, medical emergencies, or other safety concerns (such situations that could cause a person to trip, slip, or become injured). The team strategically utilizes tactics that allow it to operate without being a hinderance or distraction to the worship and ministry being provided during service.

The Safety Team consists of a team leader, assistant team leader(s), members, and probationary members. The size of the Safety Team at your church will depend upon the immediate needs and may be amended with growth. As the team cultivates members, so too will be the need for additional assistant team leaders. The structural requirements of your team may necessitate that some team members be designated to operate in a specific role/position. For example, a team member may be designated to operate a radio that connects that team member with other ministries. That Safety Team member, of course, is not going to function in a low visibility capacity because any reasonable person will observe the radio and identify the team member as being affiliated with the church.

Another example of a specific position that a team member may be assigned is to monitor cameras. If your church utilizes security cameras and radios, the same person should be designated to monitor them both. That way the person monitoring the cameras can communicate observations via radio to other ministries utilizing radios and via text messaging to the Safety Team. Having one-person act in this dual responsibility is the most efficient use of a Safety Team member. However, it does not have to be a Safety Team member in that role. Anyone can be trained in how to monitor cameras and properly dispatch radio and text messages appropriately. Whoever fulfills this role at your church has the same fundamental function as the rest of the Safety Team and Force Multipliers. That is, they are to observe and communicate suspicious activity in order to increase the overall security and safety for everyone at the church.

Another role that a member of the Safety Team may occupy is that of a low-visibility asset assigned directly to the pastor. If this is the case, that team member will remain on the team communications but not participate in a surveillance of suspicious persons. They will assure that they are in the know of what is going on but remain with the pastor through the service. A Safety Team member serving in this role is performing executive protection not surveillance. SLS recommends that if you have the assets available, at least one overt Force Multiplier and one covert Safety Team member be assigned to the pastor. Anyone serving in a role of executive protection must not only fulfill all the requirements to serve on the Safety Team, they must also be directly approved by the pastor.

In order to enhance the security of the entire church, the SLS Tactical Strategy utilizes a combination of high- and low-visibility elements *Acting* to *Deter, Avoid,* and *Mitigate* threats. High-visibility (overt) elements are an important part of the strategy. They work as a deterrent to criminal activity. The presence of the overt elements (uniformed law enforcement personnel and Force Multipliers) declare that security is being conducted. But it is not done in an overbearing way. A salient characteristic of the overt elements is their welcoming demeanor. Everyone serving must be hospitable and loving towards the congregation and guests while operating

SLS Tactical Strategy

in *condition yellow* to observe suspicious activity. If not, they may become an obstacle to reaching the lost and thus work outside the framework of the Great Commandment and Great Commission.

The Safety Team is the conduit of communication between entities.

The low-visibility element of the SLS Tactical Strategy is the covert Safety Team. The Safety Team provides the capability to conduct mobile surveillance without creating a distraction to the service. The use of a covert team is essential to protect the integrity of the service and maintain a welcoming atmosphere. With that in mind, imagine the following hypothetical situation. In it, the church *does not* have a covert Safety Team when a suspicious person enters the church.

In this scenario, the greeters notice a suspicious person. However, because they have a responsibility to greet guests, they are hesitant to leave their post. Additionally, they have not been instructed as to whom they should contact if they observe a suspicious person. So, they scramble to notify someone on the staff. In the terms of the OODA loop, they *observed* a suspicious person, *oriented* themselves to that person, made a *decision* to tell someone, and *acted* by attempting to flag down a staff member.

The greeter continues to fulfill their responsibility as a greeter while attempting to get the attention of a staff member. Eventually, an associate pastor comes over. In the meantime, the suspicious person has moved out of sight. The greeter advises the associate pastor that she saw a suspicious man wearing a blue jacket acting very oddly. The associate pastor asks where the suspicions man is now located. The greeter replies, "I last saw him walking down that hallway." Because the person's whereabouts are uncertain and there is a sense of urgency, the associate pastor does not get additional information. He begins to walk in the direction of the hallway that the greeter pointed to.

The associate pastor, who is wearing a shirt that clearly identifies him with the church, hastily walks down the hallway searching for the suspicious man. As he moves past the entrance to the sanctuary, he grabs two ushers (also clearly dressed in a way that identifies them with the church) and tells them to join in the search for the man. Without hesitation, they obey the associate pastor's command and leave their posts.

Unfortunately, now no one is at the doors escorting guests to their seats. A minor inconvenience, but one that should not occur. The sudden unexplainable absence of the ushers is observed by the lead usher. He, therefore goes to the doors to fill the vacated position. Meanwhile, the associate pastor and "drafted ushers" are moving with a purpose down the hallway. As they continue to look for the suspicious man, the briskness in their walk and the stern looks on their faces are noticed by guests. A minor distraction for the guests, but one that should be avoided. Suddenly, all three notice the suspicious man as he emerges from the rest room. The three awkwardly find themselves walking towards the suspicious man. As they pass him, he clearly observes that they were looking at him. The associate pastor and two ushers turn their heads as they pass by him. They observe the suspicious man walk into the sanctuary through a side entrance.

The suspicious man enters the sanctuary through one of four entrance points. This is a side entrance that is commonly used by guests. The man quickly takes an aisle seat in the second row just as the service is about to start. The suspicious man is now seated alone and making no effort to talk to anyone. Soon thereafter, the service begins just as the associate pastor and ushers enter the sanctuary. They walk in through the same side doors that the suspicious man used. Together, the three observe the subject and assemble towards the back of the sanctuary.

Although they can see the suspicious man, they are not in a position to respond if he does something nefarious. As they attempt to formulate a plan, members in the congregation observe them uncharacteristically standing together. The concerned look on their faces is evident to the members of the congregation watching them. *They are becoming a distraction to the service.* One usher detects this and suggests that they split up and sit around the suspicious man. It is a hasty *ad hoc* plan but seems to make sense as no other options were blueprinted.

The three men walk towards the aisle where the suspicious man is seated. All three sit in different aisles, one usher in front and the other two behind the man. Although they attempt to make it look as if they are joining the congregation, that fails and they further disrupt the service. There is no way to hide the fact that the three men, an associate pastor and two ushers oddly walk down the aisle together and position themselves in the area around the man. Their activity clearly is out of place and has *further distracted the congregation*. Even the suspicious man perceives that the three are fixing their attention on him. Apprehension is high all around. The associate pastor, ushers, suspicious man, and the congregation all are feeling it. The service is clearly being disrupted.

Within a moment, the man's wife walks down the aisle and sits next to him. Immediately, tensions lighten but the man clearly conveys his discomfort about the three men. He tells his wife that he first observed them in the hallway. She looks and spots all three looking in their direction. This is further distracting the congregation.

The congregation is not the only ones picking up on the activities of the associate pastor and two ushers. Other ushers, not knowing what is going on, have detected that something is out of place. Hence, they too have positioned themselves in the section where the couple is seated. By this point, the lead pastor has noticed that something is wrong. Both he and his congregation are distracted.

Although everyone at the church, from the greeter, staff member, and ushers had good intentions, they have clearly disrupted the service. The back story to this example is that the couple was on their third visit to the church. They drove together, but the man's wife dropped him off before she parked the car. In fact, he was driving, jumped out of their car, and hurried into the church. She then moved into the driver's seat and parked the vehicle.

The man urgently rushed into the church because he had a pressing need to use the bathroom. Therefore, the man's wife proceeded to park their car while he rushed in. What the greeter saw was indeed suspicious. In the end however, it was explainable. The unorganized reaction clearly made the couple feel unwelcomed. In addition, many aspects of the service were disrupted. *This outcome is unacceptable.* We, the people serving, cannot be a distraction to the service. People are trying to focus on their relationship with their Creator and we cannot be a hinderance to that.

Many problems occurred in the aforementioned situation. The greeter did a good job of seeing something that was out of place. However, she did not know how or to whom she should speak to about it. *She was situationally aware but functionally lost.* This caused a delay and a sense of urgency for the associate pastor to find the suspicious person. Therefore, he only got a piece of the story. The lack of a Safety Team meant that an associate pastor and two ushers were taken away from their areas of responsibility to surveille a suspicious person. They did so without knowledge of how to conduct a surveillance. Due to the fact that all three had no training, experience, or blueprinted plans, and because they were clearly identifiable as church members, this was a recipe for disaster. Their lack of competence created a distraction to the church service.

This is absolutely not acceptable. The vast majority of suspicious people observed in the church will turn out *not* to be threats. Therefore, unorganized inefficient responses will create distractions to service affecting more than just the person being surveilled. It is not just an inconvenience. A distraction to service causes an interruption to peoples' worship. The quality of their lives, the conditions of their hearts, and their relationship with the Lord may be affected by a preventable distraction. In this example, everyone was trying to do the right thing and prevent a suspicious person from attacking the church. However, their response was abysmal.

In order to enhance the security of the church you must have a covert Safety Team that utilizes Force Multipliers to observe and communicate suspicious activity. This is the only way to cover the church in condition yellow and conduct surveillance without creating a distraction. Consider the following response as an alternative to the previous situation. What if the situation played out like this instead?

The greeter observes a man she does not recognize hurrying into the church building. He doesn't make eye contact or respond to her greeting. He is determined to walk past her and is clutching his jacket against his lower stomach. As a Force Multiplier who has been trained to observe *red flags*, she realizes that something is not right. She immediately communicates what she saw to a covert Safety Team member. The

Safety Team member observes the man before he makes it to the hallway. She continues to greet guests and fulfills her role as a greeter. Her observations have been passed on to the Safety Team. Her situational awareness and observation of red flags was on target. She communicated that information effectively to the Safety Team and never missed a beat greeting guests as they came in. As a Force Multiplier, she performed admirably because she has been empowered and trained on what to observe and how to communicate it.

The Safety Team member begins to follow behind the suspicious man. He is able to catch up and quickly uses his phone to take photo of the subject as he walks down the hallway. The Safety Team member texts the photograph of the man to the Safety Team with the message: "S1 [an abbreviation for suspicious person 1 or subject 1], just walked into the bathroom." Immediately, other Safety Team members head towards that side of the church. Since they are in plain clothes with no identifiable markings associating them with the church, they appear as guests. They easily blend in with other people who are walking about the church.

The Safety Team members surveille the subject at a pace that is no different than other people in the hallway. Prior to getting to the bathroom, one Safety Team member enters the bookstore where she can observe the bathroom entrance and exit. She has taken an advantageous surveillance position as she blends in with other people in the bookstore. Another Safety Team member steps just inside the doorway that leads to the sanctuary. He also has pre-positioned himself advantageously. These members are conducting mobile surveillance and have taken up temporarily fixed positions of observation. They do this to be strategically set up where they can cover any directions that the subject goes.

The original Safety Team member that initiated the surveillance has not been observed by the subject. He enters the bathroom and realizes the man went directly to a stall and closed the door behind him. He observes this from in front of a sink where anyone using the bathroom would commonly stand. The Safety Team member updates the team with a text that says "S1 in stall 2." The Safety Team member begins to wash his hands in an attempt to blend in with the other people in the bathroom. Shortly thereafter, a second Safety Team member enters the bathroom and stands in front of a urinal. This too is a location where any guest, staff member, or church member would normally be. This allows the first Safety Team member to leave the bathroom as the second Safety Team member takes the *eyeball*. This is a designation taken by the person who has *eyes on* the subject being surveilled. The transition of the eyeball from one member to another allows for continuous observation of the suspicious person without being detected. The two team members have effectively maintained surveillance of the suspicious man without being noticed.

Subsequently, the man comes out of the stall, washes his hands and exits the bathroom. The Safety Team member in the bathroom does not immediately follow the suspicious man out. Rather, he passes the eyeball to the team member who was pre-positioned in the bookstore. She watches him exit as he heads towards the sanctuary doors. As he enters, a Safety Team member texts the team "S1 into the sanctuary" but she does not immediately follow him in. She meets up with the Safety Team member who is now exiting the bathroom. Together, they proceed down the hallway and bypass the sanctuary doors.

There was no need for the Safety Team members to follow him into the sanctuary and risk burning the surveillance or creating a distraction. This is because of the advantageous prepositioning of a Safety Team member who setup inside the sanctuary. He knows what the subject looks like from the photo that was texted to the team and he knows that the subject just entered the sanctuary via the text message. The Safety Team member inside of the sanctuary takes the eyeball and maintains surveillance without anyone in the congregation knowing what is occurring.

The Safety Team member pre-positioned in the sanctuary observed the suspicious person enter and sit alone on an aisle seat. He sends the team a message, "S1 right side, aisle seat, second row." Another team member is now seated behind and to the right of the man. He immediately texts "I have a good eye." The eyeball has been passed and a team member in the sanctuary proceeds to sit in the first row between the suspicious person and the pulpit. He has taken a position of advantage in case the man tries to move towards the pastor. He does this without looking at the man and creating suspicion. This team member has all the intelligence that he needs via the text messages which includes a photo of the subject.

At this time, two Safety Team members (one male and one female) enter the sanctuary together from a set of doors on the opposite side of the auditorium. This allows them to look at the subject without appearing to be out of place. It also allows them to scan the congregation for additional threats and locate advantageous places to sit. Because they strategically entered from a location that allows them to scan for the best possible place to sit to surveille the subject, they have time to do this without looking suspicious.

They walk in and sit on an aisle two rows behind the suspicious person. They appear as a normal couple to the congregation and communicate their position via text message to the team. Successfully, the Safety Team has positioned members around the subject without ever being detected by him or creating a distraction to the service.

The suspicious person's wife now enters the sanctuary. The Safety Team members observe her as she sits next to him. The husband and wife smile at one another and laugh off the "urgent need to use the bathroom" that caused him to jump out of the car. The Safety Team member with the eyeball texts the team that a woman is now sitting next to him and their conversation appears normal. *No additional red flags have been observed and the situation is de-escalating rapidly.*

A couple of moments later the pastor asks guests to greet one another. Taking advantage of this opportunity to make contact with the couple but not look out of place, the Safety Team member sitting in the front row turns and walks over to the couple. He introduces himself and engages them in conversation. There is a specific purpose to his greeting. He is looking for intelligence. Are there additional indicators that lead to additional red flags or does it appear that things have de-escalated? No additional red flags appear. As their conversation continues to be normal and not indicate any additional red flags, the Safety Team member's concern rapidly diminishes.

The Safety Team member finishes his conversation and sits back down. He texts the team that everything appears good and that he will remain in the sanctuary for a while to preserve the appearance of a normal service. The other team members are able to exit the sanctuary as they see fit and resume their duties. One team member contacts the greeter and champions her situational awareness and updates her on what occurred. Later, that greeter is able to talk with the couple and joke about him *rushing* into service. Although she does not talk about the Safety Team, she uses the opportunity to converse with the couple and provide additional information about the church.

Unlike the first example, this surveillance was a success. No one, not the person being observed, his wife, nor the congregation was disturbed. The Safety Team handled the situation and correctly concluded it without having to notify church staff, the law enforcement officer, or the pastor. *Nobody in the church knows that the team was watching a suspicious person.* The Safety Team rightfully determined that the red flags initially observed did not amount to anything. The integrity of the worship environment was preserved while the safety and security of the church was maintained. Success!

† † †

The security ministry should reinforce the vision of your church. The Safety Team should not only enhance the overall safety throughout the church, but do so in a way that fosters the life-giving message of the Gospel. As demonstrated in the previous examples, good intentions are not enough to do this successfully. A vision, sound tactics, and a commitment to stewardship, outreach, and discipleship are required. Tactically, the flexibility in utilizing a covert Safety Team allows team members to operate with fluidity. This flexibility created by the ability to blend in with the congregation is not just for conducting a successful surveillance, it is to maintain the integrity of the worship environment.

A Safety Team that is overbearing, confrontational, or distracting does not allow the congregation to focus on the service. Many churches who have a "security team" utilize it in a way that is counterproductive. Overt only teams can fall into this category. If an uninvolved person can identify who the team members are, then that team is overt no matter how creative they try to get with their appearance. Overt teams lack the ability to perform efficient surveillance without becoming a distraction. For example, if three members wearing sport coats and ear pieces attempt to do the same surveillance that the associate pastor and ushers did in the example above, the results would be the same. The team would be compromised and a distraction to service would occur.

In addition to the low cost and empowering nature of the SLS strategy, it is scalable among different size churches. It can be employed at any local church regardless of the size, service times, or location. Of course, the uniqueness of each local church requires a specific plan to implement the SLS Tactical Strategy. A church with a congregation of 1,000 in one building will not require the same number of team members as a church of 4,000 people located in multiple buildings. Although most churches will only need one law enforcement officer present during service, that is not to say that other churches will be adequately served by one. The quantity is based upon the specific needs. The tactical strategy of using an overt law enforcement presence, with a covert Safety Team and functioning Force Multipliers does not change from church to church. It is scaled appropriately to the needs of each church.

The church's Emergency Preparedness Plan will reflect the philosophy of the SLS Tactical Strategy with the specific implementation directed by the Safety Team leader. The philosophy does not change whether implemented on a Sunday service, Wednesday night service, or for a special event. Due to the logistical differences between events, the implementation of the tactical strategy simply adjusts. For example, on a Wednesday night service, the Safety Team may only need to cover 50% of the area that it would normally covered during a Sunday service. Hence, the tactics remain the same but adjustments are appropriately made to the number of personnel serving and the area being covered.

Just as different size churches will have different needs, equally sized churches may also have differing needs based upon how they function. The size of a Safety Team serving during an event or regular church service is determined by the area that it covers and its specific function within that area. For example, if one church has security cameras that cover many areas of the church, it will not need as many personnel serving as an equally sized church without cameras. This is because one person viewing multiple screens can do the work of multiple people on the ground. However, security cameras in no way eliminate the need for a Safety Team or the overt presence of a law enforcement officer and Force Multipliers. Both are still needed to deter, avoid, and mitigate threats. Cameras are not able to replace mobile team members who can adjust, assess, interact, and react to threats. They are merely a tool to be used to increase the Safety Team's efficiency.

† † †

Safety Team members must be able to play two roles. First, they serve to observe and communicate suspicious activity. This is achieved through the function of covert surveillance. For the Safety Team, the ability to conduct surveillance without being detected is paramount. Therefore, team members must be dressed in a way that does not identify them as part of a church ministry. A low-visibility appearance allows them to perform surveillance by blending in with the congregation. By avoiding detection, the low-visibility surveillance ensures that Safety Team members can follow, observe, and position themselves around suspicious people without being identified. It also ensures that they do not become a distraction to the congregation. In fact, it allows them to interact with the congregation to further ministry when they are not surveilling a suspicious person. Safety Team members have the ability to blend in with the congregation whether they are focused on a potential threat or scanning the crowd while speaking with guests. This allows the team to avoid being detected by suspicious people while interacting with guests in a non-confrontational way.

Because the Safety Team functions in a low-visibility capacity and is strengthened by its ability to blend in, the team should be reflective of the congregation, *with one exception*. The Safety Team should consist only of adults. The responsibilities of this ministry require mature commitment, proper vetting, and an ability to deal with emotionally difficult issues. Team members must be vetted church members who have passed a background check. They must be able to enter children's areas of the church and interact with first responders. Therefore, minors should not be members of the Safety Team.

Without any minors on the team, how does the Safety Team blend in with a group of children? The question is flawed. It assumes that the church is permitting children to be in areas unattended by adults, which should not occur. With that being stated, the answer to the question begins with leadership. First, pastors and leaders over children's ministries should be trained as Force Multipliers who know how to observe and communicate suspicious activity to the Safety Team. Second, adults in leadership should always be in areas where children are present. Very rarely, if at all, should children be unattended. If adults are always present around children, then the Safety Team will have the ability to blend in and decide if and when to approach a suspicious child.

The function of the team is to observe and communicate information. When a team member detects indicators that present red flags *from a minor,* they should immediately contact a church staff member. If immediate action is deemed necessary, then the Safety Team member should reasonably act as outlined in their training and the Emergency Preparedness Plan. Each team member's decision to act is made based upon their observations and the reasonable options available. The decision to approach or talk to a child is no different than when dealing with an adult; actions must be reasonably based upon the observations, information, and options that the Safety Team member has at that time. However, as suspicion levels rise, the observations should be communicated to staff, parents, and in extreme circumstances to law enforcement. The idea is to observe problems and communicate them to the appropriate person as early as possible in order to deter, avoid, and mitigate a threat.

Overt Deterrence - Covert Observation and Communication

Thus far, this chapter has focused on the *who* of the SLS Tactical Strategy (law enforcement, Force Multipliers, and the Safety Team) and now it will move on to the *how*. Admittingly, some of the *how* was addressed in the aforementioned descriptions of the hired law enforcement officer(s), the Force Multipliers, and the Safety Team. It would be difficult to completely separate the *how* from the descriptions of each element and the hypothetical examples provided. Therefore, some of the *how* was included but only to the extent that the descriptions of the elements and purpose of the examples would convey the message intended. The remainder of this chapter will continue to address the *how* of the SLS Tactical Strategy. It will provide much needed information for the training of the Safety Team and Force Multipliers.

There are two parts of the SLS Tactical Strategy that *Act* to *Deter*, *Avoid*, and *Mitigate* threats during service. The first part is deterrence through *overt* entities. The second is avoidance and mitigation through the *covert* Safety Team. By utilizing hired law enforcement and empowered Force Multipliers, a high degree of deterrence can be achieved. The success of overt deterrence is often not known. A success rate is not measurable because nobody knows how many people did not steal something from the bookstore, break into a car, disrupt the service, or commit a violent act because of the presence of law enforcement or the volunteers serving.

Characteristics of each element of the security ministry.

Every area where people serve can be covered in *condition yellow*. The people serving provide a visible deterrence element and intelligence source. Their observations can be transferred to the Safety Team. The law enforcement presence and the Force Multipliers are two overt elements of deterrence functioning to deter attacks. Their tactical roles and effectiveness have already been well established. What is missing is *how* the covert Safety Team functions tactically.

The primary tactical function of the Safety Team is to operate in a low-visibility capacity, conduct surveillance throughout the church, and address safety issues without creating a distraction to service. Therefore, *how* the Safety Team functions centers on the tactics used to operate covertly. The following pages will offer advice in ways that your church can successfully observe and communicate suspicious activity covertly without disrupting service.

Surveillance: The Safety Team uses covert, mobile surveillance to gather information on suspicious people, objects, and activities. This tactic is an *Action* used to *Deter*, *Avoid*, and *Mitigate* criminal acts through low-visibility observation and communication. Conducting surveillance requires versatility to obtain accurate information and communicate it to the appropriate people. Therefore, the Safety Team must always be gathering accurate information to avoid over- or under-reacting to a stimulus.

The Safety Team is intelligence based. Do not underestimate the importance of gathering intelligence. All material obtained during a surveillance operation is important. Do not only focus on the red flags. *Red flags* are indicators of suspicious activity. They highlight anything that appears out of the norm. This includes items that seem out of place and actions that appear out of character. Red flags must be investigated to determine if their suspicious appearance is an indication of a problem or threat. Further investigation may lead to additional red flags or the data obtained may explain the red flag and reduce suspicion. All observations have value in determining the next course of action, whether it is alarming or not. Thus, there is a high degree of emphasis on obtaining accurate information.

A successful surveillance operation is achieved when it produces accurate information and does so without creating a disruption to the service. Each time the Safety Team conducts a surveillance the experience is beneficial. The involvement provides growth in the capabilities of the individuals and the team. Hence, the actual surveillance of a suspicious person and surveillance conducted during mock scenarios are blueprints that condition the mind by establishing patterns through repetitive experience. It also offers the opportunity to practice variations in technique. Surveillance is as much an art as it is a science. Success in each area must be achieved to properly surveil a person without disrupting service.

Effective surveillants take advantage of opportunities that are presented before them. Every team member starts with a working knowledge of the layout of the church. This is an advantage that the Safety Team has over most people who pose a threat to the church. If the Safety Team is familiar with all of the areas of the church, they have an advantage that they can exploit. For example, Safety Team members have the advantage of knowing points of entrance and exit, locked rooms, and multiple ways of getting from one location to another that an unfamiliar person is unaware of or have access to. Safety Team members can use this knowledge to anticipate routes, take positions of advantage, and locate suspicious persons if they are lost during surveillance.

Safety Team members dressed to blend into the congregation can also make use of different types of cover. Knowing the layout of the church, areas of concealment, and blending into crowds will facilitate this tactical advantage. Cover, in the context of mobile foot surveillance in the church, commonly refers to obstacles including non-involved people who provide some degree of concealment of the surveillant from the subject(s) being observed. Heavy cover would refer to numerous people being in close proximity. No cover would indicate that the eyeball and surveillant have nobody in-between or immediately around them. Cover allows for the surveillant to blend in and not be the sole focus of the subject. Cover, in the context of surveillance is not to be confused with the *ballistic* context of cover and concealment.[80]

The Safety Team should use discretion in conducting surveillance. It should not be used where a person has a reasonable expectation of privacy. In most areas around the church access is open and the church has the authority to maintain and control those areas. Therefore, there is likely no reasonable expectation of privacy. This is why it is important that the church not only use signage as a deterrent but also to advise everyone who comes onto church property that security and surveillance is being conducted.[81]

With that being established, reasonable choices must be made even on private property. For example, a large public restroom may not give a person a reasonable expectation of privacy, but it could be argued that an individual stall within that bathroom does bring with it an expectation of privacy. Therefore, the Safety Team should use discretion when a suspicious person enters into an individual stall within a bathroom.

---

[80] Concealment refers to the ability to hide behind something that bullets are able to penetrate. Cover provides a barrier that bullets cannot penetrate. However, cover that will stop ammunition such as a 9mm round may offer no protection against a .223 round. Therefore, these terms must always be taken in the context that they are presented.

[81] Consult legal counsel to determine the specific laws, rules, regulations, ordinances, and opinions regarding the reasonable expectation of privacy that apply to your church. Since the author, SLS, and affiliates are not legal advisors or offering legal advice, all decisions and actions taken by the church should be presented to the church's legal counsel before any form of implementation of the presented recommendations.

If the totality of the situation, including the amount red flags observed, warrants substantial concern that the person in the individual stall is a threat, then law enforcement should be involved. The bottom line is, always act professionally, do not conduct surveillance from a vantage point that a normal person would not be able to observe the suspicious person, and do not hesitate to get law enforcement involved when necessary.

When the team becomes involved in a surveillance, it is important to confirm that they are observing the correct person. This is why an accurate description of the suspicious person is required and communications through text messaging work efficiently. Safety Team members surveilling a subject should not mimic the suspicious person's movements. If you have the eyeball on a person who is seated, and the subject suddenly gets up, do not immediately do the same thing. Rather, *hand-off* the eyeball to a surveillant who is in the direction that the subject moves to. Then take advantage of the opportunity to move to another advantageous position.

During surveillance it is important to exploit the Force Multipliers and the mobile ability of the covert Safety Team. *Pre-positioning* is the strategic placement of Safety Team members and Force Multipliers from other ministries to provide comprehensive coverage in a designated area of the church. Force Multipliers will already be positioned in areas that function best for their ministries. However, their positions are fixed. *Fixed positions*, often referred to as stationary surveillance, is the establishment of an observation post. The advantage of this is that it assures high traffic areas, such as points of entrance and exit, and sensitive areas have continuous coverage. The use of ushers and greeters, for example, allows for the Safety Team to have additional eyes and ears in high traffic areas.

Some fixed positions are permanent; others are stationary. A permanent example is a camera attached to the wall. It is unable to be relocated when a surveillance is being conducted. Generally, ushers, greeters, and Force Multipliers are assigned

SLS Tactical Strategy

a position to be and thus are fixed. However, in a situation that warrants it, they can be moved. However, this is taking them away from the assigned position that they are serving in their specific ministry. Safety Team members are mobile surveillants and can assume fixed positions as needed. For example, they can advantageously pre-position themselves in fixed positions in anticipation that the subject they are surveilling moves into that area. This is part of the philosophy that says if you are conducting surveillance and do not have the eyeball, move to an advantageous position. The fluidity of the covert Safety Team allows this to be done without looking out of place or creating a distraction to the worship service. As you can see, there is a lot of moving parts to surveillance. The keys are to be professional, appear "normal," always be able to identify who you are and why you are there, move to advantageous positions, and pass of the eyeball often to avoid detection.

† † †

Surveillance is a fluid, ever-changing, team operation. Always be prepared to *receive or pass the eye* to another Safety Team member. The greater the variation in surveillants the more likely the integrity of the covert surveillance will be maintained. Tactics that aid in this variation include: Tailing, Leap Frogging, and Paralleling.

Tailing is a term used to identify a surveillant who is observing the subject(s). It is often referred to when surveillants are conducting a mobile surveillance. Tailing is also commonly referred to as shadowing, following, or simply surveilling.

Leap Frogging is a process of using multiple surveillants to vary who is closest, ahead of, and serving as the eyeball. This variation is done to reduce the frequency of encounters and observations of specific surveillants when the Safety Team is following a subject that is mobile. A surveillant can pass ahead of both the suspicious person and other surveillants in order to get to an advantageous position. This technique involves fluidity and anticipating the direction the person being observed is going. During a surveillance, leap frogging can also give a tactical advantage as it allows the team to pre-position people in a bathroom, lobby, sanctuary, or parking lot in order to facilitate the passing the eyeball.

Paralleling is the use of a parallel route when the subject's direction of travel is anticipated. This allows for trailing surveillants to follow the general direction of the subject without being in his/her view. For example, if the subject is walking down a hallway and being followed by the eyeball, a trailing surveillant may cut through the sanctuary while heading in the same direction of the subject. This allows the trailing surveillant to be pre-positioned in the sanctuary in the event the subject enters or gets ahead of the subject if s/he continues down the same path. This tactic also creates an opportunity for the paralleling Safety Team member to take over the eyeball. This gives relief to the surveillant who was following down the hallway and provides variation in the people that the subject may see near him/her.

When conducting surveillance, consider the proximity of each member of the team to the suspicious person. *Loose* and *tight* are relative terms that describe the proximity to the subject being surveilled. How close a Safety Team member needs to be to the subject is determined by the value given to the red flags indicating suspicious activity. There is no pre-set distance that a team member must maintain to fall into either category. Every situation brings with it many variables in addition to the red flags that will determine what is *loose* and what is *tight*. This is a prime example of how the art and science of surveillance work together.

Be aware of surveillance detection techniques that a subject may use. Examples of these countermeasures include:

- Looking past an object (like over their phone, a flyer, or other item)
- Entering a room and immediately coming back out
- Reversing direction abruptly, turning a corner and stopping without reason
- Purposely going into an unoccupied room
- Using mirrors or other reflective surfaces for observation
- Changing the rate of speed that the person walks for no reason
- Going down a hallway that dead ends with doors that they have no intention on entering
- Reversing direction for no apparent reason
- Sitting down for only a moment and then getting up or changing seats
- Changing physical appearance
- Walking surveillance detection routes

Additional countermeasures include the use of a decoy or a distraction. A *decoy* is the use of another person with a similar appearance to counter surveillance. This is rare, but if the Safety Team sees this tactic being used, it brings with it an abrupt red flag indicating possible pre-planning and coordination. Law enforcement should immediately be notified and both the suspicious person and decoy should be surveilled. A *distraction* is a purposeful event designed to attract attention and divert observed concentration away from the threat. If someone is observed using any of these or similar techniques, law enforcement should be immediately contacted.

If you are the eyeball, do not be sucked into a room just because the person you are surveilling enters it. A better option is to pass the eyeball to another Safety Team member who can enter. A third Safety Team member can *post up* outside of the room to pick up the suspicious person if they come out. In a large room, the new eyeball can relay information that will dictate if the team needs to stagger into the room or move ahead to more advantageous positions to pick up the surveillance if the person being observed exits the room.

This scenario is very common when a person under observation enters into a small room. As the person enters, generally the surveillant with the eyeball will pass it off to another person if available. That person can pick up the surveillance of the suspicious person inside the room and switch out if it proves to be tactically advantageous. When properly conducted, the varied eyeball will allow the Safety Team to maintain observation of the suspicious person without being detected.

Determining when to start, continue, and stop surveillance involves discretion. This requires flexibility, critical thinking, and proper analysis. Surveillance requires the highest level of situational awareness, spatial awareness, self-awareness, and spiritual awareness. It requires a relaxed state of vigilance while in *condition yellow* and increased effort to appear typical while in *condition orange*. When surveillance is being conducted and no suspicious person is on the radar, the Safety Team member must be in *condition yellow*. However, when a suspicious person is observed, they transition to *condition orange*. The team members must remain relaxed even though they have a condensed focus on the suspicious person. Even in a heightened degree of condition orange, the Safety Team must function covertly to prevent a distraction to the worship service.

In the rare occasion that the Safety Team would have to move from operating covertly to overtly, it should be done so with the assistance of uniformed law enforcement. This is why it is important to have established relationships with law enforcement and have a uniformed law enforcement officer at the church during service. The mission of the Safety Team is to observe and communicate information. Having a uniformed law enforcement officer at the church reduces the time it takes to communicate that information and the likelihood that a member of the Safety Team would have to take an overt action to prevent a crime.

When a team conducts a surveillance, it is important that a minimum of three people is used in order to protect the integrity of the surveillance and not create a disruption to the church service. A one-person or two-person surveillance is extremely limited in its ability to accomplish these goals. In a one-person surveillance, constant observation has to be made by the sole Safety Team member. That person has limited flexibility and a high likelihood of being detected. A single surveillant has no assistance to pass the eyeball to or rotate out of being in the suspicious person's line of sight. A one-person surveillance is in essence shadowing the subject.

The key to a successful surveillance is flexibility to maintain constant observation without being detected. Even with two Safety Team members, flexibility is very limited. Having two surveillants does allow one Safety Team member the opportunity to pass the eyeball off to another. However, it is a back and forth that can only go on for so long before being detected. Having multiple Safety Team members becomes crucial when a suspicious person enters into a room or uses countermeasures to detect surveillance. Remaining undetected is exceptionally difficult when only two surveillants are used.

A three-person surveillance provides the minimum number of assets to have the flexibility needed to be successful. The ability to be flexible and vary the surveillant's proximity to the subject reduces the risk of losing track of the suspicious person. It reduces the frequency, location, and time that the subject will observe a team member. The variation of Safety Team members taking the position of the eyeball greatly protects against detection. Therefore, a minimum of three people should be used to surveil a suspicious person in order to avoid being compromised, creating a distraction, or losing the person the team is surveilling.

If the subject being observed is lost during a surveillance, it should be communicated to the team. However, this is not a reason to discontinue the surveillance. If this occurs, the Safety

Team should use the last known location of the subject and their familiarity with the church to begin searching to reacquire the suspicious person. Once located, this should be communicated to the rest of the Safety Team. If done discretely and through the use of text messaging, this will be well communicated and documented in the text message chain. This chain will provide accurate, time stamped information of each observation.

Clothing: Members of the Safety Team should make every attempt to act naturally while conducting surveillance. The first action to take is to maintain an ordinary appearance. This means blend in with the congregation. Clothing, facial features, mannerisms, and interacting with people at the church need to camouflage the Safety Team member into the general congregation. This is why the Safety Team's attire is more about function than fashion.

As a team that is focused on low-visibility surveillance, it is imperative that members be able to blend into the congregation. Therefore, it is essential that clothing be consistent with the majority of the people attending church. Additionally, the clothing that the team wears should be operational. In addition to camouflaging the team member, clothing should fit to conceal equipment. For example, if a team member wears a radio, clothing should be chosen that will conceal the radio by not allowing it to *imprint* through the clothing. Imprinting is when an item, in this case a radio, is concealed beneath clothing but the outline is clearly visible. An example would be attaching a radio to a team member's belt and covering it with a tight-fitting T-shirt. Although the radio is covered, the shape is not concealed. It clearly imprints the item, identifies the person as being part of "security," and creates a distraction as people will take notice of it.

Footwear is another important item to consider when serving on the Safety Team. As stated above, clothing must blend in with the congregation and be operational. Shoes therefore should be comfortable since Safety Team members spend a great deal of time on their feet. If circumstances dictate that a Safety Team member needs to run or jog a short distance, they must be functionally-appropriate.

Footwear should not attract undue attention. Therefore, footwear must not be loud in color or create noise. Bright colors stand out and become easily identifiable. Footwear that creates noise does the same thing. When a team member is following a person, it is imperative to conceal any noise that indicates their presence. If the Safety Team member's footwear makes loud noises with each step, it will draw attention. In a noisy environment during praise and worship this may not matter as the loud atmosphere will mask the noise created by footwear. However, following a person down a hallway when the majority of the congregation is in the sanctuary attentively listening to the sermon is completely different. Every squeak, tap, clop, and trot will stand out. Noise from boots, heels, or other footwear will be a detriment to a Safety Team during a surveillance.

Another important feature of the clothing is its ability to carry many items. Clothing with ample pockets allows team members to carry and conceal items such as a flashlight, ID, phone, camera, sunglasses (as you may have to work the outside perimeter), a pen, a note pad, medical gear, and any other items you may choose to have in your possession. Each individual Safety Team will determine what items to carry. But at a minimum, no team member should be without a form of communication (phone), identification, and a flashlight.

The final item to consider is identification. There are three types to consider: Official, church, and emergency. Official identification and church identification are required; emergency identification is beneficial but optional. Each team member should have official personal identification on them. This could be a driver's license or any other credentialed form of identification. Additionally, a secondary form of identification is required. This secondary form is one that associates the team member with the church Safety Team. Because the team functions in a low-visibility capacity, the church credential should be concealable. Options to consider include printed name badges, lanyards, and church identification cards. Your team may also consider a tertiary form that comes out only in extreme emergency situations. This comes in the form of vests, jackets, hats, or sashes that clearly identify the member as being part of the security ministry or Safety Team.

Notwithstanding the third type of identification that is only for extreme emergencies, Safety Team members need the ability to produce the concealable form of identification. It is not possible that every staff member of the church will be familiar with or easily identify members of the Safety Team. This problem is amplified as the size of the church and team membership is increased. Therefore, staff and leaders of the church should know that the covert Safety Team will carry a concealed form of church identification. It is important that the Safety Team's form of identification is consistent with that of other ministries. That will make it easily recognizable, familiar, and consistent to what everyone in the church has.

People: The most important piece of equipment that you can invest in is people. If your focus is on strengthening people, decisions concerning adding resources will be easier. However, this requires that you know what your people need. Do not just think that you understand what a ministry needs. You may be an associate pastor who oversees multiple ministries but are not closely involved in any of them. If you are not a functional part of the ministry, you are disconnected; you need to acquire the boots on the ground input that only comes from those who are doing the work. Additionally, if you do not consult the people who will be using the equipment, you may end up purchasing items that they do not want or need. This will produce wasteful spending which is bad financial stewardship.

Simply put, remain within the vision of the church and consult with the leaders who will be utilizing any equipment you are considering. Determine if purchasing the items enhances the vision of the church and benefits the person serving. Do not impulsively purchase items that *seem* to make sense. Purchases must enhance the vision, support the people serving, and fit within the established budget.

The SLS strategy is people-focused not technology-focused. That is why resources must support the people serving. An item that does not help a person fulfill their role is useless. The same can be said about an item without a trained person to use it. Lt. Col. Dave Grossman appreciates the importance of people over "items." In *Warrior Mindset*, Grossman emphasizes software over hardware. The difference is that amateurs talk about hardware such as gear, or equipment while true professionals focus on software like training, preparedness, and mental readiness.[82] Focus first on people; all technological hardware must benefit the operator and enhance the vision of the church, if not it is useless.

Cameras and Radios: Every type of technological addition introduced to the Safety Team has the potential to help and hinder the team's function. Therefore, a detailed cost/benefit analysis must be conducted before the purchase of any equipment. This is a matter of stewardship both in the initial cost to purchase item(s) and the cost to maintain and upgrading the equipment. The use of portable radios by a low-visibility Safety Team can be a double-edged sword. A negative aspect of wearing a radio is that it indicates that the person wearing it is affiliated with the church. The person wearing a visible radio is not able to operate in an undercover capacity. It is common that people will attempt to overcome the obvious display of radios by the use of "covert packages." This is a misnomer as they are low-visibility at best. Covert packages include earpieces, bluetooth communications, or hidden wires. They are attempting to hide the devices but often fail miserably to completely conceal them. Consider how the use of this type of equipment

---

[82] Asken, *Warrior Mindset*, v.

will *enhance or expose* your Safety Team before making any purchases. If any of the equipment is visible, your team is in essence not a low-visibility team at all. That means its ability to function covertly, without creating a distraction to the service, is gone.

In addition to the difficulty to conceal radio equipment, radio communication itself has limitations that are often overlooked. For example, when the noise level in the church is increased, the ability to use radios is reduced. Think about how loud the music is when worship is being conducted. A person standing in an area with loud music will have trouble hearing what another team member is saying. More importantly, if a team member is standing in an area where there is a great deal of noise, they will not be able to transmit. The message that they try to send will be covered in background noise.

Consider the limitations of radio communication when deciding whether or not to purchase them. For the Safety Team, they offer a limited scope of use. Radio communication is not the primary form of communication for the covert SLS Safety Team. But for other ministries they can be since these ministries are already overt. When the Safety Team loses its ability to function as a covert entity, it loses its ability to perform surveillance in an effective way that does not create a distraction during the worship service. Therefore, the people on the Safety Team who utilize a radio will be limited to individuals with specified roles who are not operating in a covert capacity.

Let's look at some of the positive aspects of radio use. When functioning, they provide real time intelligence to what is occurring. One transmission can be sent and heard by everyone wearing a radio. This means a person serving in a location such as a children's ministry could use the radio to call for assistance and get immediate attention. The recipient of that message can immediately respond, call for assistance, or dispatch a Safety Team member via a text message to the team. In this sense, the use of radios can effectively enhance safety and a response

SLS Tactical Strategy

to an emergency. At larger churches with multiple ministries spread out in large (or multiple buildings) this is a feasible option. However, not every church has this necessity.

Another positive aspect of utilizing radios at church is the ability to provide one to the uniformed law enforcement officer(s) working the security detail. As the uniformed officer patrols the grounds, s/he will have the ability to monitor any radio traffic that is broadcast over the radio. A designated person will have to provide the radio to the law enforcement officer and retrieve it when their shift is over. Again, this may be an option for some churches, but not for all.

If your church utilizes radios for communication between ushers, greeters, or other teams serving, it is recommended that one member on the Safety Team maintain a radio to monitor traffic. This is done to efficiently get the Safety Team involved when something occurs. This would be the only person on the Safety Team with a radio. That person now is overt and may not be able to conduct effective surveillance. Therefore, you can only designate a person to fulfill this role if you have substantial assets available.

The Safety Team member with a radio monitors radio traffic and dispatches information via text message to the team. For example, if a member of the hospitality team sends a radio transmission that a suspicious person is near the nursing mothers' room, the Safety Team member who is monitoring the radio will receive the information and "copy" that transmission by stating that the Safety Team has it. More than likely, that will be the extent of the radio conversation as the Safety Team has taken over.

The team member who received the radio transmission immediately sends it via a text message to the Safety Team. They receive the information and begin a surveillance on the suspicious person. The first Safety Team member to acquire the suspicious person sets up the eyeball. That team member takes a picture of the person and sends it to the entire team.

At this point, everyone has the intel on the suspicious person and a picture of the subject. The other team members advantageously pre-position themselves to observe the subject if he goes mobile (begins walking away from his current location). They have set up *takeaways* to receive the eyeball when the subject begins to move. This allows the first team member who established surveillance to *pass the eyeball* and continue to blend in. As the man gets up and heads towards the sanctuary doors, the initial Safety Team member who took the photograph passes the eyeball off to observe the subject walk down the hallway towards the sanctuary doors. She texts "S1 heading into the sanctuary – south doors." The observation and communication is received by the Safety Team member pre-positioned inside who takes the eyeball and continues the surveillance. The team continues to observe and communicate the surveillance until it is resolved.

The point of this scenario was to demonstrate how an individual on the team with the radio can expedite the initiation of the surveillance. It also demonstrates how little radio traffic is transmitted once the Safety Team gets involved. Although the Safety Team member with the radio is not able to participate in the surveillance in a low visibility capacity, s/he plays a crucial role. This only works, however, if enough assets are available so that the observation of the subject can be done without creating a distraction to the worship environment.

As with all equipment, training is necessary to ensure its proper use. Radio communication only works if the device, the transmitter, and receiver all operate correctly. Devices have limitations created by distance, battery life, and interference by other electronic equipment. Radios are also limited by the operator's ability to effectively use them. Transmissions must be clear, concise, and accurate. Finally, if people do not listen to the radio, the transmission coming across is lost. Because of these factors, it is essential that operators know the equipment they are using and its capabilities.

Any small error can have catastrophic results; hence, training on proper use must be conducted. The training must include teaching everyone how to operate in a calm atmosphere and during emergency situations. Properly implemented, radios can save manpower, time, and lives. However, when they are not effectively utilized, radios only add to the confusion of an emergency situation.

For low-visibility Safety Teams, radio usage is limited or not used at all. As addressed above, having a single Safety Team member with a radio can be useful in providing communications with other ministries within the church. It, however, takes that Safety Team member out of a covert surveillance role. That role is a crucial part of the overall enhancement of the security and safety of the church. It is a role that can only be filled by another Safety Team member. Therefore, sufficient assets must exist to assign a person to facilitate radio communication.

Cameras are technological hardware that, like radios, must be obtained only if beneficial to the team and the vision of the church. Relatively speaking, they have less of a down side than radios. The use of electronic surveillance cameras by the Safety Team will aide it in the enhancement of the overall safety and security of the church. But in the SLS strategy cameras are not a requirement.

Camera systems have multiple functions. They exist to aid the surveillance team and serve as a deterrent. If the church chooses to integrate cameras in to their security plan, they must include positioning them on the proper platform, have an ample power source, and a sufficient recording device. The quality of the camera and the picture it records must be sufficient to identify people. Camera capability increases with cost; therefore, the need must be balanced with the investment. As a tool used for surveillance, they provide an efficient way to monitor many areas at one time by a sole operator. That operator can relay information to others from a stationary location. Cameras also serve as a deterrent. Their visible presence alerts people that they are not only being monitored, but their activities are being recorded.

Radios and cameras for many churches will enhance the security of the church. However, their capabilities and reliability are limited. Neither should ever be used in lieu of a covert, low-visibility Safety Team. Because of this, much research, thought and testing must be placed before making this costly investment. Consult the people who will be using them to make sure it will enhance their ministry and the church's vision. Also, make sure that their use will not interfere with other ministries.

Properly test all equipment before implementation. Will their use interfere with other elements of production? Will keying up a radio create interference that generates feedback into the speakers in the church? Will utilizing people to monitor cameras and radios take individuals away from other areas of service where their presence is needed? The unique characteristics of each will determine the benefit to its overall security. For some churches, it will be evident that they do not need radios or cameras. For other churches, it will be a well-placed investment.

Primary Means of Communication: The primary means of communication of the Safety Team is text messaging. Radios, as mentioned above, can be beneficial to the team if used in a specific scheme. However, the Safety Team's role is to blend in, observe, and communicate observations without creating a distraction. Keeping within this role, one of the best ways to communicate among team members is utilizing cell phones. For example, every time the Safety Team works together, a group text message should be established. This establishes direct communication between all members of the team that will not compromise their ability to blend into the congregation. Note: your church may choose to include certain individuals on the group text such as an associate pastor, the law enforcement officer, or the head usher. If there is a person designated to monitor cameras and radios, they must be included on the text as they can relay information directly to the team.

One of the greatest advantages of group texting is the ability to include pictures. For example, imagine that a Safety Team member observes a suspicious person sitting in a car in the parking lot. In one text, that team member can send a photo and advise the entire group instantaneously that s/he is watching a suspicious person. The photo eliminates the need to type a long description of the car (make, model, color) and the person in the car (height weight, skin tone, clothing). One picture immediately communicates all the information.

Utilizing a group text message also creates a time stamp that will aid in documenting an event if it rises to that level. For example, what time the person arrived, who observed the suspicious person, the suspicious person's path throughout the church and any other suspicious activity. Finally, unlike utilizing radios, most people do not need training on how to take a photo or use text messaging because it is something they do every day.

Documentation: The Safety Team is responsible for documenting suspicious activity that rises to a level where it needs to be communicated to staff. Documentation is important as it should provide clear and concise information about what occurred. The SLS strategy uses a two-step process for documenting an event. The first step involves everyone who was involved in the event to fill out an Observation and Communication Intel Report that details what they saw and what they did. This is not a synopsis of the entire event. Rather, it is just what one person's role was. This should only take 5-10 minutes to complete. Therefore, it can easily be completed before the person leaves service. This is vital as you want to acquire all of the Intel Reports on the day of the event. If not, you will have to track down the participants who have left the church service to get their input. Lacking information, especially from a person who was directly involved in the incident, will prevent you from completing the second step which is the creation of an After Action Report.

An After Action Report is a chronological summary of the event. It is created from the information collected via the Intel Reports. The After Action Report is a complete account of what occurred. It includes all the participants, their observations and actions, and a narrative that describes the event and disposition. It also documents what went wrong and what went right. Finally, it is an opportunity to seek growth from the experience. The After Action Report prevents the false information that spreads when people hear one part of the story and fill in the rest with their imaginations. It also contains everyone's role and experience who participated in the event. So, the reader gets the complete story and does not have to call someone to get their point of view. All of the information from all participants is recorded on the Intel Reports and collected by the team leader or designated person who will compile the information into an After Action Report.

The After Action Report provides an accurate account of what occurred. It is a written debriefing that can be shared with those who need to know what transpired. When properly completed, the After Action Report will comprehensively document what occurred and what the next steps are concerning the event. Below you will find an example of a standard SLS Intel Report and a SLS After Action Report.

† † †

So, what does a typical Sunday or church event look like for a Safety Team member? The answer to this question are the standard operating procedures that the Safety Team follows during church service and events. The following is a recommendation for these procedures. You may adopt this or a variant that you decide works best for your church. Once

SLS Tactical Strategy

you have created your version, make sure to document it in the Emergency Preparedness Plan and make it available to all Safety Team members.

Upon arrival at the church Safety Team members must scan the exterior of the church for suspicious persons, items, or other potential safety threats. Next, they should sign in and meet with the other team members serving that day. Once the entire group that is serving has arrived, they should pray together. Next, the team needs to establish communications via a group text message or through another app. Once this is set up, the team can break up and conduct an initial scan of the entire area of responsibility inside and outside of the church for safety concerns. As they do this, team members should make contact with staff and leaders within other ministries.

If you utilize sworn law enforcement officers, make sure a member of the team meets them as they arrive. Always brief the officer(s) and invite him/her/them into the church to establish area familiarization (A-FAM). Offer the use of the restrooms, coffee, and/or any other hospitalities that your church would offer a guest. Prior to the arrival of guests, team members should maintain a low visibility role. They should take advantageous positions of observation that allow them to view people as they arrive and enter the church. The team leader should take advantage of opportunities to conduct Operational Training Exercises (OTX) when applicable.[83] If any incidents occur, they should be documented using Intel Reports and After Action Reports (See the following examples of each). Finally, the team members should notify the team as they leave the church via the text group established at the beginning of the shift.

---

[83] An Operational Training Exercise (OTX) is a designed scenario that functions as a controlled practice session to test and improve operational skills. It will be covered in detail in Chapter 8.

YOUR CHURCH NAME AND LOGO
Observation and Communication Intel Report

Please complete this form on the day of the event and provide it to the Team Leader. If the team Leader is not available please give it to a church staff member and then provide the Team Leader with the name of the staff member you gave this report to.

Please complete this form as accurately as possible. Each person involved in the event should complete an individual form detailing their involvement in the event. It is **not** a summary of **everyone's** involvement. Rather, limit your response to your specific role.

Your name:
Date of the event:
Time of your involvement:
Your position: Please check the applicable description
Parking - ____ Usher - ____ Greeter/Concierge - ____ Kids- ____
Other Team Member- ____ Staff- ____ Service Attendee- ____
Other- _____
Event type: Suspicious Person(s) - ____ - Medical Emergency - ____
Other _____
Synopsis of your role in the event:
- How did you first become aware of the situation?
- Who provided you with information?
- What did you observe and do? Include people's actions, demeanor, and movement.
- With whom did you communicate?

Any other important information you can provide.
If additional space is needed please use the back of this page.

SAMPLE:
After Action Report
Date of Event: 20 January 2019

Event Type: Mobile and Static Surveillance of a suspicious person.

Synopsis: On this date an unknown individual demonstrated suspicious characteristics that caused members of the Serve Team to observe him while on site. This included the interior of the building within the sanctuary, common area, and the bookstore. Members of the Safety Team and Ushers conducted mobile and static surveillance of the individual. This initiated outside of the building, proceeded inside, and concluded outside of the building. The surveillance initiated during the transition between services and concluded before the end of the second service.

Individuals involved and aware of the surveillance: James Bowden (Safety Team), KC Williams (Safety Team), Michael Williams (Church Member -juvenile), Diego Lopez (Usher), Andre Masters (Usher).

Details: During the transition between first and second service, at 1035 HRS Williams observed a suspicious individual (further described as S1) wearing a satchel lingering outside of the church building. S1 appeared to be alone and walked back and forth from the West to the East side of the building. S1 stopped numerous times and took photographs of the front of the church. While this was occurring, Williams contacted Bowden who was inside of the foyer. Bowden proceeded to assist Williams with low visibility surveillance of S1 outside of the building.

At 1041 HRS, S1 walked from the East side of the church towards the front doors and entered into the building. Once inside, Williams and Lopez observed S1 in the bookstore (1045 HRS). At 1047 HRS, S1 went from the bookstore into the main sanctuary where Bowden observed him. S1 sat towards the back of the Sanctuary close to the center aisle. Bowden informed Masters who then assisted with the surveillance.

Bowden and Lopez observed S1 take numerous photographs of the inside of the sanctuary during praise and worship. Prior to the end of the music, S1 exited the sanctuary and proceeded out the front of church (1052 HRS). Bowden and Williams followed S1 and attempted to get a description of the vehicle the he was driving. However, S1 walked down the east side of the parking lot towards Round Stone Lane. He then proceeded east on Round Stone Lane until he walked out of sight (1056 HRS).

At 1125 HRS, Bowden and Williams were retrieving the church flags and parking cones when they noticed S1 walking northbound on Route 26. This was approximately 30 minutes after he was last seen walking east on Round Stone Lane. Bowden and Williams bottlenecked S1 at the main entrance of the parking lot. They made it appear as if they were retrieving the cones as S1 walked by. Bowden approached S1 and greeted him. S1, still in possession of the satchel smiled at Bowden. He then mumbled something unintelligible. S1 did not stop walking as he said something in a foreign language to Bowden. S1 continued to walk north on Route 26 until out of sight at approximately 1129 HRS.

Disposition: S1 exhibited unusual behavior but left without incident. S1 was not observed making contact with anyone on his own. He was carrying a satchel that appeared to be out of place with the way he was dressed. The photographing of the front and inside of the church is alarming. Also, walking up and down the streets around the church raises additional red flags. This behavior is out of character of members of the congregation and that of guests. It is unknown if S1 is able to speak English or not. S1 did not want to stop to talk despite smiling at Bowden when he greeted him. S1 should be monitored for both suspicious behavior if he is seen at the church again.

Service Team members and staff should take note of his activities and anyone who appears to be a companion of his. There are numerous possibilities as to what S1's intentions are. They range from being a church planter gaining information, to a person with an unknown-based malicious intent. Because of the suspicious activity all contact with S1 should be documented and shared with the church staff. There is a heightened urgency for this due to the holiday season. The attached surveillance photographs should be shown to the church staff to see if anyone can identify him. All members of the Safety Team and the Ushers should be made aware his description.

Takeaways: Negative: Only one member was serving on the Safety Team during the second service (Williams). Bowden was serving in another ministry when informed of the suspicious person. He was able to assist in the surveillance and coordinate with the Ushers. At a minimum, the Safety Team needs (3) three people serving in a low-visibility capacity at each service. This allows the Safety Team to maintain continual observation of suspicious persons and communicate up the appropriate channels. Although things worked in this event, it is not ideal or efficient.

Positive: Information was quickly relayed to the appropriate people. Teamwork between the Ushers (Overt) and Safety Team members (Covert) worked very well. No incident occurred, and the congregation's worship experience was not interrupted or disrupted by S1 or the team member's surveilling him.

It should be noted that the presence of S1 did not cause reason for other areas of the church (Kids, Youth, or other Service Team members) to be alerted. His actions, although suspicious, did not reach a level to support "sounding an alarm." Appropriately, the other sections of the church were NOT advised thus avoiding the creation of a heightened sense of alert which would have taken away from the worship experience. Future interaction may necessitate additional dissemination.

Incident Injury Report

This report is to be used when needed as a supplement to the After Action Report.

Injured Person's Name:
Date and Time of the Incident:_
Incident Injury Report Completed By:_

Mark the location(s) of injuries referred to in the Intel Reports and After Action Report.

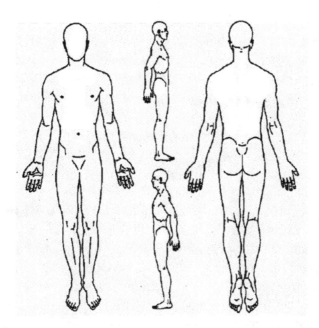

Chapter 7

Red Flags and Pre-Assault Indicators

———⋙∘⋘———

"May the favor of the Lord our God rest upon us; establish the work of our hands for us."
Psalm 90:17

Training Force Multipliers and Safety Team Members

*S*ecurity Ministry Basic Training is required of everyone serving as a Force Multiplier or Safety Team member. This includes the previously covered topics of situational awareness, conditioning the mind, the OODA loop, cognitive blueprinting, properly communicating suspicious observations, and the Christian Warrior Mindset. This chapter adds two items to the list: identifying red flags and pre-assault indicators. The ability to recognize red flags and pre-assault indicators will increase reaction time when an attack occurs. An increased reaction time is the goal of the security ministry as it allows for a greater chance to avoid or mitigate the damage during a critical event.

Red Flags and Pre-Assault Indicators

Red flags are indicators of suspicious activity. They highlight anything that appears out of the norm. This includes items that look out of place (such as suspicious bags, packages, or emails) and actions that appear out of character (including conscious and subconscious behavior). When anyone at church identifies a red flag, they must be investigated to determine if it is an indication of a problem or threat. Through further investigation you will find additional red flags or discover the initial red flag is a false alarm. The observations that are made and information that is obtained will determine the next course of action.

Pre-assault indicators are also commonly referred to as pre-attack indicators. Pre-assault indicators are red flags that a person may exhibit signaling an attack. A person may exhibit pre-assault indicators consciously or sub-consciously. Most people live their lives not looking to identify this type of red flag. But they should. Just as storm clouds, lightning, and wind indicate a thunderstorm is near, a person looking into car windows, watching for people who may see them, and concealing their hands may indicate a burglary about to happen. Being aware of red flags is a characteristic of operating in condition yellow. By watching for red flags, people serving at church are less likely be caught off guard. Therefore, they will increase their reaction time and find themselves in a better position to *Act* to *Deter, Avoid,* and *Mitigate* an attack.

By being situationally aware and familiar with pre-assault indicators you can effectively blueprint contingency plans and increase reaction time. When you observe a red flag, the System 1 mind searches for a blueprinted pattern to relate it to. Since the System 1 mind noticed the indicator before an attack ensued, it is primed with a planned response. In addition, observing a red flag before an attack gives the System 2 mind the opportunity to get to work creating additional contingency plans specific to that situation. When a red flag is noticed, the System 2 intellectual hero researches options and creates additional blueprints for the System 1 action hero to access if needed. By observing pre-assault indicators prior to an attack, Systems 1 and 2 *Act* efficiently to *Deter*, *Avoid*, and *Mitigate* a threat.

It doesn't matter what type of attack is coming. It may be a theft, embezzlement of funds, active shooter, or planned disruption to a service. By educating and empowering the people serving to identify suspicious activity and take the proper action before the attack occurs, they will increase their reaction time and make better informed decisions. As each person increases their security, they enhance the overall safety of the church.

I am sure you have heard people say: "the attack came out of nowhere!" From their perspective, it very well may have. Often people are victims of an attack and truly did not have a chance to defend themselves. By operating in condition yellow, you lessen the likelihood that you will be in that predicament. However, if you choose to live in condition white, you will *never* notice the attack coming. Part of the condition yellow mindset is to observe pre-assault indicators that people reveal prior to an attack. Many attacks that appear to randomly come out of nowhere, actually had many warning signs.

Humanity fears the random attack. For example, society dreads the shark attack because it comes "out of nowhere," or the spider that went unnoticed as it crawled into a shoe. We fear the unexpected earthquake, the lightning strike, and contaminated food. You cannot make yourself 100% secure from experiencing any of these. The randomness and lack of warning increases our feeling of vulnerability. Because these attacks are somewhat by chance and without bias, we are all indeed susceptible to them.

For some, this unavoidable vulnerability leads to hypervigilance. Hypervigilance will produce chaos in your daily life. One cannot spend a lifetime indoors to avoid lightning strikes, never enter a building because of it collapsing during an earthquake, or stop eating to prevent possibly consuming contaminated food. The randomness of these types of attacks is different from attacks from another human being. When a person generates an attack, it is rarely random. There is almost always some degree of planning involved with conscious and subconscious actions that give us clues that the attack is coming. Sure, you may find yourself at the wrong place at the wrong time, but even then, human attackers tend to exhibit warning sings. It is these signs that people involved in the security ministry want to look for.

Active shooters, robbers, thieves, etc., conduct varying degrees of planning. Some planning may involve research, training, and occur over a long period of time. However, some may be conducted in less than a minute as a person sees an opportunity to commit an attack and creates a quick plan to initiate the first step. In both of these examples the perpetrator will exhibit cues that provide a warning of their criminal intent. The warnings are not always blatantly obvious or observed by the victims, but in hindsight, when people are studying what happened prior to an attack, they are uncovered. If the church security ministry makes an effort to identify pre-assault indicators it may increase reaction time to avoid and mitigate attacks.

De Becker demonstrated that danger from humans can be more complicated than danger from sharks. Simply put, to be safe from shark attacks, stay out of the water. It is not as simple with people. However, what you need to know about how to be safe from people is in you too. It is enhanced through experiences learned throughout life.[84] Experience and training is all we need to enhance our overall security and that of the church. This is where the slow thinking System 2 intellectual hero must be motivated to work. This means identifying red flags and blueprinting contingency plans for the System 1 action hero to access.

Now, before we look at a list of pre-assault indicators, it must be made clear that there is no specific number of red flags

---

[84] Gavin De Becker, *The Gift of Fear* (New York: Dell Publishing, 1997), 344.

which creates a threshold that must be observed to indicate a pending attack. For example, a man pointing a firearm in the parking lot towards the church does not need further investigation; an attack is underway! A man sitting alone near the entrance of the church wearing a hoodie and tapping his feet rapidly exhibits multiple red flags but does not indicate that an attack in underway. As a member of the security ministry you must work to not overreact or underreact to either scenario. A lone red flag may be enough of an indicator of an attack just as multiple red flags may not.

Balancing over- and under-reacting to red flags comes with training and experience. Take the second scenario for example. Over-reacting to the man sitting alone exhibiting multiple red flags could cause you to rally multiple team members and a law enforcement officer to approach him. Maybe this young man was just waiting for a friend to arrive whom he wanted to go into church with. On the other hand, maybe this person is indeed planning to walk into the church and begin executing anyone he encounters. If you over-react, you are chasing away the person whom we are trying to protect. If you under-react, you have paved the way for a tragedy to occur. Every decision you make is balancing the Pastor's Paradox – How much security is too much verses how much is too little.

Although every case is independently different, the answer to the question of what to do to avoid hyper- vs hypo-reaction is to constantly be assessing and obtaining accurate information while always being ready for an imminent attack. For this young man sitting alone and exhibiting multiple red flags, advise the Safety Team who can set up in positions to observe him without appearing as a force approaching him. Prior to doing this, advise the law enforcement officer of the suspicious person the team is looking at. Once everyone is covertly in place, have one member approach him in a non-confrontational way that is consistent with the way anyone serving at the church would greet a guest. Of course, other team members are around but they are blending in with the rest of the people at the church. As the Safety Team member interacts with the young man s/he must be constantly looking for additional red flags while being ready for an attack. The information that s/he obtains may dismiss the initial suspicion or help to de-escalate any pre-attack tension the subject has.

This scenario presented two possibilities. First, this young man is a person who is about to attack the church. If this turns out to be the case, the Safety Team has placed itself and the law enforcement officer in a position to avoid a direct hit and mitigate the attack. The second possibility is that the young man is waiting for his friend to arrive so they can go to service together. If this was the scenario, the team operated in a way that determined that the red flags he exhibited were explainable. Equally important, they did so without creating a distraction to the worship environment or making the young man feel unwelcomed.

Each time a red flag is observed it must be taken in context and investigated for intent. The red flag will either be corroborated or dismissed as more intelligence is obtained. Some of the more prevalent red flags that indicate possible malintent are listed below. They have been broken down into two categories – those to be looking for when people arrive and attend church and those that people may exhibit when interacting with you. Train everyone serving at church on the following pre-assault indicators and always be obtaining accurate intelligence while remaining ready for an attack.

Red Flags

Red flags to look for when observing subjects at the church:

- Unusual Driving: The subject pointlessly drives around the parking lot or building before parking. This is can be an indicator of conducting pre-assault surveillance.

- Delayed Exit of the Vehicle: This can be an additional indicator of pre-assault surveillance. It may indicate a time of mental preparation or the subject working through the decision point of committing an attack.
- Suspicious Clothing: Does the clothing worn by the subject seem out of place? Is it overly loose fitting, providing the ability to conceal items? Does the clothing seem out of character for the climate or culture of the church? If so, this may be a red flag that arouses suspicion.
- Repeated Adjustment of Clothing: Does the subject oddly fidget or readjust their clothing? This may be an indicator that the subject's clothing is not functioning correctly because it is concealing an item such as a weapon.
- Fixation on an Item Being Carried: If the subject is suspiciously paying out of the ordinary attention to an item being carried, it may indicate a subconscious attachment to that item. This red flag indicates that the subject's mind is focused on that item and whatever its intended use is.
- Repeatedly Enters and Exits the Vehicle: If a person is seen entering and exiting a vehicle repeatedly, it may indicate indecisiveness. If that person is considering an attack, they are still in the decision phase. They may be calculating additional information they have observed and orienting themselves to it.
- Concealment of the Hands: Observing a person's hands is crucial in identifying pre-assault indicators. The hands are used to break into cars, steal purses, grab kids, fire weapons, and so forth. The hands also contain fingerprints which provide for the unique identification of a subject. If a person is obviously concealing their hands, that subject is exhibiting a red flag that must be investigated.

- Head on a Swivel: This is a subject who is constantly checking his/her 360-degree awareness. They look around often using their head and eyes to scan the area around them. If a subject exits a vehicle and walks to the church exhibiting this type of situational awareness it will stand out as being uncharacteristically high for a normal person attending service. If they are about to commit a crime, this is a way of scanning the environment for obstacles to their attack. This is one reason the overt presence of a law enforcement and the highly identifiable Force Multipliers is a critical part of the security ministry.
- Signs of Alcohol or Drug Use: The subject exhibits the effects of being under the influence of drugs or is inebriated.
- Focused Attention: This occurs when a person fixates their attention on a specific location, person, or item. For example, if a subject exits a car with a focused attention on the place that they will enter the church. As they move towards the entrance, they may walk briskly with an unusual determination to enter the church. This may be an indicator that the decision-making process of the OODA loop has concluded, and the subject is already in the action phase.
- Isolation: People that purposefully avoid interaction with others at the church are isolating themselves. This coupled with additional red flags increases suspicion. An example is a person sitting alone and concealing their hands, fixating on an item they possess, excessively tapping their feet or hands, etc.
- Suspicious Location: This refers to a person being in a place at a time that appears to be out of the ordinary for them.

Red flags to look at when interacting with a person:

- Inconsistencies of Verbal and Non-Verbal Cues: When speaking with a person who has exhibited suspicious behavior, you must ask yourself, does what the subject is saying match up with their body language? If not, this is red flag. If a person is sweating profusely and you ask them, "Can I get you a bottle of cold water to cool off," to which the subject responds that they are not hot at all, then the verbal and non-verbal cues are not congruent. Thus, this is another red flag.
- Focused Attention: Focused attention occurs when you are talking with someone and they uncharacteristically focus on you but not what you are saying, or they are pretending to be conversing with you but are intently focused on another person, location, or item. This generally occurs when the subject is committed to or about to commit to the attack. They have reached the state of decision. All they have to do is act. De-escalation techniques are limited and preparation must be made to avoid or mitigate a pending attack.
- Thousand-Yard Stare: This occurs while talking to a subject and they appear to be looking through you. When a person is in this state, it is difficult to communicate with them. Therefore, de-escalation techniques are extremely limited. Subjects in this state have mentally checked out and are very dangerous.
- Verbal Aggression: This occurs when a person elevates their voice and/or uses language that is abrasive, intimidating, and often offensive.
- Nervousness: This can indicate discomfort or an interruption of their plan by speaking with you. Nervousness can be exhibited by fidgeting, tapping of their feet, sweaty hands, tension, and elevated heart rates.

Red Flags and Pre-Assault Indicators

- Disconnected Communication: This, in addition with nervousness, can indicate that the person is distracted from your greeting or conversation.
- Excessive Overbearing Conversation: This is an unusually dominant from of talking that makes it difficult to have a normal conversation with the subject.
- Excessive Questioning: The subject is uncharacteristically asking questions that in and of themselves raise red flags of suspicion.
- Blading the Body: This is a repositioning the body into a combative stance. Blading occurs when the subject places their strong side foot slightly behind them. This rotates the body and indicates that the subject is preparing for an offensive or defensive attack. This can be a posture a person takes preempting an attack (an offensive cue) or in anticipation of an attack (a defensive cue).
- Flexing and Fist Clenching: These actions serve the purpose of psychologically pumping the body and mind up to fight. Physiologically, during a heightened state of arousal, vasoconstriction pulls the blood from the extremities and moves to the vital organs. Pumping the body up can force greater circulation of the blood. Clenching the fists is a natural response indicating that the subject is mentally and physically preparing for an attack. An additional red flag related to this is the clenching of the teeth.
- Stuttering, Trembling, and Shallow Breathing: These are indicators of agitation and stress in the subject.
- Prolonged Responses: This occurs when a subject takes unnecessary time to answer basic questions. It is an indicator of distraction and disconnection. It may be a red flag for suspicious activity.
- Avoiding Eye Contact: In a church setting where eye contact is welcoming and normal, a subject who is

purposely avoiding it is likely indicating that they are hiding something. It is similar to hiding their face. In and of itself, it may not be an indicator of an attack but, it is a red flag that should be noted.
- Posturing: In some people this is a physiological reaction that demonstrates dominance. It can also be an indicator of an attack. Examples of posturing include standing tall, broadening the shoulders, and puffing up the chest. Each is an attempt to appear larger and stronger in stature. NOTE: Another form of a change to posture is one exhibited just before a person physically attacks someone they are talking to. These pre-assault indicators are lowering the head, tucking the chin, adjusting or removing clothing, licking one's lips, and touching one's face or head.
- Warming up with rhythmic movements such as pacing back and forth, or bobbing up and down, etc.: These movements are an attempt to prepare the body for attack. It is similar to an athlete hopping, bouncing, stretching, or making other movements to warm up and prepare for exercise. All are an attempt to loosen up, prime muscles, and oxygenate the body for action.

Once you have established your Safety Team, it becomes their responsibility to teach the people serving as Force Multipliers to better safeguard the church. They take ownership over the safety and security of the congregation and essentially manage a ministry that belongs to God. They are always focused on the *one,* while training others to protect the *ninety-nine.* The Safety Team should teach an overview of what is in this book focusing specifically on Chapter 3 and the content of this chapter. In addition, they must instruct the Force Multipliers on how to communicate what they observe to the Safety Team.

Having a Safety Team at the heart of the security ministry that provides training assures that they are in regular contact with the other ministries. Tactically, this is a crucial connection between the layers of security at the church. Additionally, the interaction between the Safety Team and Force Multipliers forces people serving within the church to engage with each other. This will surely intensify the fellowship and discipleship among church members who may not regularly associate together.

Chapter 8

Safety Team Operational Training

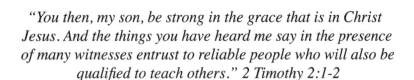

"You then, my son, be strong in the grace that is in Christ Jesus. And the things you have heard me say in the presence of many witnesses entrust to reliable people who will also be qualified to teach others." 2 Timothy 2:1-2

Concept

The Safety Team requires specific instruction on tactical operations and leadership, including the ability to train others. This is in addition to the Security Ministry Basic Training that everyone serving should receive. Specific Safety Team instruction should include: tactical training in surveillance, covert/low-visibility operations, de-escalation, and team observation and communication techniques. Of course, your church can include additional training in each area and advanced training in areas such as: defensive tactics, the use of force, use of weapons, medical care, and so on. However, before embarking on any additional advanced training, set a firm foundation with Security Ministry Basic Training and Safety Team Operational Training.

Safety Team Operational Training builds upon the Security Ministry Basic Training.

The Safety Team leader will be responsible for planning, conducting, and implementing team training. This is why it is important to establish a team leader early on and get that person up to speed on the SLS strategy. Once that person is knowledgeable and comfortable to instruct, Security Ministry Basic Training can be taught to the Force Multipliers and Safety Team. A question often asked is: If we are starting a security ministry from scratch, should we train the Force Multipliers at the same time as the Safety Team or wait until the Safety Team is up and running so they can instruct the Force Multipliers? The answer is: it has been done successfully both ways. Remember, Security Ministry Basic Training is for everyone serving. The Safety Team receives its Operational Training after that. The plus side of training the Force Multipliers as soon as possible is that you immediately increase their situational awareness and empower them to be part of the security ministry. Unfortunately, they will be observing and communicating information to a Safety Team that has not been taught how to react. Therefore, they may perform surveillances with a higher likelihood of being a distraction to the worship service. This is not a risk that most churches are comfortable with.

Because of this, the ideal situation is to train everyone serving (the Force Multipliers and Safety Team) in Security Ministry Basic Training and follow that up with Safety Team Operational Training. This ideal approach involves a lot of factors that have to come together. For example, you need to get everyone together at one time for a full day of training. This often proves to be very difficult since the majority of the people serving as Force Multipliers or Safety Team members are working jobs, taking care of families, and living busy lives. Their schedules may make it impossible to find a time where everyone can be gathered together.

Another approach that is less than ideal but can effectively work is to train the Safety Team in Security Ministry Basic Training and Safety Team Operational Training first. Then, with a competent Safety Team in place, they can train the Force Multipliers at a formal training session or as opportunities present themselves during service. In reality, the latter is the most likely scenario for most churches. For example, a five-minute conversation on a Sunday during service with a person serving in any ministry can pave the way for them to become situationally aware. Simply letting them know that a functioning Safety Team exists and that is who they are to direct any suspicious activity towards will get the ball rolling in the right direction. Their situational awareness and ability to identify suspicious activity will increase through future training and interactions with the Safety Team. Both of these approaches will work. In each case, an additional opportunity for instruction will come as new team members come on board and the team continually trains to increase its ability.

† † †

How does the team leader who is new conduct Safety Team Operational Training? First, they must know *what to teach* and *how to teach* it. All training, including tactical training, is as much about people as it is about the technique being taught. Every instructor, trainer, and leader must want to see their student(s) grow in ability and attitude. This is why the Safety Team leader must conduct training sessions that focus on bringing out each person's greatest potential to perform operationally. Because no one ever attains perfection, training sessions are an opportunity for individual growth regardless of skill level.

Success in training is determined by achieving an increase in the condition of the person being trained. Of course, standards must be set (and achieved) but progress is the first goal. Every bit of progress achieved is a victory to be championed. This will lead to standards being met. While on that path, accountability is important. Thus, at the end of every training session, the instructor should determine if the team (and each individual) increased their aptitude as a Safety Team member.

The team leader must set up the training for success. Training sessions, including meetings, exercises, and briefings must be a positive use of time. Unproductive training is not only a waste of people's time, it crushes passion, potential, and faith in leadership. This is why it is essential that you make sure that each training session and team meeting demonstrates respect for people's time. That can be done by sticking to the scheduled meeting times, making sure that the information provided is valuable, and that the training is structured.

Two examples of improper training are ones that waste people's time and negative training. Wasting time, as mentioned above can be crushing to morale. As bad as that can be, negative training is potentially even more destructive. In an effort to avoid negative training sessions, Grossman outlines three key principles for training. These principles are used by elite instructors in military special operations and law enforcement SWAT communities. They are: 1- Never "kill" a warrior in training. 2 - Try to never send a loser off your training site. 3- As a trainer, never talk trash about your students.[85] Each one of these principles must be followed during the formal training of the Safety Team.

Principle 1: The first principle, *never kill a warrior in training* counters the poor training given by instructors who teach people to die during a training scenario. Killing a warrior in training occurs when a person makes a mistake and the instructor "kills them" during the scenario.[86] In the context of combative training, this often occurs when a person is shot and is told to assume that they are dead.

Once they are *killed* in training, they lose the ability to continue to learn as they are effectively removed from the scenario. Hence, if you get shot, you are sent to the sidelines to wallow in your sorrow while other participants continue to learn. Rather than lose this opportunity to grow, wouldn't it be better to train on what to do if you get shot? Or, how to stay in the fight and continue to learn through the training scenario? What about care under fire where the team also can train on how to treat a wounded teammate? At a minimum, the person who is "dead"

---

[85] Grossman, *On Combat,* 136.

[86] This does not include times when instructors purposefully have a student roleplay being shot, injured, or killed as part of a scripted scenario-based training exercise.

should be allowed to continue to observe the scenario even if they are not an active participant. Sending someone to the sidelines to pout does nothing to empower them. It is purely bad instruction by poor instructors. The instructors who "teach" this way do not understand that they are creating a far greater problem than they realize.

Killing a person in training and removing them from an opportunity to learn conditions the student's mind to die. For example, if a poorly conditioned student is shot during an actual critical event, they will revert to their previous training experience. Then they will recall that "training said" once they are shot, they are dead. Therefore, the cognitive science side of this is that the System 1 side of the mind says, "I'm shot, this has never happened to me before, what can I do?" It accesses the only previously-established pattern filed away which came from the poor training that taught if you get shot, you are dead. The mind then concludes, "I am going to die." Once the mind has decided it is going to die, the fight to live is lost. Simple actions and techniques that could save a life are never even attempted because of a *lie* in the person's mind that came out of poor training.

Negative training has the potential to kill warriors who otherwise would survive. This often used and detrimental technique teaches defeat. It imparts how to lose rather than how to win. Do not just play to win, train others to win! Every opportunity in training is a chance for growth. Therefore, as an instructor you must never "kill" a warrior in training. When someone does something wrong, use it as an opportunity to grow. Continue on and increase their ability to perform. If mistakes are going to be made, especially crucial ones, it is far better to make them in training than during a critical event.

Principle 2: The second principle is to avoid sending *losers* home after training. If people leave training sessions feeling like a loser, those thoughts will be reinforced over and over again each time they remember that experience. For example, on the way home, they will think about what they did wrong. They will try to figure out what is wrong with them and why they are inevitably not capable of being successful. This destructive path leads to mental lies about their ability to perform. They will psychologically repeat the training failure over and over again without the mistake ever being repaired. Unfortunately, the System 2 mind is blueprinting these *negative* patterns and they will be accessed by the System 1 mind during a critical event.

As an instructor, this type of poor training infuriates me because it mentally conditions people to failure. It is an evil scheme that uses a combination of bad instruction techniques and bad instructors to destroy people's confidence and purpose and thus, their potential. The devil came to steal, kill, and destroy, but Jesus came to give life (John 10:10). Do not be an instructor who steals potential and creates losers. Rather, be an instructor who brings life!

One way that bad instruction occurs is when people's failures are exposed without providing correction. When this happens, the instructor destroys their student's ability to grow. When the team leader (or other instructor) is teaching, individual and team failures should be exposed and adequately corrected before leaving the training session. Students must comprehend what went wrong and experience how to do it right. If a student does something wrong, correct it and then have them perform it properly. By doing so, you are creating a positive mental pattern. You are making their System 2 intellectual hero blueprint the proper way of handling a situation and thus providing the System 1 action hero a plan to use during a critical event. Do this and your students will go home empowered and not defeated. That is how to instruct victoriously!

When teaching, instructors should build upon victories that reinforce what was done correctly. This positive instruction makes the student mentally build upon each victory instead of mentally killing himself/herself. Whereas bad training leads to mentally conditioning students to believe that they are failures, positive training creates encouraged students. A student who is defeated in training will fear coming to the next session because that student will dread being exposed again as a failure. However, the victorious student will arrive at the next training session prepared to build upon what they have learned.

<u>Principle 3:</u> Finally, a leader who trains others is held to a higher standard than the other members of the Safety Team. Although warriors often joke and make fun of one another, a Safety Team leader cannot do this when instructing a team where that type of relationship has not been formed. Warriors in the military and law enforcement that have grown close together have forged a bond that allows for this type of dynamic. Over time this may also occur among the members of the Safety Team. But, as a leader, especially in a training environment, you must maintain control and build respect and trust which will allow for that type of camaraderie to grow.

Furthermore, it is important that you never joke about someone's mistakes. Do not belittle team members who are trying to learn and grow. *Having fun* and *making fun of* are two different things. Having fun yields positive results, making fun of is often detrimental to growth. Your job is to correct the mistakes they make and build upon their successes. This approach will sharpen the team members (and yourself) during the process (Prov 27:17).

A growing team will experience issues that will need to be adequately addressed. Some issues will be good and others bad. Addressing them is a part of the team leader's responsibility. This is another reason why it is important to discover the person for this position rather than plugging a person into it. For example, if something negative occurs and a reprimand is needed, always punish in private. However, when a reward is deserved, give praise in public. As a leader, trainer, and instructor you must maintain a standard that others can rely on in good times and in bad. The success achieved in the training environment will translate to the type of actions performed during an emergency situation. This is why training should always be conducted professionally and produce growth in capability.

By following the three principles that Grossman has provided: never kill a warrior, don't send losers off the training site, and never belittle your students will set you up for successful training sessions. Additionally, you must provide the proper training environment. This requires that the setting and atmosphere be conducive for success. This includes the location, size, and function of the room and building that you will use. The atmosphere must be one that welcomes tactical and spiritual growth. People need to walk into the training location and be greeted with a feeling that they are valued and that they are going to grow.

Grossman recommends creating an environment where your people want to train. He advises creating a training environment where the warrior spirit is nurtured and the warriors want to train.[87] When you conduct a formal training session, the members of your Safety Team will be volunteering their time and counting on you to provide instruction. They will arrive with a longing to serve and grow in Christ. This ministry is their calling and they are giving their time to serve under your leadership. Be a good steward of their time. If you set the right tone, you will be greeting the students with an attitude for growth and success. In the end they will depart having received a good return on the time that they invested.

Formal Training: Stewardship, Outreach, and Discipleship

There are two types of training sessions that the Safety Team will participate in: Formal and On the Job Training. Formal training sessions are team training sessions that are

---

[87] Grossman, *On Combat,* 136.

conducted quarterly. Each session should consist of a meeting that reviews the procedures and responsibilities of team members, a debriefing of the events that have occurred since the last training, and specialized training that is unique to that particular quarter. Having a formal team training session every three months provides an opportunity for the Safety Team to grow together in *stewardship, outreach,* and *discipleship.*

The Safety Team can only be fully functional if it is balanced upon a foundation of Stewardship, Outreach, and Discipleship.

During the meeting, the team leader must reinforce the stewardship aspect of enhancing the safety and security of the church by providing the team members with clarity on their roles and responsibilities. It should include the standard operating procedures and address any changes or new procedures that are being implemented. For most of the Safety Team members, this will strengthen what has already been taught to them. For new team members, this will be their initial formal training session. Therefore, the instruction has to be comprehensive.

The team leader should walk through what a typical day looks like from the moment a team member arrives at the church through the end of the time that s/he is serving. In the end, everyone should leave the formal training session knowing exactly what their scope of responsibility entails.

Formal training should also solidify the tactical strategy utilized by the team. This includes how to operate in a covert capacity, training Force Multipliers, and proper documentation of events through the use of After Action Reports. The team should debrief and discuss suspicious events that occurred since the previous quarterly training and do so from an objective position. Look specifically at the event, what went well, and where improvement is needed.

During the quarterly training, the team should also discuss any concerns or announcements coming from the church staff as well as upcoming special events. Finally, each quarterly training should provide the team with a specialized training topic that is not addressed every quarter. For example, one quarter may focus on medical mitigation training, another quarter the training may center on non-verbal indicators of attack, and another quarter may focus on de-escalation techniques.

Quarterly training is a great opportunity to bring in subject matter experts to speak on these topics. This includes contacting first responders and inviting them to be guest instructors. For example, have the fire department/EMS come in and provide first aid training for the team. This is part of enhancing the safety and security of the church and the sustained outreach effort to the first responder community. It also demonstrates the due diligence that the church is taking to provide professional training. Quarterly training therefore will consist of a meeting, debriefing, and specialized training focused on *stewardship*, *outreach*, and *discipleship*.

Concerning outreach, quarterly team meetings should include a discussion on the how the team is interacting with the first responder community. In order to develop relationships, it is important that the team knows the name of the off-duty officer(s) who serve during service. Find out if anyone has spoken with the first responders and determine if there is a ministry need that the team can fulfill. Discuss any upcoming outreach opportunities that they can be involved in. Finally, affirm the Safety Team will take the lead in outreach to first responders and be there to support them through traumatic events. This includes providing support if a first responder is injured or killed in the line of duty.

Quarterly team meetings must have a discipleship element. It should reinforce the spiritual growth of the team. The team is generally outward-focused through their stewardship responsibility over the congregation and through the outreach to the first responder community. But the team must also look inwardly as well. This is the discipleship aspect of the training session.

Through discipleship the Safety Team must focus on its spiritual growth. The Safety Team as a whole must be attentive to the needs of the individual team members. As a group of men and women focused on *situational awareness,* they must not forget the importance of *self-* and *spiritual* awareness. How is each member doing in the battlefield of life? How is each member doing in regard to their walk with Christ? Quarterly meetings therefore must function as a Bible study/small group fostering spiritual growth and concern for the individual needs of the team members. This reinforces the importance of setting the right atmosphere for spiritual and tactical growth.

On the Job Training: Stewardship, Outreach, and Discipleship

Conducting the quarterly formal training sessions is essential for the Safety Team to operate efficiently. However, since the team is comprised of people serving as volunteers and not co-workers, it will be difficult to get everyone together for multiple formal training sessions more than once a quarter. This is complicated by the fact that most team members work all week and serve on Sunday. To overcome this obstacle, SLS has found that training be conducted in two ways: First, as was previously established, through quarterly sessions for formal training. Second, training each Sunday in the form of *On the Job Training* (OJT). Together, formal sessions and OJT will provide an opportunity to reinforce standards and tactics weekly, while growing in specialized areas quarterly. Therefore, if a member of the Safety Team serves one Sunday a month and attends a quarterly training session, that member will never be out of touch with the function of the team and the mission of the church. The team concept of *stewardship*, *outreach*, and *discipleship* will never be distant from that team member.

Every time the Safety Team serves during a service it is designed to enhance the security of the church and foster relationships with first responders. However, you can only interact with the law enforcement officer for so long before you become annoying! Also, there is not always a suspicious person that needs to be surveilled. Therefore, in order to maximize the use of time, the team should take advantage of the downtime to improve tactical skills. This is part of the OJT that should occur during service. It is extremely beneficial for new team members who are learning the tradecraft. It also provides the seasoned veterans an opportunity for refining their skills and improving their leadership ability.

Operational Training Exercise (OTX)

OJT tactical training during service is ideal because the environment is not artificial. By conducting training while service is ongoing, you provide a realistic setting to run an *Operational Training Exercise (OTX)*. This is a designed scenario that functions as a controlled practice session to test and improve operational skills. It includes a person posing as a suspicious subject and allowing the team to utilize their tactical skills in observation and communication.

If the team only trains on an "off day," they face an unrealistic setting where the church is empty. In that situation, there are no cars in the parking lot, no people in the sanctuary, no worship, no message, no noise, and no Force Multipliers serving. It does not provide the proper realistic environment to refine skills. But during an ongoing service, the environment is real.

By conducting an OTX, you will effectively remove the downtime that occurs during a worship service. By creating and running a training exercise, the team becomes focused on the scenario and is actively scanning the church. Of course, while running a mock scenario the team is constantly looking for actual safety concerns and addressing them when need be. At any time, the training scenario can be terminated, and the team's attention fixated on the actual suspicious activity.

An OTX is created to assess and enhance the operational capabilities of the Safety Team. It is important that the entire team understands that it is a training scenario before it is initiated. If the mock scenario is being conducted during service, the leaders of other ministries who may be involved must also be aware of the training exercise. It is imperative that everyone is on the same page and that no-one reacts as if the scenario is anything other than a training. The team leader conducting the OJT must make sure that the OTX never becomes a distraction to the worship environment. This is another benefit to conducting training while service is ongoing.

Furthermore, an OTX is a scripted scenario run by the team leader. Therefore, planning the training exercise to avoid a disruption to service is essential. For example, a training scenario during service will never involve a person approaching the pastor, alarming the children's ministry, incorporating a loud and obnoxious person, or any other variable that would disturb service. Scenarios during service are limited to use of covert surveillance to observe and communicate suspicious activity.

Therefore, the scenario should not disrupt service in any way. Successful scenarios conclude without anyone knowing that the team was training. Below is an example of a scenario that you can run.

OTX Scenario – Suspicious Person in the Parking Lot:

During a worship service, the team leader assesses that there is down time and sees an opportunity to conduct an OTX. Therefore, the team leader informs the Safety Team that they are going to conduct a training scenario through the group text message that was established when they assembled before service. *Every member* must acknowledge that they understand that the scenario is a training exercise. The team leader must also inform the ministry team leaders they deem appropriate for the scenario they have designed. For this scenario, the team leader will inform the parking lot team and usher team.

Once everyone is notified and all team members have acknowledged the training exercise, the team leader initiates the exercise with a text message. That message must clearly say "TRAINING EXERCISE" followed by the beginning of the scenario. In this case, it reads, "Suspicious person – east side parking lot." The team leader plays the role of the suspicious person and stands near a car in the parking lot. Included in the team leader's message to the group is a picture of himself and the message S1 (Suspect 1). This provides the team intel that *he* is S1, the subject of the surveillance. The team leader ends the text message by sending a message stating: "Begin Training Exercise." This initiates the OTX scenario.

It is important to note that the exercise created by the team leader has an identified end point. The team leader has determined how this exercise will end well before it begins. This is done to control the exercise and prevent any disruption to the ongoing worship service. The Safety Team has no idea how the exercise will evolve, but the team leader knows that he is going to conclude it by walking out the front doors of the church and entering his personal vehicle.

What transpires between the initiation and conclusion is more fluid. The team leader playing the role of the suspicious person must present a viable training scenario for the team and make sure that the exercise does not disrupt service. Training scenarios require a good plan and a proficient instructor who can run it successfully. OTX's are a vital part of the OJT that the team implements. But never conduct an OTX with a person not comfortable in leading it.

Returning to the training exercise, the team leader walks up and down one of the aisles in the parking lot allowing time for the Safety Team to acquire him. In an effort to better observe the subject, one Safety Team member goes out to his car and gets in. By doing this, he is able to take a picture of S1 loitering near cars. Via text message he sends the photo to the team. While this is transpiring, other Safety Team members advantageously pre-position themselves inside of the entrance of the church. This allows them to observe the person without being detected. The team leader wants to push the scenario inside, so he walks towards the front of the church. This movement is indicated by the Safety Team member in the car that has a good eyeball. Since the other team members have advantageously pre-positioned themselves, it does not matter which way S1 goes when he enters the church, a Safety Team member will be able to assume the eyeball in all directions.

S1 enters the building and moves towards the café located just inside the main entrance of the church. A Safety Team member is there acting as if he is on social media. But in actuality, he is surveilling the subject. From this position he texts the Safety Team: "S1 in the Café." The other team members, all out of sight, re-position themselves to locations where they can pick up the eyeball if S1 gets up and leaves. Therefore, when S1 moves towards the sanctuary, the team member sends a message of this observation. In the message he indicates that S1 did not purchase anything in the café. As S1 enters the sanctuary, he immediately sits in the back. The Safety Team member who pre-positioned herself in the sanctuary now takes on the eyeball. She texts the team: "S1 back row section 2." She observes that he is suspiciously tapping his foot rapidly and looking around the sanctuary. The other Safety Team members covertly reposition themselves based on S1's current location.

Less than two minutes after sitting down in the back of the sanctuary, S1 leaves out the same doors he entered and moves directly towards the exit. The team observes and communicates this. One team member exits a side door of the church allowing him to be in the parking lot without having to follow directly behind S1. That team member begins talking with a member of the parking team. Their conversation is a *cover* to make it look like they are not concerned with S1. They laugh and do not look directly at S1 who is now walking down a different parking aisle. They observe him as he gets into his car. Members of the Safety Team notate the vehicle he is driving and the license plate. At this point, the team leader playing the role of S1 texts the team: "END OF TRAINING SCENARIO" and each team member acknowledges.

The total time of an OTX like this will take 10-15 minutes. When you are participating in one, it will seem like it lasted much longer. Fortunately, the time and information are captured on the group text message. Once the scenario is concluded, the team leader lets the other ministries know that the training scenario has terminated. Finally, the Safety Team gathers for a quick debriefing by the team leader.

The team leader conducts the debriefing and deems the training exercise a success. The surveillance was efficiently conducted without a disruption to service. The group text message has created a timeline of the actions of S1 including photographs. Had this been a real scenario, each team member would fill out an Intel Report to be used in the creation of an After Action Report. The team leader (or designated person) then prepares an After Action Report which will be provided to church staff.

Safety Team Operational Training

During the OTX example above, S1 exhibited numerous red flags. Each of these should be included in the After Action Report and reported to the entire team. They are important details to be documented and shared with the members of the Safety Team. If S1 were to return to the church, the team would observe him to determine if his suspicious activity continues or diminishes. If, hypothetically he was to return and exhibit additional red flags, those observations may necessitate informing other ministries and law enforcement.

This above scenario was conducted successfully. A post-scenario debriefing of what occurred will prove to be as valuable an experience as the exercise itself. This is due to the discussion and team growth that occurs while the experience is still fresh in their minds. During the OTX, each member of the team experienced numerous micro-scenarios, observed and identified red flags, and processed through many OODA loops. Both during the exercise and in the conversations at the debriefing, the team members' System 2 minds blueprinted patterns for the System 1 mind to use in the future.

For example, the positions that the team members took while observing S1 created patterns of reference that can be quickly accessed in the future. For instance, a team member who took a good position to observe S1 may utilize that same location for an actual event. Also, less advantageous positions that were taken become *lessons learned* through the training exercise. They will be avoided in the future when an actual suspicious person is being observed. By practicing their ability to conduct surveillance and by participating in a comprehensive debriefing, the team is able to sharpen their skills. By cognitively blueprinting prior to an attack, team members are making the System 2 slow thinking intelligent hero work hard to create plans and patterns for the fast-acting System 1 action hero to use. The OTX experience, training, and cognitive blueprinting, will make every team member better equipped for actual situations.

† † †

The combination of OJT and the quarterly formal training sessions is essential to the Safety Team. Through this combination of ongoing training, team members will consistently grow in their tactical proficiency (the stewardship to protect the congregation), interaction with the first responder community (outreach), and Christian growth (discipleship). Additionally, the formal training will strengthen camaraderie within the team which will foster sustained internal ministry.

Characteristics of the two types of Safety Team training sessions.

There cannot be a separation between the tactical training and the growth in ministry as each reinforces the other. Formal training sessions provide a Bible study, complex training topics, and camaraderie-building that can only grow in that environment. The OJT experience provides consistency and practical application, which bridges the gap of time in between formal training sessions. All training must conform to the SLS strategy and thus, begin in prayer and maintain a focus on *stewardship, outreach,* and *discipleship.* Failure to do so will lead to the breakdown of the team, a disconnection with the vision of the church, and the SLS mission to enhance the security of the church while fostering a sustained outreach to the first responder community. Every training, be it the formal quarterly training or an OJT session must maintain a focus on the *one* and the *ninety-nine.*

Before digging deeper into the unique position that the Safety Team has in reaching the first responder community for Christ, this chapter is going to conclude by addressing Safety Team tactical considerations. This information is part of the Safety Team Operational Training but also can be provided to the Force Multipliers. The more knowledgeable and prepared the church is, the greater the likelihood it will be able to *Act,* to *Deter, Avoid* and *Mitigate* attacks.

Tactical Considerations

Appearance: The ability of the Safety Team to function properly relies heavily on its ability to blend into the congregation. It is essential that members not only dress to appear as part of the congregation, but also act in a similar fashion. Therefore, wherever team members are operating they should appear to fit in with the context of that location. Team members should talk with other team members and congregants as they normally would if they were not serving on the team. Of course, they do this while being *situationally aware* and functioning in *condition yellow*.

Safety Team members serving who find themselves awkwardly alone should utilize their environment to aid them in blending in. Appearing to read a book or using a cell phone are examples of ways to accomplish this. A Safety Team member who takes a surveillance position facing the main entrance doors to the church will successfully blend in if they are seated appearing to read the Bible, using their phone, or watching a television monitor than a person who is standing up against a wall like a sentry. A lone individual who appears to have no reason to be standing by the wall near the doors looks very out of place. You cannot afford to look suspicious. If you do, you are creating a red flag! In order to serve effectively, Safety Team members must blend into their environment through clothing they wear and the actions they take.

Note: Force Multipliers have a different role as they serve as overt deterrence and therefore should be highly visible. The clothing, lanyards, name tags, etc., that they wear should identify them with the church. Each Force Multiplier must represent their ministry in appearance and demeanor. Therefore, they should be very welcoming to guests and positioned in advantageous locations around their ministry that allows them to observe and interact with as many people as possible. With that being said, their actions must allow them to blend into their overt role. When watching a suspicious person, they must use their position to not look out of place. Rather than blending into the congregation, they must be able to observe a suspicious person by upholding their role. A member of the hospitality team must appear welcoming and friendly even when operating in condition yellow.

Footwear: Safety Team members will spend a lot of time on their feet. They will stand watch and walk throughout the inside and outside of the church. Therefore, it is important that it wear comfortable shoes that are styled in a way that fits in with what the congregation wears. Footwear should be functional and not draw attention to the team member.

Positioning: Before service begins, Safety Team members should pay close attention to points of entrance and egress. These areas funnel people into the line of sight of multiple layers of observation. If a person uses an entrance to the church that is not intended for the general congregation, that is a red flag that a Safety Team member should investigate. Safety Team members should take positions of advantage that allow them to see as many guests as possible as they arrive at the church.

During service, Safety Team members should concentrate on the main sanctuary, children's ministry, parking lot, bathrooms, and other vital areas you deem essential to your church. As members walk about the church, they should focus on areas where Force Multipliers are not present. As service begins, many Force Multipliers will retract into their ministries and be focused on their responsibilities. Because of this, surveillance by the Safety Team is needed in the areas around their ministries.

In the main sanctuary, Safety Team members should augment the Force Multipliers who are already serving. Team members should sit in positions that allow them to observe large sections of the congregation and be able to get up and leave without creating a distraction. If the team is operating with enough assets, a Safety Team member can be assigned to serve in a fixed position inside of the sanctuary (or other locations, as this is just an example). This person will maintain their focus on the sanctuary and be prepared to take the eyeball if a subject under surveillance enters. This pre-positioned asset will allow the Safety Team members who are surveilling the subject to use less conspicuous entrances to the sanctuary when they set up their positions of observation.

Phones: Phones provide the primary form of communication for the Safety Team. They allow the team to communicate their observations in text messages. By doing this, team members will blend into the congregation and do not create a distraction to the service. Information can be shared individually or through group messaging. Using phones to communicate is the most efficient way to share accurate information. A single picture of a suspicious person shared through a group text will provide an accurate description of that person's face, clothing, and location. The message also creates a chronological list of what was observed and by whom. When an incident occurs that needs to be documented through an After Acton Report, the time stamped text messages facilitate the process.

Flashlights: Flashlights are tools that provide multiple uses. They are able to illuminate dark areas, signal for help by distinguishing the user among a crowd of people, and illuminate an area where attention needs to be focused. They can also be used as effective weapons when need be. During an emergency situation, be it weather, medical, or criminal, a flashlight is an essential tool to have.

Functional Clothing: The clothing that the Safety Team wears should blend in with the congregation. In addition, consider loose fitting clothing as it will reduce the amount of imprinting by items carried and concealed. It should also function to conceal flashlights, medical gear, radios, and other items that your church decides to have the members of the Safety Team carry.

Medical Gear: Every church should enhance its available medical gear to go beyond basic first aid. At a minimum, this should include tourniquets, pressure bandages, and an AED. The amount of the gear per church and bag is determined by the size of the church and the amount of buildings it has. In addition, each team member can be carrying individual medical gear to supplement larger packs pre-positioned in areas throughout the church. Do not confuse this with a first aid kit. These are for medical mitigation of a life-threatening injury.

Weapons: The purpose of the Safety Team and Force Multipliers is to observe and communicate information to *Act* to *Deter, Avoid,* and *Mitigate* attacks. It is not to function as an assault team. The amount of vetting, training, proficiency, cost, and oversight for any type of armed react-team is not feasible for most churches. This is why the presence of a professionally trained law enforcement officer with weapons such as firearms, batons, "tazers," and the ability to call additional resources should be present during service. Suspicious observations made by the Safety Team should be communicated with the law enforcement officer early on as they are a crucial part of the overall safety and security of the church.

In addition, individual states regulate what type of weapons can be carried by its citizens. This includes those that can be carried and concealed on a person. These regulations must be consulted to make sure that no team members are illegally carrying weapons. The church must operate within the laws that govern its location (Rom 13). Carrying weapons, specifically firearms is regulated differently throughout the fifty states. The laws that govern them must be adhered to.

If a church decides that it wants to endorse its Safety Team members in carrying weapons, it must consult with a legal advisor who can determine what is allowed and what is prohibited via federal, state and local laws, ordinances, and regulations. The church should also make sure that continual training standards are created and met. The church must consult with its legal advisor and insurance provider to decide on what, if any, weapons can be carried by anyone serving in the church. They will be able to advise the church on options and how that will affect the church's insurance policy. They will also be able to determine the standard of initial training and continual training that members carrying weapons should receive. Any weapon's policy and subsequent standards of training that the church establishes should be listed in the Emergency Preparedness Plan and provided to everyone serving on the team.

The church must also consider the role of weapons biblically. Insight can be found in Luke 22:35-38; John 18:10-11; Luke 22:49-53; Luke 3:14; 1 Cor 10:33; and all of Nehemiah chapter 4. The determination to use or not use weapons must be made by the pastor of the church and each individual person serving. The purpose of the SLS strategy is to take *Action* to *Deter*, *Avoid*, and *Mitigate* threats. Weapons can surely be used to accomplish this and having a law enforcement officer present assures you that you will have at least one person present who is armed.

You also have to consider that other guests and off duty police officers may be armed. The first group will likely be armed without anyone knowing. They present a complication for the church and law enforcement as their abilities, training, and cognitive reaction to a threat are not known. These individuals are solely responsible for their actions. The second group consists of the off duty law enforcement officers attending service. Through their respective agencies, they are trained in the proficient use of firearms and how to respond during emergencies. If they take any law enforcement action, they will be doing so as a law enforcement officer and not a part of the church. They receive accredited training through their agency in the use of force. Therefore, for many reasons SLS recommends that when a law enforcement officer joins the team it be outlined that if they legally carry weapons (including firearms) while serving, the actions that they take will be done in their law enforcement capacity.

SLS recommends that each church consult with its legal and insurance advisor before making any determination on a weapon's policy. The SLS strategy recognizes that many congregations contain law enforcement officers. Those officers should be identified and approached by the Safety Team for two reasons. First, to determine if they are called to the Safety Team ministry and secondly to assist the church with outreach to the first responder community. Off duty law enforcement officers serving on the Safety Team or as Force Multipliers provide an opportunity for the church to have a trained armed line of defense. If the church determines that a reason exists (biblically, legally, insurance policy provision, the vision of the church, or otherwise) that non-law enforcement members serving in ministry should not carry weapons, the church can still greatly enhance security through the use of the Safety Team, Force Multipliers, and a hired law enforcement presence.

Gloves: Safety Team members should take precaution when dealing with situations that present exposure to bloodborne pathogens, urine, feces, saliva, infectious organisms, or other forms of contamination. Emergencies may create situations where Safety Team members will have to assist victims prior to the arrival of first responders. Therefore, each Safety Team member should carry or have immediate access to protective gloves.

Sun Glasses: Safety Team members will operate inside and outside of buildings. Part of their area of coverage will include the parking lots, playgrounds, and walkways. Therefore, Safety Team members should have sunglasses on them when going outside. In addition, polarized sunglasses greatly aid in reducing glare. They make it easier to see through the windshield of vehicles where the angle often creates a high amount of glare.

Forms of identification: This topic was touched on in Chapter 6 but will be reviewed here due to the importance of Safety Team members carrying two forms of identification. The first is a primary form such as driver's license. The second type of identification that they should carry is a Safety Team identification. This form helps to identify Safety Team members to other ministries and law enforcement. It can be supplemented with the primary form of identification if need be. Having a recognizable form of identification that can be displayed when necessary and supplementing it with an official form will avoid confusion.

A third type of identification is an option that some churches may choose to employ. It involves purchasing a garment that only is displayed during emergencies when the team needs to be overtly recognizable. A building evacuation where the team is assisting direct the flow of foot and vehicular traffic is an example of this type of event. This tertiary identification comes in the form of a brightly colored vest, sash, hat, shirt, or other easily recognizable article that conveys "security" or

"Safety Team." These are only utilized in rare situations where there is not a need for covert members of the team. Because these articles are not easily concealable, they are less likely to be carried by the team and thus stored in a separate location where the team can retrieve them from if needed. Of course, there is a cost that will be associated with implementing this form of emergency identification. Thus, a cost benefit analysis should be made.

While serving, all team members must carry their official and church identification. Since the Safety Team operates covertly and does not wear anything overtly identifying them with the church, neither form of identification should be openly displayed. However, while serving during church services, they are constantly traveling in and out of numerous areas throughout the church. A Safety Team member may go into a Bible study or repeatedly go down a hall leading into the children's ministry. These actions may appear out of place and of course will be minimized. Having proper identification will alleviate any concerns that people serving in that ministry may have.

Do not create a special form of identification for the Safety Team that is different from that which other ministries use and easily identify. Being able to produce an identification that is consistent with that offered by the church will alleviate misunderstandings. This allows the Safety Team to operate without creating a distraction to service and readily identify themselves when needed.

<u>De-escalation Techniques:</u> The purpose of making contact with a person who has exhibited suspicious activity is to acquire information, determine why the person appears suspicious, de-escalate tension, and change behavior from threatening to non-threatening. During this contact, you want to determine if the actions observed actually are red flags or something that can be explained. If explainable, the attention given to the person's suspicious activities ends. However, you must also be looking to identify any additional red flags exhibited during the contact.

In cases where the red flags are confirmed, the immediate action is to de-escalate the situation. Not knowing what is going on in the subject's life, what their mindset is, and what their intentions are places you at a significant disadvantage. Therefore, as you gather additional information by speaking with the subject, you must make sure that you do not add to an already tenuous situation. Of course, the degree to which the red flags create an alarm will determine how the subject is approached, by whom, and if law enforcement becomes involved. Each case presents its own circumstances and requires a unique but reasonable response.

Speaking to a person who has raised multiple red flags must be done with caution while pursuing a specific objective. Your goal is to gain information and, if necessary, de-escalate the tension. However, you must always be prepared for an attack. At any time the person may attempt to harm you or others. Not knowing what their intention is makes this a difficult state of affairs for everyone involved. Because of this, you must always consider your safety and the safety of others when interacting with a suspicious person.

When speaking with a person who may seek to harm the church, the people in it, or you, the objective is to obtain information and create a change in their behavior. If their intent is malicious, then try to de-escalate the situation. Work to change their behavior away from being a threat. This includes de-escalating any intent to harm themselves. Of course, when a person appears to be a threat, obtain the additional resources, including law enforcement, when necessary. If this is a matter that law enforcement does not take over, you can continue to influence the subject's behavior away from malevolence by: praying for them, observing their behavior, listening to what they are saying, being empathetic to their position, developing a relational rapport, and influencing them to affect a change in their behavior. Let's look at each of these tactics further.

Pray first! Now, this does not mean go up to the suspicious person, restrain them, and forcibly pray over him. Rather, start with a short prayer asking for the Lord's intervention. Even if this is just you saying, "Jesus help," it is beneficial. God already knows what you are praying for before you ask. But by initiating this prayer (which takes less than a second) you place yourself in a position of peace. As you recall, starting from a position of peace and not fear is a salient difference between secular security and the SLS strategy. From a position of peace, you can overcome the negative aspects of fear with faith and be wise in your decision-making before even contacting the subject.

Observing non-verbal cues and listening to their story will calm the situation. As long as they continue to talk with you, they are not committing an attack. So, you must be willing to listen to them no matter how crazy their story is. Second, this delay buys time for other people to come to you. If things go badly, those additional resources (Safety Team members, Force Multipliers, law enforcement, etc.) will help mitigate an attack. Finally, by listening to what the person is saying you may be able to start a dialogue that further de-escalates the situation. When speaking to the subject, be an active listener who continues to observe their non-verbal cues and allows them to talk.

When speaking with a person, use tactics to foster a dialogue. Look for opportunities to speak. Listen to what they are saying and do not immediately give them advice or try to solve their problems. Encourage them when they are speaking by saying "uh huh," "yeah," "ok," and nodding your head. By doing this you are acknowledging that you are listening, even though you may not agree with anything they are saying.

For example, think of the television reporter who is conducting an interview and holding a microphone in front of a person who is speaking. The reporter appears to be actively listening by nodding their head as the person talks. In actuality, the reporter may not agree at all with what the person is saying. Their goal is to obtain a sound bite from the interview. Like the reporter, you too have a specific goal and that is de-escalation. In trying to de-escalate a situation when a person is venting, rambling on, or just talking (no matter how irrational it may sound), be the "reporter" while you gather information, develop rapport, and get additional assistance.

When communication allows, be empathetic to their situation. Being empathetic means that you convey that you understand and are aware of the concerns they have. Although empathy demonstrates being sensitive to their position, it does not mean that you agree with them. It also does not mean that you are sympathetic to their situation. They may be completely wrong, but your goal is not to win an argument. Rather, you are striving to produce a behavioral change to de-escalate the situation. Do not fall into the trap of being led into an argument. In 2 Tim 2:23 we find good advice concerning these tricks: "Don't have anything to do with foolish and stupid arguments, because you know that they produce quarrels." Avoid arguing but use empathy to establish rapport and counter conflict.

There are a few simple ways to move towards behavioral change by being empathetic. The first is by rephrasing what they have said and repeating it back to them. For example, if the subject is complaining about how he hates his boss and that there is a lot of stress at his job. You can respond by saying, "work can be very stressful and unrewarding." This type of communication is non-threatening and demonstrates that you are listening to what they are saying. Another way is by using the last few words that they said in a way that begins your response. Using the same example above, you can say, "I too have dealt with the stress of a bad boss at work, but I got through it." Being empathetic will bridge the confrontational tension that can arise when a person is approached (and being investigated) by a member of the Safety Team. Even though you are focused on de-escalation, you must always be ready to deal with a person who turns violent in an instant. Be vigilant as you tactfully take advantage of the opportunities they provide by being empathetic to what they are saying in order to produce a positive behavioral change.

Once you have developed rapport with a person, it is likely that they will be open to listen to you. They may not agree with you or follow your suggestions, but at a minimum they have developed enough of a relationship to listen to what you have to say. This is a huge step towards being able to influence their behavior. For example, when you ask questions, ask open-ended ones. Allow them to talk, vent, and let off some steam as they move in a positive direction. As they divulge information to you and you determine that it is a time to respond, summarize what the person has said and use it to introduce questions. This will increase the rapport that you have established.

As rapport increases, so too will your influential ability. Ideally, this will lead you to a point where you are able to de-escalate the situation. However, this does not always occur. Some people will not talk to you at all and thus diminish your ability to de-escalate the situation. But if they allow you the opportunity, then you have a chance to influence their behavior. Influencing their behavior away from conflict is the best outcome to what could be a terrible situation.

Training the Safety Team in basic de-escalation techniques has many benefits. First, it can alter the direction of events away from the subject seeking to harm the church. It also demonstrates the due diligence that the church is taking to resolve potentially dangerous situations peacefully. It is important to remember that you must always be prepared to act if the subject chooses to threaten or attack someone at the church. In the rare instance that they do and it becomes immediately apparent that they are doing so, *passive de-escalation is over*! You must actively respond to protect yourself and everyone in the church! When a subject chooses to attack, defensive action is the only option that the subject allows you. In the vast majority of circumstances attacks do not occur and the aforementioned de-escalation techniques will be very beneficial.

The Dance: The dance refers to the constant adjustments that Safety Team members perform during surveillance. In order to observe a suspicious person while blending into the congregation, each person will have to artfully find ways to do this in an everchanging environment. Therefore, before ending this section, let me provide you with an example of *the dance*. For the purpose of this illustration, imagine that you are a member of the Safety Team operating in a low-visibility role.

It is twenty minutes until service begins and guests are arriving. You and the other Safety Team members have already completed your standard operating procedures and are spread throughout the church. Each of you has taken advantageous positions to monitor people as they arrive. You have assumed a fixed position in the front lobby which allows you to watch the main entrance doors. You see that a friend of yours is talking with another man. Therefore, in order to blend into the congregation, you take advantage of the situation and walk over to your friend. Your goal is to engage in a conversation that assists you in blending into the environment.

As you walk towards your friend, Nathan, you set yourself up for success. Understanding that if you just walk right up to him you will be in a bad position as your back will be to the main entrance. Therefore, you purposefully proceed to a point that allows you to turn to greet Nathan. This advantageously places him between you and the doors. From this position, you can have a conversation and be able to look past him to observe guests as they arrive. He introduces you to his friend, Cliff, who shakes your hand before heading into the sanctuary. You are effectively blending in while observing the main entrance of the church. This was your first step in the dance.

As you and Nathan talk about the family and the upcoming church mission trip to Guatemala, you observe a person carrying a tube walking towards the church entrance. While looking over your friend's left shoulder, you get a clear view of the face of the person with the tube. Immediately you realize that you do not recognize him. As he enters, he makes an immediate right and walks towards the information table. As he moves, you now find yourself watching him over Nathan's right shoulder. This was the second dance step.

As he walks past the information table, you have to adjust your body position to observe him as you continue talking with Nathan. So, you slightly blade your body to observe the subject. Another dance step taken by you. Unconsciously, Nathan adjusts his body position as he feels awkward standing offset to you. This was his first dance step. Now, repositioned, you are able to blend into the congregation and use your friend as visual cover as you continue to observe the subject.

The subject now sits down on a chair while clutching the tube rather than placing it on the floor beside him. Having observed these red flags, you have moved from condition yellow to condition orange. The subject is now on your radar and you need to initiate a surveillance by communicating this to the rest of the Safety Team. This is easier said than done because you are in the middle of a conversation. You must find a way to cut the conversation off without being rude, get a photo of the subject, text the team the information, and maintain the eyeball. You must do all of this while appearing normal, blending in with other guests, and avoiding anything that would create a distraction to the worship environment.

You pull out your phone while in conversation with Nathan and look at it, another dance step. You smile and apologize to you friend as you say that you have to go and will catch up later, another dance step. You send a text to the team "S1 seated in the lobby" as you calmly walk away from your friend, another dance step. As you walk towards the subject to take a picture of him, you run into your friend, Evan, who just arrived with his family. You greet him and shake his hand as you move past him. Yet another dance step. As you move closer to the subject, you take a quick picture of him and send it to the team. While doing this, you move to a new position where you can maintain the eyeball. More dance steps. This dance continues until the surveillance is concluded. Every dance step is made in condition yellow as you are taking *Action* to *Deter*, *Avoid*, and *Mitigate* an attack.

This is just one elementary example of a dance that can occur. The possibilities are endless and require Safety Team members to be artful while serving. Admittingly, this example occurred under ideal conditions. But what if the person exhibited numerous red flags that needed immediate attention? What if it wasn't a friend that you were talking to but a first-time guest named Allison? What if she has engaged you in questioning about becoming a member of the church? How do you artfully cut that interaction off mid-conversation? In this situation you have a dilemma. As a Safety Team member serving, you have a suspicious person that you need to observe. You have a responsibility to protect the *ninety-nine*. But what if the first-time guest you are about to sever a conversation with is the *one* who is *lost* and needs to be rescued? You cannot just brush that person aside.

As you can see from the example above, you have to deal with the Pastor's Paradox on both a large and small scale. You have to cognitively blueprint these scenarios so the System 1 mind has a plan to act upon. Tactically, Safety Team members should always be ready to introduce a person they are talking with to someone else. Accordingly, if a pastor or leader in the church is nearby, be aware of it. You may have to take advantage of their presence and introduce a guest to them as a cover. If you have to suddenly move, you can grab that person and introduce them to the guest as you walk off. It may be awkward for a split second, but if you do it smoothly, they will focus on each other and not your immediate absence.

It is not always easy to blend into the congregation while observing the people attending the church. As a Safety Team member, you will find yourself constantly repositioning and dancing to blend in. Additionally, as you converse with people, you will find yourself only partially paying attention to what they are saying as you are scan the congregation for threats. You will always have divided attention as you scan for threats and text with other Safety Team members. While conducting surveillance, you will exhibit numerous actions that will seem out of place to the people with whom you interact. In order to do this effectively, you need to blueprint scenarios, remain fluid as you work to blend in, and be vigilant as you artfully overcome the difficulties of being on surveillance.

Remain fluid! This means being able to go with the flow of the atmosphere and adapt to the changing environment around you. Never put yourself in a position where it would be hard to jump right into a surveillance of a suspicious subject at a moment's notice. While serving, you will always be dancing. Embrace it and enjoy it! Sometimes you will have to dance your way into a place where you can blend into the environment, and at other times, you will have to dance your way into a surveillance. Remain fluid and constantly be blueprinting while in condition yellow.

† † †

This chapter has covered a great deal of material related to Operational Training for the Safety Team, in both a formal and OJT setting, and the importance of "never killing a warrior," never sending losers home, and the importance of not belittling students. It also covered the impact of establishing the proper training environment where the team is primed to grow tactically and spiritually. As stated, the SLS strategy requires that all team training be based on the core principles of *stewardship*, *outreach*, and *discipleship*. This will ensure that the team stays within the vision of the church, takes ownership over the ministry, reaches out to first responders, and grows in its relationship with Christ.

Properly incorporating scenario-based training while members of the Safety Team serve is crucial for the team's growth in proficiency. This is accomplished through conducting OTXs to sharpen the skills of the team and train new members. These exercises allow the team to test their mental capabilities as well as tactical considerations of appearance, functional clothing, tactical positioning, various types of gear, and the importance of de-escalation techniques.

As you develop and maintain your security ministry and Safety Team, do not overlook the importance of continual training. It is essential to promote a functional team that can pursue the *one* and protect the *ninety-nine*. The combination of formal training every quarter and continual OJT as members serve will ensure that the team stays aligned with the vision of the church and overcoming the Pastor's Paradox. The Safety Team must be committed to serve the Lord by enhancing the security and safety of the church (stewardship), bringing the Gospel to the first responder community (outreach), and Christian growth (discipleship). Focus in these areas during training sessions and make sure that training is educational and life-giving. Finally, because litigation always looms, always document and maintain a record of formal and OJT training sessions.

When conducting a formal training session, consider the following format to empower the Safety Team in *stewardship*, *outreach*, and *discipleship*. The agenda should include:

- Begin in prayer and impart a story, verse, or topic from the Bible to set the tone of the meeting. The Safety Team should function as a church within the church.
- Reinforce the SLS strategy of Action to Deter, Avoid, and Mitigate threats.

- Champion the successes achieved by the team in tactics and in evangelism since the previous quarterly meeting.
- Highlight and review security/safety events that have occurred.
- Plan, prepare, and organize for upcoming ministry events.
- Provide a briefing on information that the church staff would like to be brought to the attention of the team.
- Conduct specialized training (each quarter should have a focus – medical mitigation, surveillance, risk management, and Operational Training Exercises, etc.) and utilize guest instructors such as local first responders. This will further the effort of the team to maintain outreach to the first responder community.
- In order to maintain proper communication between the church and the team, address issues that need to be taken to the staff and provide them to the staff member who is the direct point of contact with the team.
- Initiate new members by praying over them and celebrating their official transition from probationary member to team member.
- Enjoy the time together as a team and disciple one another.
- Close in prayer.

Chapter 9

Outreach to First Responders

"Therefore, go and make disciples of all nations, baptizing them in the name of the Father and of the Son and of the Holy Spirit." Matthew 28:19

Strategy

Unfortunately, most people do not see the connection between a functioning church security ministry and evangelical outreach. The failure to recognize the connection between the security ministry and reaching the first responders who are within the ministry's sphere of influence has hampered evangelism in this area. Even with churches who have a designated security ministry of some sort, outreach to the first responder community is often overlooked. In the SLS strategy, the Safety Team takes on the responsibility to pursue a sustained outreach to the first responders. If your church currently has a security ministry and outreach is not part of its DNA, you are missing an evangelical opportunity.

The partnership in security with first responders necessitates that the church shares the Gospel with them. This should

Church Security and Outreach

occur through the relationships developed with the law enforcement officers serving during worship, the first responders who are part of the congregation, and by reaching out to the local police, fire departments, and EMS personnel. If you have no relational interaction with first responders, initiate it with those who are in your congregation. A ministry that is not involved with reaching the lost is not following the Great Commission. Do not have a security ministry that is fulfilling the stewardship obligation to protect the church but not actively working to reach the lost.

First responders are the Safety Team's targets for outreach (1 Pet 4:10; Exo 35:10; Rom 12:3-11; 1 Cor 14:12) and their partners in providing a safe worship environment. Make an assessment of your local church's current security strategy to determine if it fosters a sustained outreach to first responders. Peter wrote: "Each one should use whatever gift he has received to serve others, faithfully administering God's grace in its various forms. If anyone speaks, he should do it as one speaking the very words of God. If anyone serves, he should do it with the strength God provides, so that in all things God may be praised through Jesus Christ. To Him be the glory and the power forever and ever. Amen" (1 Pet 4:10-11). There is no separation of the use of gifts and talents to enhance security and proclaim the Gospel. Therefore, the members of the Safety Team should use the gifts they have gracefully received to enhance security and speak the Gospel to first responders. Driven by their Christian Warrior Mindset, the men and women of the Safety Team are the sheepdogs who rely on God's strength to protect the *ninety-nine* at home and actively pursue the *one* who is lost.

Outreach is a vital element to Christianity. Jesus directly commanded the disciples to embark on a worldwide mission to share the Gospel. Jesus said, "All authority in heaven and on earth has been given to me. Therefore, go and make disciples of all nations, baptizing them in the name of the Father, and of the Son, and of the Holy Spirit, and teaching them to obey everything I have commanded you. And surely, I am with you always, to the very end of the age" (Matt 28:18-20). This is commonly referred to as the Great Commission. It, along with the Greatest Commandment (Matt 22:36-40), make up the timeless, fundamental mission for Christians. In Matthew 22:36-40, Jesus replied to a Pharisee who asked about the greatest commandment in the law. Jesus said: "Love the Lord your God with all your heart and with all your soul and with all your mind. This is the first and greatest commandment."[88] These commandments form the framework that the security ministry must operate within to love God, love people, and reach the lost. Overcome the Pastor's Paradox by pursuing the *one* and protecting the *ninety-nine*.

Outreach: External Ministry – *poreuomai*

Every member of the Safety Team is called to pursue external outreach. Although the team is dedicated to protecting the *ninety-nine*, it is equally responsible to pursue the *one*. In fulfilling the Great Commission, a salient attribute of the Safety Team is targeted outreach. Jesus commanded the disciples to "go" and "make disciples." In Greek, the word "go" is *poreuomai*. The context is *to go* reach the lost and make, *matheteuo*, disciples of Christ. The church Safety Team is intrinsically in a key position to go and reach first responders for Christ. This is due to the like-mindedness, rapport, and relational interaction between the Safety Team members and first responders, who either attend or serve at the church. The first question you have to ask is, are you maximizing these relationships? The second question you must ask is, does your church have a year-round sustained outreach ministry to first responders?

---

[88] Matt. 22:39 continues: "And the second is like it: 'Love your neighbor as yourself.' All the law and the Prophets hang on these two commandments."

Outreach: Maximize Existing Relationships

Every church automatically has an existing relationship with the first responder community. Unfortunately, for most churches, that relationship falls short of what it could be. For example, most cities and counties have police, firefighters, and EMS personnel assigned to cover the geographic area that encompasses the church. Hence, the church/first responder relationship has already been established simply due to geography. It is proximity that determines the first responders who will come to an emergency situation at your church. Proximity also creates occasions of interaction between the church and first responders as they mutually attend community events. Each of these events offers an opportunity for outreach.

Is the extent of your church's outreach to first responders limited to the occasions when paths cross at these events? Hopefully not. With the likelihood that your church has first responders in attendance, you already have a place where interaction is occurring. This is a good starting point as it grows to further contact at holiday events, festivals, concerts, and other community activities.

Very few churches have a *sustained* outreach to first responders. A sustained outreach means that there is regular interaction between the church and the first responder community throughout the year. Many churches have a limited outreach (once, or maybe twice a year) but not a sustained ministry. One of the most common forms of outreach to first responders involves an event-based relationship with an annual community outreach initiative. Unfortunately, there is little follow-up or continued collaboration after the event. In essence, the church shows up to honor first responders, gives items for further contact, and leaves. This is a sincerely good gesture and the Lord does work through these events. However, rarely is there intentional interaction again between the church and the first responders until the next annual event. As productive as these events can be, they are not efficient in establishing sustained relationships.

Outreach: Taking Ownership

Relationships are about people and not entities. For example, geography has forced entities like the church and the police department to have a relationship. But what about the people? Do the law enforcement officers know any members or staff at the church? Maybe, but probably not. So, when a 911 call from the church is placed, does the first responder think about the location they are responding to or is there a person that first responder thinks of? Is the church/first responder relationship limited to the interaction between institutions or are there true relationships involving the people within these entities?

In the SLS strategy, this chasm is bridged by the Safety Team. By its own features, the Safety Team is positioned to create a sustained partnership. The team and first responder community share a common calling to serve and protect. This *like-mindedness* helps develop rapport between the groups. For example, both groups are full of sheepdogs. Earlier I wrote about how being a sheepdog is like being an outsider of the flock. The Safety Team members and many first responders share this characteristic. They each live a situationally aware lifestyle and are always concerned about what is lurking in on the other side of the wood line. Because of this, the officers may be more receptive to hear the Gospel from a Safety Team member than a stranger they cannot relate to. Although the first responder's priority concerning the church may be protection, the Safety Team bridges the gap as it sees protection and outreach as equally important.

There are many examples of how that gap is bridged through the year. Those bridges are what foster a sustained relationship. As part of their standard operation procedures, the team interacts with the law enforcement officer(s) who work the security detail at the church. They develop relationships through their interaction and conversations. Because most of the officers providing security on Sunday are working an overtime detail, the officer you see may change from week to week. Although this means less repetitious interaction with specific individuals, it also means that you can make contact with numerous officers. Because the team acquires the officer's cell phone numbers as part of their standard operating procedures, this creates a contact list that can be utilized at Christmas and Easter to invite the officers to attend service. Additionally, another way the gap is bridged throughout the year is when the Safety Team requests officers, firefighters, and EMS personnel to bring their professional experience to the quarterly training sessions. By doing so, they continue to partner with the first responders in securing the church while engaging them as they share the love of Christ.

Since the team has taken ownership of the ministry, they take that responsibility outside of the walls of the church. For example, if a Safety Team member crosses paths with a police officer at a gas station they should introduce themselves, thank the officer for their service in keeping community safe, and invite them to church. Who else is better to do this than a vetted member of the Safety Team with a Christian Warrior Mindset to pursue the *one* and protect the *ninety-nine*?

It is possible to establish a sustained ministry to first responders. With a Safety Team that has a foundation of prayer and stewardship it will occur. Therefore, when the annual "outreach event" occurs, the Safety Team will lead the effort to serve the first responder community. They already have established a relationship with them and will take ownership of the logistics of the event.

For the person who is organizing any churchwide outreach to various locations and projects, they will be happy to know that one area already has a team set up to handle the logistics. There is no need to look for volunteers as the Safety Team will take ownership over the team. There is no need to reach out to the fire department, police department, or sheriff's office because the Safety Team will contact the people they know at each location. If you are the person who is coordinating an outreach event, wouldn't it be nice to know that an entire team of individuals serving at the church already has an established relationship with those you are targeting and are willing to facilitate that aspect of an outreach event?

An ongoing relationship between the Safety Team and first responders will create a continual cycle of ministry and partnership that shares the Gospel and enhances church security. Ideally, relationships will be established where first responders come to Christ, become members of the church, serve on the Safety Team, and provide training to the team. This is a byproduct of enhancing the security of the church while evangelizing the first responder community. For a pastor, the SLS approach to security and outreach provides the opportunity to be a good steward over security while ministering to the first responder community. The SLS strategy is the solution to the Pastor's Paradox as the security ministry is pursuing the *one* while protecting the *ninety-nine*.

Keys to developing the relationships that will foster a sustained outreach ministry to first responders:

- Hire off/extra duty officers for the enhancement of church security and safety.
- Have the Safety Team interact with them by meeting with them before service, acquiring their phone number to call in case of an emergency, invite them into the church for coffee, refreshments, the use of the bathroom, and develop an area familiarization (A-FAM) within the church (which will aid them if a critical event occurs).
- Develop relationships with the officers who serve regularly.

- If a tragedy occurs involving the local first responders, contact the officers you have a relationship with. Through them the church can offer pastoral care and other assistance to those who were affected.
- Ask first responders to attend and teach at the Safety Team quarterly training sessions.
- Invite the first responders who work the security detail to church events.
- Always send a text invitation to the first responders for Christmas and Easter services.
- Honor the service and sacrifice that first responders make to the community.
- Identify members of the congregation that are first responders and approach them to consider joining the Safety Team or providing training to the Safety Team.

Outreach: Internal Ministry – *koinonia*

There is another ministry that a Safety Team must take ownership of. This involves the internal ministry between the members of the team. As seen in the above paragraphs, in the Great Commission the command *poreuomai*, to "go" is directed at an external outreach. However, *koinonia*, the Greek word for fellowship, underscores an internal relationship between members of the team.

When used in the original Greek, *koinonia* refers to a very close relationship. It goes far beyond the term fellowship that is commonly used today. *Koinonia* refers to a close bond. It is such a close union that it can refer to family and marriage. It is therefore easy to conclude that it is a tight association based upon a partnership where people can grow together. Applying this term to the Safety Team indicates a bonded group of individuals who possess the Christian Warrior Mindset and are sincerely growing in Christ together.

As mentioned earlier, every Safety Team training is focused on *stewardship*, *outreach*, and *discipleship*. Over time, relationships will foster, and the members of the Safety Team will become bonded together in purpose and growth. Much like what occurs in Bible studies and small groups, people humble themselves to the Lord, and the Holy Spirit works within the group to convict, counsel, and grow individuals.

As the Safety Team is forged together, members will continually sharpen each other as they go through life together. They will hold each other accountable and grow closer to the Lord both as a team and individually. The Safety Team effectively becomes a church within the church. This internal ministry is an attainable goal in the SLS strategy. The end product is to have a functional Safety Team that enhances the security of the church, fosters outreach to first responders, and creates disciples for the Lord. Through *stewardship*, *outreach*, and *discipleship*, the Safety Team will serve to pursue the *one* and protect the *ninety-nine*.

† † †

The most common way that many churches approach outreach to first responders is through a single (often annual) outreach event. As the preceding paragraphs point out, single events alone are not effective in fostering sustained ministry. However, they can be part of a *sustained ministry strategy*. Events like this should be encouraged with the Safety Team taking the lead. Because it can be a successful part of the sustained ministry to first responders, the remainder of this chapter will focus on how to conduct a successful event as part of the SLS strategy.

When an outreach event has a specified team that targets first responders, the goal should not center on conducting a successful event. Rather, make it a goal to initiate sustained outreach. Be more focused on the people than the event. The

Safety Team's existing relationships with the first responder community provides an avenue into planning the event. An outreach event to first responders can be anything from selecting a time to deliver items, providing them with breakfast, or coordinating a community function sponsored by the church. Whatever the event type, the Safety Team should take the lead and incorporate anyone serving at the church with a desire to support the mission.

The Safety Team must take ownership over forging a team to serve. This is the *outreach mission team*. It will consist of members from the Safety Team, but likely will also incorporate members of the church with a desire to serve the first responder community. It is recommended that you do not have a staff member leading the outreach mission team if the Safety Team is fully capable of doing it. Empower the Safety Team members to lead the outreach event with proper church oversight.

The following information is a four-phase approach to conducting an outreach event targeting first responders. It focuses on people over projects when considering strategy, education, launch, and debriefing.

Education: The Mission, Audience, and Training

Create a clear vision for your event that defines goals, responsibilities, and expected outcomes. This will set the stage for **Phase 1 – Strategy**. Designate a single person to be the event team leader supported by other members of the Safety Team. This person does not have to be the Safety Team leader. Actually, it is beneficial if someone else takes on the leadership opportunity so they can grow in that area.

Once the event type, vision, and outreach mission team leader have been determined, you can zero in on the event location and time. The established relationships between the Safety Team and first responders will facilitate this and help avoid making scheduling mistakes. You must consider that first responders work shifts, unique hours, and additional assignments. Therefore, schedule the date and time of the event to maximize interaction between the team and first responders.

This ministry is about building relationships. In order to foster a successful event between two entities, you must include the people from both groups. Therefore, have a designated member of the Safety Team contact a member of the Command Staff, a Chaplain, or others who can aid in the coordinating the date, time, and location of the event. This is important as it demonstrates that you are not only taking into consideration the dynamics of the first responders, but that you are also going the extra mile to be a good steward of the church's resources. You don't want to plan your outreach at a time when the department is already having a major event. That would be a wasteful endeavor that could have been avoided through proper planning.

Once you have your location determined, target your outreach for maximum effectiveness. One way to do this is to conduct an advance on the location to make sure that you can work adequately within the area that is going to be used. Look at how the event will play out, consider parking, traffic, restrooms, and other basic considerations that if overlooked will lead to less than adequate results. Also, it is important to have a contingency plan ready in case something unexpected happens at the last minute. You are targeting first responders who by nature of their profession respond to unexpected emergencies. If an unexpected emergency was to occur during your scheduled event, it will alter your effectiveness. Therefore, have options available by creating contingency plans.

Once you have the logistics lined up, proceed to **Phase 2 – Education**. In order to bridge the Gospel to first responders it is important to educate your mission team on sharing the Gospel and about first responders. If your mission team is not ready to conduct the outreach mission, they may not be effective. For example, first responders regularly deal with death, violence, public hatred towards them, suicide (both in the public and within their ranks), traumatic injuries sustained on the job, extremely high stress levels, and the fact that they are in a career that could take their life at any time by way of being shot, injured, or exposed to a communicable disease. Your team needs to know this as it will allow them to better communicate with them.

First responders are in a career where opening up to others is culturally looked down upon. Therefore, some of these men and women desperately need assistance, but fail to get it because of fear of losing their job or being chastised. They desperately need the Gospel, but it needs to be presented in a way they will be open to hear. Plus, the mission team member must understand that first responders may not be very open due to pressures that are created by their jobs. Educate the team so they know that this is a common response. Experiences like this do not indicate that the mission team is being ineffective. Many first responders have very solid walls that they have built up due to all the violence, death, tragedy and stress that they have endured over their career. Present the love of Christ and let Him tear down those walls!

Within **Phase 2 – Education**, there are two areas to focus training the mission team on. The first is on the *mission*. The second is on the *audience*. Finally, the team must be provided with *training*.

Education Part 1- The Mission:
If you do not know the mission, how can you achieve success?
1. Make sure that everyone knows the mission team's purpose is to show the love of Christ (Colossians 3:17).
2. There may be opportunity to share the Gospel; therefore, you must *provide your team training in sharing the Gospel*.
3. Encourage the mission team to provide an opportunity to build relationships that foster sustained ministry.

Education Part 2- The Audience:
If you do not know who you are talking to, how can you communicate effectively?
1. Educate the mission team on who first responders are. Do not limit your audience to police officers and firefighters. Consider the Dispatchers, Evidence Technicians, Crime Scene Investigators, Forensic Scientists, Administrative Personnel and Community Volunteers. All of these men and women are part of the first responder community.
2. Educate the mission team on how the unique job demands, both on and off duty, create ministry opportunities. First responders are servants who face evil every day. Consider how this affects them in ways that people outside of the first responder community do not relate to.
3. Reinforce to the team that most first responders chose to enter into their careers to help others. Although they do help people, their efforts will be insufficient and unfulfilling without Christ.
4. Educate the mission team on the human side of first responders. Very rarely will a first responder ever fulfill their life/career goals, expectations, or self-image. Most first responders do not know the void that exits without Christ. They will try to fill it with their career, but like everyone who tries to fill this void with something other than Jesus, they will fail.

Education Part 3 – The Training:
If you do provide training, how can you expect people to know what to do?
1. Conduct training for the entire team.
2. Seek mutual education and camaraderie building (Prov 27:17).
3. Pick a venue that allows for focus and growth.

4. Solidify the Team Leader – (supported by the staff).
5. Identify prospects for future leaders (sustained ministry and growth).

Make the training session you conduct effective. It is imperative that *everyone* leaves the training understanding the core principles of the education phase including the *mission* and the *audience*. A successful Phase 2 is the only way to set your team up to successfully communicate the Gospel to first responders.

Phase 3 – Launch contains the all activities on the day of the event. It begins with a *preoperational briefing* and runs through the conclusion of the event. At the preoperational briefing, be sure to emphasize the team's commitment to engage. Be mission-focused. First responders have a tendency to be receptive to purpose-driven people. Therefore, at the preoperational briefing, it is important to amplify the team's motivation. Since you have already educated the team, you can now focus on energizing them as they head out.

Do this by accentuating the team's purpose to establish rapport with first responders. Remind them of the unique job that first responders have and how they risk their lives for serving the community. The mission team members should represent themselves as servants of the Lord focused on reaching the first responders that they meet. They can share with them how God's light penetrates into the corrupted, lost world that they spend a large part of their lives in. The team should remind the first responders of how His light can be seen in their careers and home lives. They should focus on how first responders have gifts and talents to use for His glory. Finally, commit the team members to sustain this ministry throughout the year. Ask members to take ownership of the event and further occasions for outreach. This is an opportunity to discover people who are prospective members of the Safety Team and future mission team leaders.

It is important to provide mission specific items to give to the first responders that the team encounters (and leave behind for those who they were not able to contact). These items should be *relatable* and *relevant*. Before you purchase items, consider that your target audience will consist of government workers. It is common that they have policies that will place them in a difficult position if they openly possess religious materials while at work. Many employees of government agencies feel pressured not to display anything that represents their faith and fear repercussion if they do. Therefore, if the church purchases thermoses that have a Christian logo, Bible verse, or other overtly Christian imagery, the employees may be reluctant to use them at work. Be a good steward of church resources and make wise decisions on what you provide first responders. Talk with them on your team and within your congregation as to what they feel will be effective. Do not assume that you know what a good item will be. Research before you purchase. An item that they will be reluctant to accept due to their agency's policies or political pressure is not a good expenditure. If the first responder does not have the item with them to remind them to focus on Christ while batting evil in the dark and dangerous world that they work in, then what good is it?

Rather than making costly purchases of objects that will not be used, purchase effective and practical items. Many first responders will maintain items with them that remind them of their faith. They often conceal these items in their office, patrol vehicles, or in their gear or clothing. One of the greatest gifts that I received from a church was a small laminated copy of Psalm 91. I keep it with me while working. Consider the difference and effectiveness of the purchase of a single $8 thermos that a first responder may not keep due to an agency policy versus purchasing a 25-cent laminated copy of Psalm 91 that they will likely place somewhere relevant to their job. Obviously, the latter is a cost effective and useful item to purchase.

Do not forget to have a link to your church's website and/or the address on the items. Provide a clear way for the first responders to contact the church. You don't need to spend money on coffee mugs, thermoses, hats, shirts, or other items to impress first responders. Those type of items are generally not going to make an impact. All you need is God's Word presented in a practical way with an avenue to contact the church. Some of these ideas may not work for outreach to other communities, but these suggestions have proven to work with first responders.

During the outreach event it is important that the mission team leader is cognizant of obstacles that may occur. First, as stated above, an emergency may occur and you may be left with little to no first responders to speak with. This is where the contingency plans come into play. If this happens, focus on prayer over the first responders, over the emergency that has occurred, and that the first responders will be receptive to the items that you leave behind. Encourage the team to write personal notes to the first responders and let them know that you are praying for them and their families.

Another contingency that the mission team leader must plan for are obstacles of ineffectiveness. Generally, these are self-perceived by the mission team and actually, false perceptions. Therefore, the mission team leader must be focused on assisting team members by encouraging and reminding them of the education and training they received concerning the mission and the audience. This return to their training will motivate them and keep them on focus.

Finally, the event must carry with it the atmosphere that was established in the preoperational briefing. Therefore, the team should be encouraged to be mission-focused in an upbeat and enjoyable way. This is also a great time to encourage members of the mission team to interact with each other. Although the focus is on the first responders, never become so event focused that you fail to observe people in the ministry. Although the target is first responders, the ultimate goal is growth in Christ. Ask the Holy Spirit to work among the mission team as well. One thing that I have learned is that Kingdom projects only succeed when they are people- focused. The project should never be more important than the people.

As the event concludes, encourage the mission team to leave the location in a better condition than it was when the team arrived. This means clean up in a way that serves the host. Additionally, strategically leave behind the items such as food and personal notes that you have for reaching the first responders. If you partner with the children's ministry ahead of time, you can have them create thank you cards while in class in the weeks leading up to the event. Collect them and bring them with you to leave for the first responders. This is very effective, especially with those who were not there. Finally, pray with your team at that location and leave together. This is your opportunity to leave as one team on a very positive note. Often, as events conclude members of the team tend to trickle out one by one. This leads to a sense of the team members going their own way before a debriefing. Therefore, debrief at the location of the event, or rally the mission team at the church, staging area, or restaurant where the debriefing can occur. This is the last "image" that the team will experience as part of the event and is the heart of phase 4.

Phase 4 – Debriefing: After the event concludes, it is important to conduct an operational debriefing. Its purpose is to recap the event and to set the threshold for a sustained ministry. Regardless of where you conduct the debriefing, do it on launch day! Do not skip this step. You will not get another opportunity like it once everyone leaves. The information that needs to be shared is fresh in people's minds and hearts. If not addressed promptly, it will likely be lost over time.

The debriefing should be succinct. Ask people what they saw and what they did. The team leader should identify areas that need improvement but do not attempt to fix complicated problems at that time. A greater emphasis should be on appreciation for the team that served and celebrating victories. Encourage people to share their positive experiences for everyone's benefit. Finally, find out if any follow-up needs to be made and facilitate them.

A second debriefing should be conducted for church leadership by the mission team leader. This can be in person or in writing. Regardless of which way better serves communicating the results of the event, it should be done in a timely manner. This strategic debriefing should provide an honest assessment of the vision, the event, and the mission team. Determine if the ministry was a good fit for each member who served. Assess how you can further develop members of the team within that ministry and consider future leaders. Make note of every positive aspect and the areas that need improvement. Doing this will help set up the next event's team leader for success.

Finally, integrate the results with the Safety Team during the next formal training session. For the Safety Team members who did not take part in the outreach event, it will bring them up to speed as they continue to foster relationships with first responders. It will also assist them in discovering new Safety Team members from the volunteers who attended the event. Some of those volunteers may have discovered a desire to reach first responders with the Gospel. This may also call them to the security ministry. Whether they become part of the Safety Team or not does not matter. If they have a heart to reach the first responder community, they will be partners with the Safety Team in the sustained outreach pursuing the *one*. Outreach events conducted in this way increase the relationships with the first responder community and foster growth among team members. For the Safety Team and other members of the church who participate, this type of event produces *stewardship*, *outreach*, and *discipleship* and brings the love of Christ to those who are on the frontlines battling the worst that society has to offer.

An outreach event like this, coupled with numerous contacts with first responders throughout the year, will create a sustained outreach ministry. Below is a list of some of the interactions that the Safety Team and church should have with first responders throughout the year.

- Targeted Outreach Event
- Request a free site survey of the church performed by police and fire departments to assist in security planning.
- Ensure weekly interaction of Safety Team members and the law enforcement officer(s) serving at church.
- Identify and engage the first responders in the congregation to develop relationships, discover members for the Safety Team, and create points of contact for outreach to their agencies.
- Provide updated church floorplans and room descriptions to the first responders on an annual basis.
- Invite first responders in to speak and provide training (particularly during formal quarterly training sessions).
- Invite all of the officers personally who were hired to cover services to the Christmas and Easter celebrations.
- Meet with church staff and local first responder Command staff for lunch and community relationships.
- Coordinate with first responders on how the church can assist in response to weather events (floods, fires, hurricanes, tornados, etc.) and other emergency situations.
- Take advantage of the opportunity to interact with first responders at community events such as parades, festivals, and celebrations.
- Identify and honor "local heroes" from the first responder community at the church.
- Have a first responder appreciation service where the heads of the local agencies are invited to attend.

- Be the arm of the church that not only reaches out to first responders after a tragedy hits, but already has a relationship with them.

These are just some of the examples of the interactions that the Safety Team can have throughout the year. A successful outreach event coupled with a Safety Team that has continual interaction with first responders will develop relationships. The point of these relationships is to share the love of Christ and point the first responders to Him. It is a partnership in enhancing the security of the church and sharing the Gospel. The Safety Team has the opportunity to overcome the Pastor's Paradox by pursuing the *one* while protecting the *ninety-nine*.

Chapter 10

Active Shooter

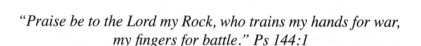

"Praise be to the Lord my Rock, who trains my hands for war, my fingers for battle." Ps 144:1

In this final chapter of the book, I will address the topic of surviving an active shooter. According to the United States Department of Homeland Security (DHS), an active shooter is defined as: An individual actively engaged in killing or attempting to kill people in a confined and populated area; in most cases, active shooters use firearms and there is no pattern or method to their selection of victims.[89]

Even if your church has established a functioning security ministry and *acted* to take measures to *deter* and *avoid* an attack, one still may ensue. A determined assailant who does not care for their life or the lives of others may still commit an attack despite the actions you have taken to prevent one. If this occurs in the form of an active shooter, you must accept that you have been thrust into a fight for your life and your only option is to *mitigate* the damage. Action is necessary to

---

[89] United States Department of Homeland Security, October 2008, *Active Shooter How to Respond,* 2.

save your life and the lives of others. Fortunately, the concepts provided in Security Ministry Basic Training and Safety Team Operational Training will better position those in the church to survive and help others.

When an attack ensues and shots are fired, everyone involved begins cycling thorough the OODA loop. With each additional shot a new stimulus is introduced potentially causing you to reset your OODA loop each time. Additional stimuli will come from the screams, destruction, chaos, carnage, and countless other factors that may come into play. Each observation makes it difficult to orient to the stimuli and decide what action to take.

Most active shooters last less than 15 minutes. But for the people involved, it will seem as if time has stopped. Everyone who experiences the critical event is a victim, not just those who are shot or physically injured. You can never fully prepare for this type of event. The people who have training, are operating in condition yellow, and are utilizing blueprinted contingency plans will have the greatest likelihood of surviving. These people will be best positioned to survive, help others, and mitigate the damage of the attack.

The standard reaction to an active shooter recommended by the DHS requires an *immediate response*. They have determined that an immediate response will increase the likelihood to survive an attack. One report that looked at the Virginia Tech massacre noted that some students had a delayed response. The report states: "During the Virginia Tech shooting, individuals on campus responded to the shooting with varying degrees of urgency. The [study affirms a] delayed response or denial [will occur]. For example, some people report hearing firecrackers, when in fact they heard gunfire."[90] You can fully expect that this will occur to some degree at every active shooter incident.

---

[90] U.S. Department of Education, et al. 2013. Developing High Quality Emergency Operation Plans for Houses of Worship. Washington, DC: U.S. Department of Homeland Security, 29.

Earlier we looked at some of the psychological and physiological reactions that may occur during a life-threatening event. At times, the mind will choose to deny the attack and "brush off" what should be identified as gun shots as fireworks. This may not always be purposeful, it may come out of the ignorance of a mind that is not operating in condition yellow. A lack of understanding what is occurring in the area leads to a lack of information. Moreover, that lack of information is filled by imagination. For many, the imagination will create explanations that are in denial of what is actually occurring. "That's not gunfire, it's just fireworks."

In the SLS strategy, this underscores the importance of the material taught in Security Ministry Basic Training: always be in condition yellow, situationally aware, and ready to *act*. Although an immediate response is indeed necessary, being situationally aware will improve the likelihood that you will be able to take an *Action* to *Deter*, *Avoid*, or *Mitigate* the threat. This position is strengthened from the SLS biblical basis of overcoming fear, increasing faith, and obtaining godly wisdom that allows us to operate from a position of peace not fear. As the following paragraphs will demonstrate, what occurs during an active shooter requires immediate and continuous *Action* to *Deter*, *Avoid*, and *Mitigate* the attack.

You must commit yourself now to survive an attack and revert to that position when the chaos of the attack comes. Plan what you and the others with you will do if an active shooter occurs. If you find yourself present during an active shooter, the first blueprint that your System 1 mind should find is, *Jesus provides peace; you will survive, now take action!* The next blueprint that the System 1 mind should find is this strategy: *Escape by actions to Evade, Hide, and Fight*. Once you have found safety begin to *Recover*. This strategy brings with it the assumption and determination that you will win, you will survive, and you will recover!

Evade

When you determine that an active shooter is at hand, your primary goal is to escape. Your highest likelihood for survival is avoiding contact with the shooter. Therefore, *focus on evading the threat in order to escape.* If you are situationally aware, you may observe pre-assault indicators and other red flags before the first shot is fired. You may see the shooter exit the car and make his way towards a building allowing you to act before the shooting begins. Your objective is to survive by evading the threat and escaping the area. If an active shooting occurs do not blindly *run*. By reacting with flight and not paying attention to where you are running, it is possible that you may trip over obstacles, run into a room that leads to a more dangerous position, or run directly to the threat. Operating in condition yellow means that you are being situationally, spatially, self-, and spiritually aware. You are not running blindly in a frantic state obliviousness to what is going on around you. Condition yellow places you in a position where you have the greatest likelihood of evading and escaping the threat.

However, if you find yourself on the "X" taking fire without cover, then yes, you can run to seek cover. But you are only doing this because your only option is to get off the "X" or die. When the lethal attack is targeting you, there is no time for the System 2 mind to formulate a plan for the System 1 mind to execute. Therefore, System 1 will take over with the only known plan which is either do nothing (freeze) or react by running (or some other form of *flight*). Nevertheless, if you are *not* directly on the "X," taking a second or two will increase your situational awareness and ability to plan a safe movement to evade the threat and find safety. You may have to run to safety, but do not do it blindly. Grab your phone if possible and move. When it is safe to do so, silence you phone and continue to escape to safety.

While trying to evade the threat to escape, you may find a time when you realize that the location you are currently in is safer than moving to another position. Of course, that can change in a second. But this is not an instance where you are sheltering in place or barricading yourself in. You are evading the threat and waiting for an opportunity to move so you can escape. If circumstances change and you are afforded the opportunity to move to a better location, do so with your head up and eyes open. Visualize your exit path and stay low. Use cover (ballistic protection) and concealment (protection from view) to aid in your escape. Be ever vigilant as you move to evade detection by the shooter and escape the attack. Help others escape but do not stay behind if they refuse to go with you.[91]

Hide

You may find yourself in the situation where you are not able to escape by moving. The proximity to the threat may place you in a position where it is more dangerous to move than to stay in place. If this is the case, you may choose to fortify your position and wait for rescue. If feasible and doing so will not draw attention to you, take steps to barricade yourself in place.[92] DHS recommends the following steps to be taken if you need to hide during an active shooter:

- Lock the doors.
- Barricade the doors with heavy furniture.
- Close and lock windows and close blinds or cover windows.
- Turn off lights.
- Silence all electronic devices.

---

[91] Information used with permission of Firebase Combat Studies Group: *Active Shooter Best Practices*.

[92] Ibid.

- Remain silent.
- If possible, use strategies to silently communicate with first responders.
- Make signs letting rescuers know you are there.
- Hide along the wall closest to the exit but remain out of view of windows, other rooms, hallways, etc.
- Remain in place until cleared by identifiable law enforcement[93]

Fight

If your attempts to avoid the threat by evasion or hiding fail, you must mitigate the attack by fighting. You may have to fight as soon as the attack comes, while you are attempting to escape, or if you have barricaded yourself in a room and the shooter forces entry. In preparation for this contingency, arm yourself and take an advantageous position that will allow you an opportunity to fight. If the shooter confronts you, your focus will narrow, and your heart rate will rise. You will hit *condition red*. Fortunately, from Security Ministry Basic Training, you know the adverse effects that come with *condition red*. Thus, you will not be surprised by them and will be able to overcome the negative aspects as you focus on defeating the threat.

If someone is attacking you and trying to take your life, you must fight back with everything you have. If they are attempting to kill you, they are trying to end your life, prevent you from going home to your loved ones, and go past you to kill others. You may not have chosen to be in this position, but they placed you there and you have to mitigate the damage. To save others' lives and your own, you may have to end theirs. Therefore, condition you mind for that possibility now. That way you will not

---

[93] U.S. Department of Education, et al. 2013. Developing High Quality Emergency Operation Plans for Houses of Worship. Washington, DC: U.S. Department of Homeland Security, 30.

have to overcome it if you find yourself in this horrible position. Your action may take their life, but your inaction may allow the attacker to take yours and/or another person's.

If an attacker brings the fight to you, don't roll over; become the family dog that sees a threat and engages it with the commitment to win. When you are forced to fight, use whatever means are at your disposal to attack the shooter. This can range from weapons to objects that can be used as weapons (chairs, fire extinguishers, coffee mugs, knives, firearms, etc.). Your objective is to disrupt, incapacitate, and neutralize that threat so you and others can survive.

A study that looked at 41 active shooter incidents that *ended* before law enforcement arrived, found that potential victims stopped the attacker in 16 instances. Furthermore, the study found that 13 of those cases resulted in the attacker being physically subdued.[94] You must mentally prepare now, cognitively blueprint now, and be ready to use force if necessary, to protect your life and the lives of others. Seek to disable the attacker's ability to see, breath, or use a weapon.[95] Be aggressive and use all means necessary as you fight to win.

Safety Team members should periodically obtain active shooter training during quarterly training sessions. Then, they can impart their knowledge and strategy to mitigate the effects of an active shooter to the Force Multipliers. During an active shooter, everyone present is a potential victim. Therefore, SLS recommends that the congregation be provided with

---

[94] U.S. Department of Education, et al. 2013. Developing High Quality Emergency Operation Plans for Houses of Worship. Washington, DC: U.S. Department of Homeland Security, 30.

[95] Information used with permission of Firebase Combat Studies Group: *Active Shooter Best Practices*.

information from the church about surviving an active shooter. This can come in a form that works best for your congregation. First responders are well versed in active shooter training and can provide literature, links to websites, and free formal training (if the Safety Team has established a relationship with local first responders). You may also want to impart what you have adopted from this book to the congregation.

Approaching the congregation may present challenges. It is a subject that certain people will not want to address. Remember, there are sheep who do not want to know that the wolf exists. When you approach the congregation about surviving an active shooter, you are the sheepdog that is reminding them of the wolf. This opposition does not diminish the fact that leaders have a stewardship responsibility to inform them on how to be successful in order to save lives. The way that individuals choose to act during an active shooting is up to them. The best thing you can do is prepare them to act.

The active shooter training should include how to respond to the police as they arrive. First responders will be heading into an evolving, chaotic, dangerous, and confusing situation. They will be running towards the danger and placing their lives at risk in an effort to save others. Therefore, the police, fire, and EMS personnel will be highly vigilant as they arrive on scene. They have to quickly assess every person; looking at each one as a potential threat. Therefore, it behooves victims to take action to facilitate a safe rescue.

If you find yourself in this potion, obey all commands given to you by law enforcement. Keep your hands up with the palms open and clearly visible. This helps indicate that you are not a threat or carrying a weapon. Do not run directly at an officer unless instructed to do so. Officers may need to engage a threat and you do not want to place yourself in a potential crossfire. Finally, provide any information that you have about the number of shooters, location, and physical description.

Recover

After any critical event, be it weather related or criminal, the community looks to the church to help with recovery. Victims from the community seek the church in need of mental, physical, and spiritual support. However, when an active shooter occurs at your church, *you* are the victim. Despite being a victim, it is in the nature of the local church to take on a leading role in aiding others. Although this will occur, you must remember that the church needs to recover too. Therefore, if your church is a victim, openly embrace the aid that will come from other churches; partner with them in your recovery.

Every critical event, be it a hurricane, medical emergency, or shooting needs to have a designated recovery effort focusing on both the short-term and long-term condition of the people involved. I have experienced how poorly the attention given to the people involved in the events becomes over the long term. It is important that the church has a contingency plan outlining the areas that it should prepare for; considering long-term and short-term recovery efforts.

The U.S. Department of Homeland Security *Active Shooter Recovery Guide* provides some valuable information regarding post-event recovery. It is not designed for churches nor does it address recovery efforts from a Christian point of view. Nonetheless, it does have insightful information that can be beneficial to the church. Some of the following information was taken from that plan.[96]

SLS recommends that the church consider including a short-term and long-term recovery strategy in the Emergency Preparedness Plan.

---

[96] United State Department of Homeland Security, Active Shooter Recovery Guide, August 2017, 8.

- Incorporate a *short-term recovery plan* to address the immediate needs after the event concludes.
- Consider identifying a designated assembly area for care and reunification of family and friends. The Safety Team can assist with this as it will also identify assembly areas for other types of evacuations (fire, bomb threat, suspicious package, etc.). If your Safety Team utilizes a tertiary form of identification such as a brightly colored hat, sash, or vest that is easily identifiable, use them to help direct and corral people.[97]
- Use social media to assist with providing information. Be clear, concise, and affirming in the social media communications. Avoid posting any photographs or information that is not confirmed. Be sensitive to the scene. Even a photograph that does not have people in it may still be inappropriate. For example, a photograph of the entrance of the church after the event may not contain any people. But if the photograph displays a child's bottle on the ground that belongs to a victim, everyone who recognizes that bottle will be further affected.
- Assist in the reunification of families and the retrieval of personal belongings. People will be coming out of the church and most of them will have left personal items inside. Also, if the parking lot is part of the crime scene, they may not be able to access their vehicles until the scene is released. If that occurs, the church should help facilitate the recovery process by coordinating the effort with law enforcement.
- Incorporate a *long-term recovery plan* that begins once the facility has been turned back over to the church by

---

[97] Note: The Safety Team must utilize two forms of identification: An official ID such as a driver's license and a Safety Team ID that is consistent with any other ministry at the church. A third form is optional as it specifically is used for high visibility situations.

local first responders. This includes leaning on outside churches for assistance.
- Work with federal, state, and local agencies to engage victim assistance programs. The agencies who respond to the scene will likely provide short-term assistance, but, it will disappear over time. Therefore, spearhead the movement to get long-term assistance through their agencies.
- Offer *and attend* grief counseling. People will respond differently to the event. Some will not want or need counseling while others will need it for years. Seek experts in post-traumatic stress and counseling who can assist people through this process. Don't just rely on what your church can do. Remember, you too are a victim.
- Beware of post-incident scams. According to DHS, "The aftermath of some active shooter incidents has seen the formation of fraudulent charities and other scams that may re-victimize those affected and the general public who wish to contribute to a legitimate charity. In addition to seeking money, some of these solicitations may be 'phishing' for personal information."[98]
- Prepare for litigation and the judicial process. The Safety Team must utilize the Intel Report and create a comprehensive After Action Report to document the event. Also, it is safe to assume that many of the people involved in the event will be part of the judicial process. Victims may have to testify to what they observed and experienced. This can be difficult, as it will "bring back" the traumatic events that they have been working to recover from. This will require additionally counseling and assistance from outside of the church.

---

[98] United State Department of Homeland Security, *Active Shooter Recovery Guide,* August 2017, 8

Church Security and Outreach

- Document all planning, action, and provision that the church takes concerning short-term and long-term recovery.

You must address the short-term and long-term effects of a critical event. In *Crisis Survival Guide: Facing Crisis Finding Hope,* Kris DenBesten writes:

> A crisis can build slowly like a hurricane or strike rapidly like a tornado wreaking havoc in our lives. Sooner or later we all will face the storms of crisis. Yet, there is a shelter — A safe refuge — In the midst of every storm. It is here provision for the journey from facing crisis to finding hope is found.[99]

Just because the emergency situation has concluded and you are in the recovery phase does not mean that your crisis is over. As you continue down your path to recovery, draw closer to God. You must *Act* to *Deter*, *Avoid*, and *Mitigate* attacks even after the shooting has stopped.

† † †

An active shooter is a low probability but potentially high-casualty event. This means that although the results can be catastrophic, the likelihood of an active shooter occurring is statistically low when compared to the other types of emergencies and crimes that the church regularly addresses. *Actions must be taken to Deter, Avoid,* and *Mitigate* each type of threat including active shooters. During a critical event such as an active shooter, immediate mitigation may involve applying a

---

[99] Kris DenBesten, *Crisis Survival Guide: Facing Crisis Finding Hope* (Text Copyright, 2011) 5.

tourniquet to stop life-threatening bleeding, or initiating grief counseling to victims that may last for years. We need to be prepared for both.

Active shooters present a deadly attack that occurs far too often in churches, businesses, schools, and other venues. The church must address the threat of an active shooter just like all other potential attacks. It must pray, plan, and prepare for an attack before one occurs. Prayer should not be used only as a last resort. Pray now for wisdom on how to *Act* to *Deter*, *Avoid*, and *Mitigate* an active shooter. Establish a security ministry that empowers the entire church through the use of Force Multipliers and a Safety Team that operate in condition yellow. Create a comprehensive Emergency Preparedness Plan. Finally, develop relationships with first responders that enhance the safety and security of the church and function as an outreach to the first responder community. Pursue the *one* and protect the *ninety-nine*.

Conclusion

*P*rotecting the local church and our guests (security) and leading the lost to Jesus (through outreach) are not mutually exclusive endeavors. Individually and corporately we can be simultaneously successful in each area. Everyone in leaderships has to face the Pastor's Paradox, which says that too much security will inhibit the ability to reach the lost while too little security leaves the flock vulnerable. As we seek the lost, we risk bringing in people who may threaten the safety of the church. In addition, if we secure the church by closing the doors to outsiders, we are ignoring our Lord's commands and the commission to pursue the lost. Our obedience to the Lord requires effort in both areas to overcome the Pastor's Paradox.

There are two fronts to the ongoing battle against evil in this corrupted world. On one front, the evil one seeks to steal, kill, and destroy the creation that we are to steward over. Failure to win battles on this front will lead to moral and physical destruction. Although the sting of death has been removed, the threat of the carnage leading up to it remains. On the other front, failure in battle has an even greater cost. The victims in this battle will not only taste death but also face eternal damnation. We have been commanded and commissioned to engage in combat on both fronts; the cost is too high to ignore one and focus on the other.

Every church has limited resources. That is why I wanted to author a book that had a strategy that is low-cost and allows the opportunity to immediately increase the security of the church while fostering outreach. It is my sincere hope that this book has provided you many avenues to overcome the Pastor's Paradox by utilizing the people that you already have serving. Through them you have the potential to immediately enhance the safety and security of your church. All you need to do is empower them! Additional training, equipment, and resources can come later. For now, focus on being people-centered and operating within the lead pastor's vision for the church. Seek the lost, be welcoming to them, but also be ever vigilant for those that you are to have nothing to do with. Be a good shepherd of the flock, serve to protect them so they can freely worship the Lord in safety and without distraction.

With everything that has been offered in this book, you can immediately enhance the security of your church. Train the Safety Team and Force Multipliers serving in other ministries in Security Ministry Basic Training. This will avoid sacrificing the mission of the church or creating an intimidating security force that causes disruption during service. Security Ministry Basic Training begins with a foundation of *prayer* and *stewardship*, and the themes of *Wisdom*, *Controlling Fear*, *Action*, and *Vigilance*. Security Ministry Basic Training is the foundational instruction that includes overt deterrence and covert observation, communication, situational awareness, conditioning the mind, the OODA loop, cognitive blueprinting, identifying red flags including pre-assault indicators, and the Christian Warrior Mindset.

Empower the people serving at the church to enhance their situational awareness, blueprint contingency plans, and operate in *condition yellow*. SLS defines situational awareness as the real time perception of the environment and the events occurring in it. This includes the three subcategories of spatial awareness, self-awareness, and spiritual awareness. Condition yellow is a relaxed state of vigilance where one has optimal situational awareness. Finally, cognitive blueprinting is a technique used to prepare the mind to act efficiently by continually creating contingency plans of action for unexpected situations. If everyone serving at your church understands these concepts, you will create a welcoming group of men and women who play an integral part in enhancing the overall safety and security of the church.

It is the goal of the SLS Tactical Strategy to maintain a welcoming worship environment while enhancing safety and security. This is achieved through the strategic use of three elements: an overt *law enforcement officer(s)*, a covert *Safety Team*, and overt *Force Multipliers*. These three elements are the *who* of the Tactical Strategy; the techniques they utilize are the *how*. By operating in their specified overt and covert capacities to observe and communicate suspicious activity, these three elements *Act* to *Deter, Avoid,* and *Mitigate* threats.

Act now to provide the Safety Team with the specific instructions offered in this book including: Safety Team operations, leadership, and how to teach others. This goes beyond Security Ministry Basic Training and is covered in Safety Team Operational Training. Topics include tactical training in surveillance, covert/low-visibility operations, de-escalation, and observation and communication techniques. Of course, your church can include additional training in each area and advanced training in areas such as defensive tactics, the use of force, use of weapons, medical care, and others areas that your church requires.

Another immediate action step that you can take is to document your effort through an Emergency Preparedness Plan (EPP). This stand-alone document provides an overview of the measures taken to enhance the security and safety of the church, guidance and accountability for maintaining standards, and effort made to reduce hazards. It is designed to take *Action* to *Deter*, *Avoid*, and *Mitigate* risks. The EPP provides direction on how to prepare for potential emergency situations. It takes affirmative steps towards mitigating risk stemming from weather, medical, and man-made emergencies. This includes, but is not limited to: preparation for active shooters, disruptive individuals, medical/health emergencies, direct threats towards church attendees and staff, internal investigations, background investigations, interviewing, collection of evidence, and referring criminal matters to law enforcement. This is a no-cost way to plan and document what constitutes your security ministry and Safety Team, specific procedures for weather, medical, and criminal attacks, and keep a chronological list of the actions taken and training provided as you harden the church against attacks. Remember, critical events are magnets for lawyers, litigation, and lawsuits. Make sure your efforts to increase the safety and security of the church have been well documented.

The wolf is out there! But so too are the lost. Be prepared to stand eye to eye against the wolf and in the end remain standing. Be also a sanctuary for the lost for in time, they may come to the Lord and enlist in His army. Then, they will stand shoulder to shoulder with you against the wolf. Each of us was once one of the lost. But the Lord carried us back to the flock. Now through His victory we are part of *the church*. We stand shoulder to shoulder with those who came before us. Paul was rescued and through God's grace joined Peter as part of *the church*. Matthew 18:16 says, "And I tell you, you are Peter, and on this rock I will build my church, and the gates of hell shall not prevail against it." As we stand together with those who came before us, *let God arise and scatter His enemies*. United in Him, let us be the church as we pursue the *one* and protect the *ninety-nine*.

Bibliography

Asken, Michael J., Dave Grossman, and Loren W. Christensen: *Warrior Mindset: Mental Toughness Skills for a Nation's Peacekeepers.* Millstadt, IL: Warrior Science Publications, 2010.

Beilby, James K. *Thinking About Christian Apologetics: What It Is and Why We Do It.* Downers

Davis, Paul K., Walter L. Perry, Ryan Andrew Brown, Douglas Yeung, Parisa Roshan and Phoenix Voorhies, *Using Behavioral Indicators to Help Detect Potential Violent Acts: A Review of the Science Base.* Santa Monica, CA: RAND Corporation, 2013. https://www.rand.org/pubs/research_reports/RR215.html.

De Becker, Gavin. *The Gift of Fear: And Other Survival Signals That Protect Us From Violence.* New York, New York: Dell Publishing, 1997.

DenBesten, Kris. *Crisis Survival Guide: Facing Crisis Finding Hope.* Text Copyright, 2011.

Dungy, Tony. *The Mentor Leader: Secrets to Building People and Teams that Win Consistently.* Carol Stream, IL: Tyndale House Publishers, Inc., 2010.

Erasmus of Rotterdam. *The Manual of the Christian Knight.* London: Aeterna Press, 2014.

Ford, Daniel. *A Vision So Nobel.* Durham, New Hampshire: Warbird Books, 2010.

Grossman, Dave *On Combat: The Phycology and Physiology of Deadly Conflict in War and Peace.* Millstadt, IL: Warrior Science Publications, 2008.

Grossman, Dave and Bruce Siddle. "Psychological Effects of Combat." In *Encyclopedia of Violence, Peace, and Conflict*, Volume 3, 139-149. Edited by Lester Kurtz and Jennifer Turpin. San Diego, CA: Academic Press, 1999.

Hawkins, Jeffery. "Five Ways to Prevent Crimes Against Churches." *Police Magazine,* (April 2012). Accessed November 17, 2018. http://www.policemag.com/channel/patrol/articles/2012/04/5-ways-to-prevent-crimes-against-churches.aspx

Kahneman, Daniel. *Thinking, Fast and Slow.* New York: Farar, Straus and Giroux, 2011.

Keller, Tim. "Vocation: Discerning Your Calling." *Church Leaders* (2018). Accessed January 26, 2019. https://www.churchleaders.com/pastors/pastor/articles/176526-tim-keller-discerning-your-calling.html/2 .

Kyle, Chris, Scott McEwen and Jim DeFelice. *American Sniper: The Autobiography of the Most Lethal Sniper in U.S. Military History.* New York: Harper Collins, 2012.

McRorie, Christina. "Rethinking Moral Agency in Markets: A Book Discussion on Behavioral Economics." *Journal of Religious Ethics* 44, no. 1 (March 2016): 195-226.

United States Department of Education, et al. 2013. *Developing High Quality Emergency Operation Plans for Houses of Worship*. Washington, DC: U.S. Department of Homeland Security. http://rems.ed.gov *https://www.fema.gov/media-library/assets/documents/33007 accessed January 15, 2019.*

United States Department of Homeland Security, October 2008. *Active Shooter How to Respond*. Washington, DC: U.S. Department of Homeland Security.

United State Department of Homeland Security, August 2017. *Active Shooter Recovery Guide*. Washington, DC: U.S. Department of Homeland Security.

Welch, Robert Welch. *Serving by Safeguarding Your Church*. Grand Rapids, MI: Zondervan, 2002.

Wheeler, David and Vernon M. Whaley. *The Great Commission to Worship: Biblical Principles for Worship-Based Evangelism*. Nashville: B&H Publishing Group, 2011.

Index

Active Shooter, 28, 91, 116-120 passim, 133, 158, 209, 325-337
ADAM, Actions to Deter Avoid and Mitigate, 5, 28, 35-48
advanced training, 151, 155, 268, 341
A-FAM, area familiarization, 249, 311
After Action Report, 155, 156, 248-255, 278, 284-285, 335
ANS, autonomic nervous system, 84, 127
badge, 43, 240
Biblical Basis, 5, 14, 49-78, 85, 327
blueprinting, see cognitive blueprinting
Boyd, John, 121-124
cameras, 13, 25, 40, 136, 147-149, 158, 213, 225, 232, 241-247 passim
children's ministry, 12, 26, 31, 114, 136, 157, 177-178, 204-205, 226-227, 242, 281, 289 321
Christian Warrior Mindset, 79-82, 93, 119, 125, 131-132, 166, 172, 181-182, 185, 256, 306, 310, 312, 340
church staff, 7, 13, 40, 178, 198, 208-211, 223, 227, 253, 284, 304, 323
clothing, 43, 207, 238-239, 247, 262, 266, 288-290, 303, 319
Cognitive Blueprinting, 98, 101, 107-115 passim, 116-132, 150, 256, 259, 274, 285, 302, 340-341

Commanded and Commissioned Warriors, 181-194
Condition Black, 58n, 102, 104-105, 126
Condition Orange, 103, 116-119, 236, 300
Condition Red, 103, 119, 330
Condition White, 28, 102, 104, 258
Condition Yellow, 75, 84, 94, 103-108, 114-120, 124, 130-132, 137, 150, 182, 201, 202, 207, 219, 229, 236, 257-258, 287-288, 301-302, 326-337, 340-341
conditioning the body, 127-130
conditioning the mind, 82, 106, 256, 340
consulting security experts, 67, 165-169
Cooper Color Code, 101-105
Copper, John Dean "Jeff", 101
courage, 55, 58, 59, 60, 63, 74, 78
cover and concealment, 95, 125, 130, 220, 230-231, 301, 328-329
covert, 15, 35, 44, 91, 148, 195, 200-203, 214-215, 219, 224-240 passim, 241-242, 245-246, 253, 268, 278, 281, 294, 340-341
decoy, 235
de-escalation techniques, 198, 264, 268, 278, 294-299
Desiderius Erasmus -twenty-two rules, 185-186
developing leaders, 190-194
distraction, 235
documentation, 149, 247, 278
establishing an Emergency Preparedness Plan, 141-146
establishing the Safety Team, 160-194
Evade, Hide, Fight, Recover, 121, 327-337
evidence, 141, 147, 152-155,
executive protection, 214
eyeball, 221, 222, 231-237, 243-244, 283-284, 289, 300, 301
Feast of Dedication, 71
Feast of Tabernacles, 71
fixed surveillance position, 220, 232-233, 289, 299
flashlights, 241, 239, 290
footwear, 238, 239, 288
Foundation of Prayer, 14, 51-63
Foundation of Stewardship, 63-78

Index

functional clothing, 290
functional design, 135, 149
gloves, 293
Great Commission
  Worshippers, 179-181
greeters, 30-31, 104, 150,
  201, 202, 207-208,
  215, 232, 243
hired law enforce-
  ment, 196-200
hospitality, 201, 243, 288
identification, 136, 239-240,
  293-294, 334
imprinting, 238, 290
incident injury report, 255
Intel Reports, 247-255
internal investigations, 141,
  151-153, 342
interrogation, 152-153
interviewing, 141,
  152, 153, 342
Jesus
birth, 70
proclaimed His Divinity 70
action during the Feast of
  Dedication 71
the Father is in Him and He
  is in the Father 71
action during the Feast of
  Tabernacles 71
miraculous signs 71
withdrew to Ephraim -, 72
lanyard, 43, 240, 288
layers of security, 134, 267
leap frogging, 233, 234

litigation, 4, 14, 26, 36,
  138-140, 151, 153, 155,
  159, 162-163, 167, 199,
  303, 335, 342
loose (surveillance), 234,
  262, 266, 290
Making Your Church
  a Hard Target, see
  target hardening
measures to harden fortification, see target hardening
medical gear, 198, 239, 290
OODA Loop, 80, 113n,
  121-132, 215, 256,
  263,285, 326, 340
Operational Training
  Exercise (OTX) 249,
  280-285, 303
tactical considerations,
  200, 287, 303
Outreach: External Ministry –
  poreuomai, 307, 312
Outreach: Internal Ministry –
  koinonia, 312
Outreach: Maximize Existing
  Relationships, 308
Overt, 15, 40-44 passim,
  135, 147, 189, 195-227
  passim, 227-253, 263,
  288, 340, 341
Overt Deterrence - Cover
  Observation and
  Communication, 227-253
Parable of the Lost
  Sheep, 8-10

349

paralleling, 233-234
parking team, 32, 201, 204, 284
Pastor's Paradox, 4, 5, 12, 14, 16-17, 20-25, 34, 38, 7n, 53, 93, 165-170 passim, 260, 301, 303, 307, 311, 324, 330-340
Paul (actions taken), 72, 73, 173
Paul and Barnabas, 72
peace, 1, 52, 54, 56, 60-63, 74, 74, 77, 78, 120, 193, 296, 327,
Peter (actions taken), 97, 174, 306, 342
phone use, 44, 102, 118, 126, 129, 144-145, 199, 220, 235, 239, 287-288, 300, 310, 311, 328
Pillar of Action, 69-74
Pillar of Controlling Fear, 55-63
Pillar of Vigilance, 75-78
Pillar of Wisdom, 52-55
PNS, parasympathetic nervous system 127
positioning (surveillance), 130, 150, 158, 212, 232, 245, 288-289, 303
prayer, 29, 36, 39-40, 50-63, 68, 69, 74, 77, 78, 80, 85, 94, 132, 162, 185, 287, 296, 303, 304, 310, 320, 337, 340

pre-assault indicators, 15, 256-267
pre-positioning, see positioning
preventative maintenance log, 143
primary means of communication, 148, 246-247.
radios, 147-149, 213, 214, 238, 241-246,
recruiting or discovering team members, 32, 161, 171-190
red flags, 15, 130, 207-209, 219-223, 227-234, 256-267, 285, 294-295, 300-301, 328, 340
Safety Team Operational Training, 15, 81, 268-304
Safety Team name, 161-165
requirements for potential team members, 178
security experts, see consulting security experts
Security Ministry Basic Training, 13-15, 31, 42, 79-132
security: gifts and talents, 10-12, 25, 31, 32, 38, 48, 65-67, 177, 181-190, 208, 306
self-awareness, 93-99, 116, 126, 127, 236, 341

sheepdog, 10, 11, 88-94, 131, 185, 309, 332
Sheep, Wolves, and Sheepdogs, 86-93
situational awareness, 40-42, 75-78, 80-93 passim, 93--132, 120-130 passim, 202-236 passim, 270, 271, 279, 340-341
SNS, sympathetic nervous system, 127-130
spatial awareness, 93-95, 236, 341
spiritual awareness, 93-94, 97-98, 236, 279, 341
suicide by cop, 40
surveillance detection technique, 234-235
tailing (surveillance), 233
The Dance, 299
tight (surveillance), 234, 238
tort, 139-140
trailing (surveillance), 234
training
Formal, 15, 139, 270, 272, 276-279
On the Job (OJT), 279-287, 302-303
ushers, 44, 112, 148, 149, 203-204, 216-232, 243
Vehicle-Borne Improvised Explosive Device (VBIED), 73
weapons,77, 78, 82, 262, 331, 332,
worship Team, 205-207
X, 73-74, 130, 153, 328

About the Author

Jason is married to his wonderful wife Heather and they have one son. Together they are partners in marriage, raising their son, and in ministry. Jason is a former Deputy U.S. Marshal, federal agent, and experienced instructor in firearms and SWAT tactics. He holds a Master of Arts degree in Theological Studies from Liberty University and a Master of Science degree in International Affairs from Florida State University. He has participated in mission trips to Africa, the Caribbean, Europe, and the Middle East. Currently Jason serves as an associate pastor at East Coast Believers Church in Oviedo, Florida.

Photograph used with permission from Dominique Andre - www.flashbang-mag.com